## Advance Praise for *India Inked*

'Sunlight is the best disinfectant ... at a time when our electoral democracy is slipping into areas of darkness, especially over money power, EVMs, and indeed the Election Commission itself, Poonam Agarwal has made a genuine effort to investigate and unravel the truth. A must-read for those who want democracy to be strengthened and our electoral process be made more transparent.'

**Rajdeep Sardesai**
consulting editor, news anchor, India Today Television;
author of *2024: The Election That Surprised India*

'Poonam Agarwal changed everyone's understanding of the Election Commission's rules during the Lok Sabha elections. Her continuous reporting helped people understand many provisions of the Election Commission, whether it was electoral bonds or Form 17C. Through Poonam's reporting, political workers also received training on how to engage with the Election Commission. In a way, Poonam's videos and reports became training manuals for the general public. She has a significant grasp of these issues. Today, as the debate about the role of the Election Commission has reignited, Poonam Agarwal's book has emerged as a major contribution to this discussion.'

**Ravish Kumar**
independent journalist and author of *The Free Voice*

'Poonam's path-breaking work on electoral bonds and the Indian electoral system is one that will be remembered for decades to come when we look back at this critical and horrifying time in Indian democracy's history.'

**Atishi**
chief minister of Delhi

'Free and fair elections are an essential feature of our Constitution. What do free and fair elections mean? Poonam takes us through our electoral process and enables the reader to better understand the range of issues. A must-read for every voter.'

**Justice Madan B. Lokur**
former judge, Supreme Court of India

'A deep dive into how and why India's electoral system, despite its historical strengths, is not quite the free and fair model of electoral democracy it is touted to be – by the reporter who first brought to light the unique hidden alphanumeric code in the scandal of the electoral bonds scheme.'

**N. Ram**
director and editor-in-chief, *The Hindu*

'History of elections, the Election Commission and the election commissioners interestingly captured by Poonam through painstaking research. A great addition to the scarce literature on a subject that touches the entire nation.'

**S.Y. Quraishi**
former chief election commissioner of India;
author of *The Great March of Democracy*

'An engaging story of how the most audacious attempts at legalised robbery of the democratic process through electoral bonds was foiled.'

**Yogendra Yadav**
political activist, Swaraj India and Bharat Jodo Abhiyaan;
author of *Making Sense of Indian Democracy*

'The book is an insightful and much-needed exploration of India's electoral process from an investigative journalist's perspective with remarkable depth and clarity especially with regard to electoral bonds and the mismatch in votes polled and counted.'

**Sucheta Dalal**

Padma Shri; journalist; managing editor – Moneylife; author of *The Scam: From Harshad Mehta to Ketan Parekh*

'Poonam's work on the electoral process and its dangers reveals her complete grasp over a very controversial subject.'

**Jawahar Sircar**

former member of the Rajya Sabha

'Poonam's investigative work helped expose the lack of transparency in the NDA government's electoral bonds scheme. This is a necessary read for those who care for the health of India's elections, democracy and development.'

**Sam Pitroda**

former adviser to Dr Manmohan Singh; author of *The Idea of Democracy*

'Poonam Agarwal has written a very comprehensive compendium on the most important democratic exercise in India. It is a significant contribution to the literature on electoral issues in the country.'

**Jagdeep S. Chhokar**

former professor, Indian Institute of Management, Ahmedabad; founder, Association for Democratic Reforms

# India Inked

# India Inked

## *Elections in the World's Largest Democracy*

POONAM AGARWAL

FOREWORD BY
ASHOK LAVASA

BLOOMSBURY
NEW DELHI • LONDON • OXFORD • NEW YORK • SYDNEY

BLOOMSBURY INDIA
Bloomsbury Publishing India Pvt. Ltd
Second Floor, LSC Building No. 4, DDA Complex, Pocket C – 6 & 7,
Vasant Kunj, New Delhi, 110070

BLOOMSBURY, BLOOMSBURY INDIA and the Diana logo
are trademarks of Bloomsbury Publishing Plc

First published in India 2025
This edition published 2025



ISBN: HB: 978-93-61315-66-4; eBook: 978-93-61313-96-7
2 4 6 8 10 9 7 5 3 1

Typeset in Bembo by Manipal Technologies Limited
Printed and bound in India by Thomson Press India Ltd

MIX
Paper | Supporting responsible forestry
FSC® C010615

# Contents

# Abbreviations

| | |
|---|---|
| ADR | Association for Democratic Reform |
| AIADMK | All India Anna Dravida Munnetra Kazhagam |
| AIIMS | All India Institute of Medical Sciences |
| AGP | Asom Gana Parishad |
| AIMIM | All India Majlis-e-Ittehadul Muslimeen |
| BJP | Bharatiya Janata Party |
| BRO | Border Roads Organisation |
| CBI | Central Bureau of Investigation |
| CAAJ | Committee Against Assault on Journalists |
| CJI | Chief Justice of India |
| CPI(M) | Communist Party of India (Marxist) |
| DEA | Department of Economic Affairs |
| DMDK | Desiya Murpokku Dravida Kazhagam |
| EC | Election Commissioner |
| ED | Directorate of Enforcement |
| ECI | Election Commission of India |
| EIU | Economist Intelligence Unit |
| EVM | Electronic Voting Machine |
| FIR | First Information Report |
| IGP | Inspector General of Police |
| IANS | Indo-Asian News Service |
| INC | Indian National Congress |
| IUML | Indian Union Muslim League |
| LTCG | Long-term Capital Gains |
| MoF | Ministry of Finance |
| MCC | Model Code of Conduct |
| MoLJ | Ministry of Law and Justice |

| | |
|---|---|
| MP | Member of Parliament |
| NDA | National Democratic Alliance |
| NEW | National Election Watch |
| NCP | Nationalist Congress Party |
| ONOE | One Nation One Election |
| PAN | Permanent Account Number |
| PIL | Public Interest Litigation |
| RWB | Reporters Without Borders |
| RPA | Representation of the People Act |
| RBI | Reserve Bank of India |
| RTI | Right to Information |
| SC | Supreme Court |
| SEC | State Election Commission |
| SLU | Symbol Loading Unit |
| SOP | Standard Operating Procedure |
| SBI | State Bank of India |
| SAD | Shiromani Akali Dal |
| TMC | Trinamool Congress |
| UPA | United Progressive Association |
| V-DEM | Varieties of Democracy |
| VVPAT | Voter Verified Paper Audit Trail |
| WJP | World Justice Project |
| WSPU | Women's Social and Political Union |

# Foreword

THERE ARE TWO KINDS of freedom struggle: one is to obtain it, the other to retain it.

The twentieth century saw the birth of many democratic nations. The twenty-first century poses before these countries and its people, the challenge of successfully safeguarding their hard-earned freedom. The year 2024 was an election year in India and many questions, concerns and warning signals emerged.

Over the years, India has surprised those who doubted its capabilities to function as a democracy because of low levels of literacy, deep-seated caste and communal divisions in society, cultural diversity and the lack of an able political leadership. India conducted successful elections and demonstrated peaceful transfer of political power. It has managed to endure the imposition of an internal emergency, during which civil liberties were suspended, and the ruling regime resorted to the suppression of dissent. Ironically, it was during this period that the slogan 'eternal vigilance is the price of freedom' gained popularity.

It has been seventy-seven years since we gained freedom from under the 'men who ruled India'. Many questions have emerged since then: Have 'we, the people' been able to retain freedom considering our own political parties and leaders have 'ruled' the country since 1947? Have the leaders done enough to empower the people and strengthen the pillars of our democracy? Have they instilled a respect for the law, or a fear of authority in the citizens instead? Have they created an India where 'the mind is without fear' and every citizen holds his head high, enjoying his freedom? Have they improved accountability, promoted transparency, curbed corruption, and encouraged citizens to ask questions – particularly about the prerequisites of democracy and the electoral process that brings leaders to power?

This book is a bold attempt to raise some of these questions by citing facts and figures gathered with courage and analysed through painstaking research, aiming to make citizens aware of issues that may be inconvenient for the establishment. Citizens have the right to question executive decisions, probe government claims and hold leaders accountable. The questions posed in this book are valid, even if they appear sceptical. Political leaders once united the people during the freedom struggle; they now seem to unite in dividing them in their own struggle to remain in power.

These questions being raised today doesn't mean that only the ruling regime is responsible for the present circumstances. The enquiries of cash, crime, caste and community, the integrity of the electoral process and political funding raised in this book must be addressed by all principal players of electoral politics. The long-term relevance of political parties depends on their ability to meet the requirements of the citizens.

Democracy is based on the rule of law. These rules contain both safeguards and loopholes. The rule of law entails the enactment of fair laws and their just enforcement. It is in the latter that questions arise regarding the quality and character of our democracy. Honest citizens abide by the law, and crafty citizens use loopholes to bypass it. Concerns of equality for all citizens remain valid despite economic progress. Is the system being steered by those who manipulate the levers of political power achieved by democratic elections?

The successful conduct of elections might be a source of satisfaction, but a democracy maintains its authority and protects citizens' rights through constitutional institutions that function with honesty and effectiveness and hold ruling parties accountable.

Parliament is sometimes 'used' to enact unequal laws; the state occasionally discriminates in enforcing the law of the land; and the judicial system sometimes leans towards recognising illegality rather than punishing it. As if this were not enough to signal the decline of democracy, there is a growing tendency among people to accept, and even applaud, this situation.

In a democracy, people are considered the most powerful. They transfer their power temporarily to elected representatives, through elections, who form a government. It would be a mockery of democracy if those representatives desire to remain in power at all costs instead of serving the interests of the people. Political parties implement different formulae to retain power, sometimes attempting to co-opt the constitutional bodies in furthering their ambition – a clear breach of trust.

Trust is an evolving relationship that is earned, not commanded by authority. As citizens become more aware, they ask more questions. Institutions and people governing them must answer the questions instead of viewing them as a challenge to their authority or credibility. It is necessary to move away from a stereotyped loyalty to a civilised relationship of ethical trust and transparent conduct.

'People get the government they deserve' is a cliche that converts manslaughter into suicide. I do not believe the people of India vote for or deserve a divisive society. They don't deserve to remain a developing country permanently. They don't deserve to live in squalid surroundings, drink unclean water, breathe toxic air, receive substandard education and struggle for decent health facilities nearly eight decades after Independence. They vote for an honest day's work and a decent quality of life – one that comes with comprehensive growth in an economy that provides opportunities to utilise their skills and talents, that is characterised by probity in public spending, and that features a responsive and accountable government machinery.

The people of India, who believe that elections are a 'festival of democracy' do not deserve to be left to fend for themselves while those in power are busy looking after their own interests. The sooner political parties realise this, the better it will be for the survival of democracy. Otherwise, other forms of governance could be waiting in the wings.

**Ashok Lavasa**
Former election commissioner of India

# Introduction

WHY ARE ELECTIONS CONDUCTED in India? How are elections conducted in India? The answer to the first question is known to all of us: elections are conducted in a free and fair manner to ensure the running of democracy in a modern nation state. With voting rights, voters get the power to elect their representatives and bring them to power to run the country. That's why the motto of the Election Commission of India (ECI), which is responsible for conducting elections to the Lok Sabha and state assemblies, is 'Every vote counts'.

But the *how* of conducting elections and the history behind Indian elections isn't known to many, including many a political party and politicians. During elections, the candidates, their parties and party members primarily focus on campaigning, collecting funds, pushing party propaganda and bribing voters which, to put in a nutshell, is done to *win* the election.

When I started reporting on and reading about elections and the ECI, I realised that many political party candidates who contest elections are not fully aware of the election processes. For instance, in the 2024 Lok Sabha elections, a huge majority of candidates and their polling agents did not know the relevance of Form 17C (containing the account of votes recorded at each polling station, number of voters who did not vote, among others) in the elections and why the polling agent must collect it from the presiding officer at the end of polling day.[1]

For voters, the elections had primarily been about casting a vote for the candidate of their choice based on the voters' wisdom and preference. Earlier, voters would listen to speeches and attend rallies of leaders and decide whom to vote for. In rural, tier-2 and tier-3 India, rallies and roadshows still make a big difference in how voters vote. Even so, listening to leaders has now become painful and traumatic as there has been a sharp rise in hate speeches and communal vitriol in these forums – India witnessed a record-breaking number of hate speeches in the 2024 Lok Sabha elections campaign.

For most journalists, elections are about reporting on rallies, speeches of politicians, development work done by a member of Parliament (MP) or a member of the Legislative Assembly (MLA) in their constituency.

---

I have been an investigative journalist since 2004. I never liked covering elections or chasing politicians for an interview or running around politicians during campaigns. I have only reported on election issues that deal with public development and welfare.

Until 2018, I didn't even imagine that my interest in knowing more about the intricacies of the election processes would open a pandora's box.

I did not know the significance of why votes polled and counted ought to match in every election. The mismatch in the electronic voting machine (EVM) figures of votes polled and counted in the Madhya Pradesh assembly elections in 2018 got me curious to know more about it. I reported on this story, and it led me deeper into the subject.

In parallel, for the first time, a former returning officer, Kannan Gopinathan, raised his concerns on the voter verifiable paper audit trail (VVPAT) by pointing out that with the introduction of the VVPAT in the voting system, the EVMs are programmed in such a way that the machine now knew which button is allocated to a particular political party candidate.[2] As a result, if a malware is uploaded in the EVMs it might corrupt the entire voting system process. This means that even if voters cast their vote for candidate A, the vote could well be recorded for candidate B.

These issues left me feeling bewildered about the entire apparatus of an Indian election. I read more on the subject and discussed with various stakeholders about issues related to EVM-VVPAT and the conduct of the ECI in carrying out elections in a free and fair manner so that it leaves no doubt in the minds of voters. I hadn't imagined that the issue that I brought up with the 2018 Madhya Pradesh assembly elections would be discussed throughout the 2024 Lok Sabha elections – mismatch in EVM votes polled and counted. You will read about these issues in Chapters 4 and 8.

In the 2024 US elections, $16 billion (around ₹1.3 lakh crore) was spent, and it was billed as the most expensive election in US history.[3] On the other hand, nearly ₹1.35 lakh crore was spent by all the candidates of various political parties in the 2024 Lok Sabha elections.[4] Of the 968.8 million registered or qualified voters, 18.4 million were in the age group of 18–19 years.[5] The polling was divided into seven phases. Elections were spread over a period of one and a half months and nearly 5.5 million EMV-VVPATs were used during the elections.

The ECI ensured that 'no voter [was] to be left behind'.[6] Thus, the polling agents walked for miles and crossed difficult terrains to set up polling booths. This tradition of inclusivity by facilitating every voter to cast their vote has been continuing since the first general elections conducted in free India.

Since 2022, the ECI has been making efforts to include particularly vulnerable tribal groups (PVTG) and other tribal groups in the electoral process. Finally, the ECI's efforts 'bore fruit with scenes of tribal groups in various states/Union Territories participating enthusiastically in phase 1 and phase 2 of the 2024 Lok Sabha Elections'. The Shompen tribe of Great Nicobar Island voted for the first time in the 2024 general elections.[7]

---

In this book, I tell the story of how elections in India are fought, won and lost, and the lengths those seeking political power go to in order to win. Chapter 1 highlights the brave and visionary efforts of our forefathers and foremothers in planning and executing election processes, which are still followed by the ECI. The foresight of India's first chief election commissioner, Sukumar Sen, to incorporate a symbol system to assist the illiterate in casting votes left such a deep impression on voters' minds that today symbols have become political parties' identities.

India remains in election mode year after year. After Independence the general and state elections were conducted simultaneously for almost three decades, but this synchronisation broke after a few state assemblies were dissolved early due to various reasons.

Once again, the demand for 'One Nation One Election' (ONOE) was reignited when Bharatiya Janata Party (BJP) mentioned it in its 2014 election manifesto. Chapter 9 examines if 'One Nation One Election' is good or bad for our country. Does the Constitution of India allow the amendments required to implement ONOE? And why is the BJP keen on this idea?

Political parties spend trillions of rupees on campaigning and organising rallies. In the age of social media, the mode of campaigning has also changed: political parties rely heavily on online platforms like WhatsApp, YouTube and Instagram to push their agendas.

Voters were subjected to a barrage of propaganda videos and memes during the 2024 Lok Sabha elections. On the one hand, social media videos, memes and news articles kept voters informed about the elections; on the other, hate speeches on religion, fake news and disinformation suffocated them. The end of the 2024 Lok Sabha elections came as a relief and freedom to many, including me, from a toxic environment.

Let's not forget the information technology (IT) cells formed by different political parties that act like election war rooms, becoming ten times more active before every election. In April 2024, just before the Lok Sabha elections, Channel News Asia uploaded a documentary on YouTube titled 'India's War on Fake News: How Disinformation Became India's #1 Threat'[8] where a freelance techie, Anil Kumar, said that he worked for the BJP IT cell whose main job is to circulate information. Freelancers were engaged by the party candidates on a pay of ₹40,000–50,000 per month, he alleged. He said 'Nationalism and Hindutva' were the primary agendas they focused on, adding that their task was to defame opposition political party leaders and spread propaganda. 'Right now Congress is our target. We make cartoons. We make memes. We make dramatic things, people like all these things.'[9]

Deepfake videos, photos and audio clips became another challenge of the 2024 Lok Sabha Elections. In fact, deepfake generated by artificial intelligence (AI) is a growing monster that has become a universal problem. Thus, we all need to keep a close watch on new AI tools and be mindful in our social media ecosystems in the absence of adequate resources to deal with the problem. In an interview with MediaNama, BOOM Fact Check shared that between 1 March and 31 May 2024, the organisation published 258 election-related fact checks. Of these, twelve were AI-generated claims, with three being deepfakes and nine being voice clones. The remaining were communal and EVM related.[10]

All political parties had two primary objectives – spreading positive messages about their party and defaming rival parties, even if it involved concocting fake videos and messages and presenting them as the truth. These war rooms work under the close supervision of party leaders. 'A team of 30–35 persons, including legal experts, carefully post the messages. Our team before posting any message gets clearance from legal experts to avoid any violation of the model code of conduct (MCC),' said Rajesh Garg, chairman of the Delhi Pradesh Congress Committee, Social Media Wing.[11] But we have witnessed in the 2024 Lok Sabha elections that the leaders of the national political parties don't worry about the MCC. What's worse, the ECI blatantly ignored highly objectionable speeches by the star campaigners of the political parties, including Prime Minister Narendra Modi, and set a bad precedent by only issuing a warning to them. In Chapter 7 I highlight the relevance of the MCC and the powers given to the ECI to implement it, including the power to register a first information report (FIR) against a politician.

In India, religion is an important factor in elections. Interestingly, the first consideration of political parties in selecting their candidates is their religion, ethnicity, caste or identity markers; other factors like popularity, the candidate's financial strength and their political graph are secondary.

Most political analysts believed that the BJP would sweep the 2024 Lok Sabha elections with the inauguration of the Ram temple in Ayodhya on 22 January 2024. In fact, the BJP was very optimistic about winning more than 300 parliamentary seats and the National Democratic Alliance (NDA) was certain they would cross 400 seats. The BJP government's slogan was 'Abki baar 400 paar' (Over 400 seats this time).

In politics there's no way to forecast the weather with absolute certainty. The judgement of the Supreme Court (SC) on the electoral bonds on 15 February 2024 came as a massive shocker to the nation when the SC pronounced the scheme as unconstitutional and struck it down. The historic judgement was the beginning of long court hearings and a tug of war between the State Bank of India (SBI) and the SC on sharing electoral bonds data with the public.

When I first exposed the unique hidden alphanumeric code in the bonds in 2018 in my investigative reportage, many politicians weren't even aware of the scheme, let alone what a big threat to democracy it was. But I was surprised when a security guard in my neighbourhood came rushing to me in May 2024 to compliment me for exposing the electoral bonds scheme. He stopped me humbly and asked my permission to speak. He said, 'Madam, aapne bahut bada kaam kiya hai electoral bond par, maine aapki interview dekhi hai YouTube par. (You have done a great job by exposing the electoral bonds scheme. I have watched your interview on YouTube).' I asked him, 'Kya aapko electoral bonds scheme ke baare mein pata hai? (Do you know about the electoral bonds scheme)?' Without any hesitation and with full confidence he explained the scheme in a few sentences: it was a tool to collect political funding in a secret manner and in return the ruling governments at the Centre and the states passed on favours to big companies. I was very impressed with him and felt satisfied that the issue had finally reached the ground level.

Until the SC judgement, this scheme, which had been in existence for almost six years, did not figure much in the larger public discourse except among a handful of people. During the 2024 Lok Sabha elections, the electoral bonds scheme became the talk of the town. I had started my YouTube channel, ExplainX, just two weeks before the bond judgement was pronounced. Once the judgement was out, I published many videos on the unique hidden alphanumeric codes, which caught the eye of journalists, politicians, judges and the public. Messages appreciating my work started flooding my X handle and YouTube channel, not just from my followers but also from many journalists, activists and academics.

At the same time, efforts were also made by trolls to discredit me as a journalist and to silence me. Some of this online trolling and targeted harassment is part of every journalist's life. It is not easy to deal with online threats, bullying and intimidation. It affects one's morale and the day-to-day ability to carry on. No one is entirely immune to it. I've learnt that beyond a point the best way to handle it is to ignore them. The trolling stops after three or four days, if you're lucky, and they move on to the next thing or target. On a lighter note, the common notion now among journalists is that if someone is trolled for their reportage, then the reporter has likely done a good job and exposed the truth.

My work bore fruit after six whole years. I was invited by the Centre for Investigative Journalism in London to deliver the prestigious Gavin MacFadyen Memorial lecture, where I spoke on the electoral bonds scheme.[12] Chapter 2 details how I exposed the unique hidden alphanumeric code in the electoral bonds. It was the biggest exposé on the NDA regime and became one of the main agenda points in the 2024 Lok Sabha elections. The opposing political parties ran with it and came up with the slogan 'Chande ka Dhanda (The Business of Charity)'.

Let's begin from the history of the Indian elections.

# 1

# The Beast That Is Indian Elections

'The ballot is stronger than the bullet.'

Abraham Lincoln

THE POWER A VOTE carries can change the lives of communities, states and nations for good or worse. The former US president Theodore Roosevelt had rightly said, 'A vote is like a rifle; its usefulness depends upon the character of the user.'[1]

Generally, that which is achieved easily is taken for granted. It is perhaps human nature to not register that which is glaringly obvious. Following Independence, India faced a great many difficulties in conducting smooth and fair elections across the country. Our foreparents worked hard to save our democracy by framing the world's longest written constitution, which declares India a sovereign, socialist, secular and democratic republic, granting every citizen of the nation justice, equality and liberty. It also gives us the power to choose our representatives in Parliament through universal adult franchise.

It is the duty of every voter to cast their vote and choose their representative intelligently. In this day and age, even casting a vote has become a matter of inconvenience for many. Some don't vote because they don't have faith in the election process, while some don't care about voting or about democracy.

The first general elections in free India took place in 1951–52, though the elective element for Indian natives in legislative bodies dates back to 1909 in British India.[2] The Indian Councils Act, 1909, was passed by the British Parliament to give approval to a scheme known as the Morley–Minto Reforms, drawn by Lord Minto, the then governor general of India, and Lord Morley, the then secretary of state for India in the British cabinet, in 1906.

This Act reserved certain seats in the legislative councils exclusively for Muslims and the representatives in these seats would be elected by Muslim electors only.[3] The Indian Councils Act continued until the Government of India Act, 1915, superseded it. The 1915 Act was further amended in 1919 to bring in the Montagu–Chelmsford Reforms. This Act gave reservation to Sikhs and created two legislative bodies at the Centre – the Council of State or the Upper House, composed of 60 members; and the Central Legislative Assembly or the Lower House, which consisted of 145 members. This Act facilitated the process of direct elections from the constituencies to both the Houses.[4]

The Government of India Act, 1919, set the stage for the election process by specifying the qualifications for voting and contesting elections and the mechanism for preparing the electoral roll. Under this Act, the first direct elections were held in 1920. Based on the Montagu–Chelmsford report's recommendation, one of the Houses in the law-making body would have members directly elected by the people. The age for voting was 21 years and for contesting elections, it was 25 years. The law also provided different constituencies, such as Muhammadan and non-Muhammadan, Sikh, European, Landholders and Chambers of Commerce.[5]

Mahatma Gandhi's non-cooperation movement launched in August 1920, before the elections, urged

Indians not to participate in the election process and called for a boycott. The election process turned violent in Lahore. A British government officer reported, 'It seems to me that these incidents are the direct results of violent speeches made by advocates of non-cooperation during the last month or two. Owing to this series of speeches, the British Government of India is now hated by the ordinary citizens of Lahore. The gift of responsible government which is being made to India is now despised.'[6]

The 1920 elections acted as a foundation for future Indian elections, although only a few Indians could exercise the right to vote. Edwin Montagu, who facilitated the 1920 elections, noted, 'The honest education of the electorate is a matter of primary importance. May one who takes an anxious interest in India's future echo the appeal that there should be no appeal to racial or religious prejudices and express the hope that, in the turmoil of an election, the great charm of Indian courtesy may not disappear?'[7]

## The First General Elections of Independent India

On 15 August 1947 India became free from British rule, but independence came with many challenges and responsibilities. It has now been over seven decades since the first general elections were held in independent India in 1951. It was a mammoth task and unparalleled in the history of humankind. India chose to give universal right to vote to citizens above twenty-one who were residents of India for at least 180 days irrespective of their caste, creed, profession or social status – unlike Britain, where the right to vote was determined by the citizens' ownership of property and profession.[8] Approximately 84 per cent of the Indian population was illiterate, which posed a major difficulty in giving all adults the right to vote, but brilliant minds behind the first general elections managed to overcome this challenge through deliberations and set the path for a strong, democratic country. It shattered the Western belief that Asians are not competent to run a government.

Before holding the first general elections it was essential to declare India a republic that entrusted every citizen living within the territory of the country the right to vote and participate in the affairs of the country. 'Every vote matters' has been the mantra ever since the inception of elections. But as you will see in the later chapters, this mantra has lost its meaning and has become a mere tokenistic mantra for the ECI.

The Constitution of India Bill, 1895 was the first non-official attempt at drafting a constitution according to historian S.P. Sathe in his book *Constitutional Amendments, 1950–1988*.[9] A Constituent Assembly composed of members from different states framed the Constitution of India. It came into effect on 26 January 1950 and the country was declared a republic. Interestingly, Article 324 of the Constitution, which created the ECI, came into effect two months earlier, on 26 November 1949.[10] An organisation can run successfully only if it has a vision and an intent to deliver on the expectations of the public. The wisdom of statespersons of the Constituent Assembly who drafted the Constitution with a pragmatic vision continues to be relevant for the modern nation state.

The number of registered voters in the first general elections was just over 173 million out of 361 million residents.[11] The geographical vastness, lack of infrastructure, unskilled labour, poverty and awareness were big challenges for the ECI. While the country was still reeling from the aftermath of Partition, many citizens who survived had also lost crucial identity documents in communal riots and while migrating from one city to another, or from one nation to another.

## Sukumar Sen: The First Chief Election Commissioner of India

In March 1950 Sukumar Sen, a member of the Indian Civil Service (ICS) serving as chief secretary of West Bengal, was appointed as the first chief election commissioner of India. He studied at the prestigious Presidency College, Calcutta, and was awarded a gold medal in mathematics from London University. He served as a district and sessions judge for nineteen years before he became chief secretary in August 1947 and also authored many books in his lifetime.

On 23 January 2020, while delivering the 'First Sukumar Sen Memorial Lecture', former president of India Pranab Mukherjee said, 'Sukumar Sen had been unacknowledged, unrecognised and unspoken for a long time. One of the reasons may be because our historical archives have very little information on who he was.'[12]

The former chief election commissioner S.Y. Quraishi said Sen's contribution in laying the foundation of a robust election management system is historic, though not adequately celebrated. In his book *An Undocumented Wonder: The Making of the Great Indian Election*, Quraishi praises Sen's astonishing work and writes, 'The nation owes him gratitude for laying the foundation of a great institution and for his superhuman effort in conducting the first general elections in 1951–52 in the most difficult circumstances with no infrastructure'.[13]

Arguably, T.N. Seshan is the most popular and praised chief election commissioner of India, known for his zeal to conduct free and fair elections. But Sen laid the foundation of the ECI, the core and the soul of Indian democracy.

The 17 February 1957 edition of a popular periodical, *Shankar's Weekly*, edited by cartoonist Shankar Pillai, called Sen 'The Man of the Week' for successfully completing India's second elections. Sen conducted the first two general elections in India – in 1952 and 1957. The magazine wrote:

> The Chief Election Commissioner became an unseen, undogmatic influence patiently judicial in his attitude to parties but insistent in regard to the machine he wielded.
>
> Where nearly two hundred million people, for the most part unlettered but politically conscious none the less, are set on choosing between one phenomenally big party and a clutter of many small and new ones, where words have to be replaced by symbols, where a corps of workers recruited ad hoc from a thousand offices with no experience of applied democracy have to face an army of agents both suspicious and persistent, the actual process of election can be very wearying.
>
> But largely due to Sukumar Sen it can be said that apart from Panch Sheela the most impressive gift we have given to Asia in the first decade of our freedom is the system of elections that has been perfected in this country.[14]

Sen was recommended by the second chief minister of West Bengal, Bidhan Chandra Roy, to PM Jawaharlal Nehru when he learnt that Nehru was looking for an able administrator to organise the country's first elections.[15]

PM Nehru wanted to hold the first general elections by spring of 1951. Hence, within a month of Sen's appointment as the chief election commissioner in March 1950, the Representation of the People Act was passed in Parliament with the hope that the country would witness the first general elections in early 1951.

Sen firmly deferred the elections until the autumn of 1951. He was tasked to put the election process in place from scratch with help from staff who did not have much knowledge about conducting elections.

In the first general elections, 489 seats of the Lok Sabha across 401 constituencies in 25 states were open for elections. Out of these, one member was elected in 314 constituencies while two members were elected in 86 constituencies: one from the general category and one from the Scheduled Castes or Scheduled Tribes category. In one constituency three members were elected. Multi-seat constituencies were established to protect seats for the backward sections of society, but the provision was abolished in the 1960s. A total of 1,949 people contested from 489 seats and each contestant was allotted a ballot box with the candidate's symbol on it for illiterate voters. The first election was held was held in 68 phases between 25 October 1951 and 21 February 1952.[16]

The elections in the Lok Sabha and Legislative Assemblies of states were mostly held simultaneously from 1951–52 to 1967.[17] This cycle of simultaneous elections was broken due to premature dissolution of some state assemblies in 1968 and 1969.[18] Article 356 of the Constitution lists a number of reasons under which state assemblies can be dissolved before the expiry of their term. If a chief minister of a state advises the governor to dissolve the Legislative Assembly and this recommendation is accepted by the governor, then the assembly would be dissolved.[19]

In its 170th report on reforms of the electoral laws published on 29 May 1999, the Law Commission of India observed, 'This cycle of elections every year, and in the out of season, should be put an end to. We must go back to the situation where the elections to Lok Sabha and all the Legislative Assemblies are held at once.'[20] I shall talk about the controversy surrounding ONOE in subsequent chapters.

Coming back to the first general elections, one of the primary tasks of the ECI was to prepare electoral rolls by conducting door-to-door surveys across the country. Sen introduced the pictorial symbols that were a part of daily life to represent political parties because symbols made it easier for the majority of voters to identify their candidate and political parties. Even today, political parties' symbols have relevance as illiteracy is still high in India. In 1951, the male literacy was 27.16 per cent and female literacy was 8.86 per cent.[21]

Each ballot box carried the distinctive symbol of a political party. The voter did not have to make any mark on the ballot paper, but simply place the ballot paper in the box marked with the symbol of their candidate. But gradually, the ECI changed the process and started printing symbols on the ballot papers.

One big challenge before the ECI was to decide the criteria to classify a political party as a national or a state party. Twenty-nine political parties claimed to be national parties. On 30 July 1951 the ECI held a conference in New Delhi which was attended by well-established national-level political parties for the allocation of distinctive symbols.[22]

The conference was attended by representatives of seven national political parties, and they reached a consensus on the following points:

1. The same symbol would be used throughout India for all the candidates of a party, both for assembly and parliamentary elections.
2. No separate symbol was necessary for a party's candidate contesting reserved seats. The party's symbol would be allotted to its candidates belonging to the Scheduled Castes and the Scheduled Tribes as well – but an additional mark, for example, a thick circle – would be printed around the party's symbol to make it easier to distinguish the ballot boxes of other candidates.
3. The name of each candidate would be written in bold on the label bearing his symbol on the ballot box allotted to him in a polling station.

4. In order to confirm the names of the official candidates sponsored by a party, each party would inform the chief electoral officer of every state of the name(s) of the person(s) who were authorised by the party to convey its ultimate decision regarding the adoption of candidates.[23]

In August 1951 the ECI allocated symbols to political parties:

1. All India Forward Bloc (Marxist Group) – Standing lion
2. All India Forward Bloc (Ruikar Group) – Human hand
3. Akhil Bharatiya Hindu Mahasabha – Horse and rider
4. Kisan Mazdoor Praja Party – Hut
5. Akhil Bharatiya Ram Rajya Parishad – Elephant
6. Indian National Congress – Two bullocks carrying a yoke
7. Socialist Party – Tree
8. Communist Party of India – Ears of corn and a sickle
9. Revolutionary Socialist Party – Spade and stoker
10. Revolutionary Communist Party of India – Flaming torch
11. Bolshevik Party of India – A star
12. Krishikar Lok Party – A cultivator winnowing grain
13. All India Bharatiya Jana Sangh – Lamp [24]

After the first general elections the political parties realised the public had started recognising them by their symbols and they requested the ECI to allocate the same symbol to their candidates at the local body elections too.

FIGURE 1.1 Designs of party symbols from the report prepared by Sukumar Sen during the first general elections

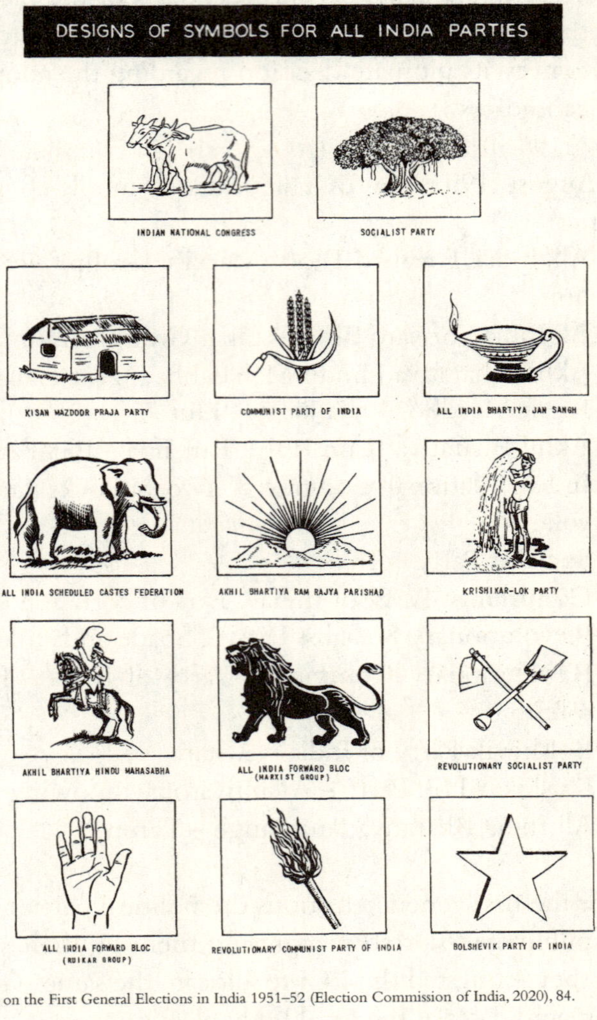


*Source:* Report on the First General Elections in India 1951–52 (Election Commission of India, 2020), 84.

It was not easy for universal adult suffrage to find acceptance in India. One of the main arguments against universal adult suffrage was the 'magnitude of the task involved'. Undoubtedly, adult suffrage demanded a herculean administrative coordination from the government due to a large public participation in the elections. Illiteracy of the voters was another important argument against adult suffrage as it required a system where an illiterate voter was able to cast their vote intelligently and in complete secrecy.[25]

Sen in his 'Report on the First General Elections in India 1951–52 Volume 1 (General)', in complete support of the universal adult suffrage, said:

> Experience demonstrates, therefore, that literacy, education, however desirable, is not an essential condition for the successful working of adult suffrage. However backward and ignorant the common man in an 'underdeveloped' country may be, he possesses in his own way enough common sense to know what is good for him. Given a simple enough system of ballot which he understands, he can be trusted to cast his vote intelligently in accordance with his own free will in favour of the representative of his choice. It is essential, however, that in order that the system of adult suffrage may work fairly and smoothly, two conditions must be satisfied: first, the conduct of elections must be strictly non-partisan or under neutral control and second, the executive government must sincerely desire free and fair elections and actively work for the same.[26]

## Material Used for Polling in the First General Elections

EVM versus ballot paper – debates on their advantages and disadvantages occur before almost every election in India.

Ballot boxes, ballot papers, indelible ink and paper seals for ballot boxes were introduced in the first elections. The challenge before the ECI was to bring in ballot boxes that couldn't be tampered with and were cost effective. In the first general elections the estimated requirement for the ballot boxes was 19,05,324 but the ECI procured 24,73,850 ballot boxes at a cost of ₹1,22,87,349.[27]

To avoid confusion during the simultaneous elections in the Lok Sabha and the Legislative Assemblies, the ballot boxes were made in two different groups of colours for the two different elections. The colours of the House of the People ballot boxes were olive green, meadow green, pale green and Brunswick green. The colours of the Legislative Assembly ballot boxes were chocolate, mahogany, teak, dark tan and bronze. Pink paper seals of specific size and design were used to seal the ballot boxes after the polling was over. These seals were made of watermarked paper and had 'Election Commission of India' printed on it.

The ECI decided to print all ballot papers centrally, and the task was assigned to Security Press in Nashik. The names of the candidates were not printed on any ballot paper; instead it had two letters indicating the name of a particular state, for instance, AS for Assam, BR for Bihar.

Sen was also responsible for the introduction of indelible ink to prevent fraud and impersonation of voters. Under Rule 22 of the Representation of the People Act 1951, voters were to allow inspection of their left forefinger to the polling officer before receiving their ballot paper. The mark made with indelible ink generally lasted for a week. This voting process continues to exist even today.

Shyam Saran Negi of Kalpa village in Kinnaur district of Himachal Pradesh was the first voter to cast his vote in independent India on 25 October 1951. He died at the age of 106 in Himachal Pradesh in November 2022. Due to difficult hilly terrains and snowbound conditions, polling at Chini (now Kalpa) and Pangi constituencies in Himachal Pradesh took place two months before the rest of the country. The ECI carried the polling material to Chini village polling stations, located in a primary school, on mules. Negi was a government school teacher at that time.[28] It took about a week to transport the ballot boxes after the poll to Chamba and Kasumpti, the headquarters of the returning officers, for the counting of the votes. Since the density of the population was low in the hilly terrains and desert areas, it was difficult to allocate around 1,000 voters in a polling station, which led to an increase in the number of polling stations. The smallest polling station had only nine voters in the first general elections.

In the hilly areas of the Outer Manipur parliamentary constituency, support of the hill chiefs was taken to obtain a supply of porters. In return, the ECI promised those chiefs a red blanket and a gun licence. In some parts of Tripura elephants were used to transport materials for the elections, but in most cases election officials had to reach their polling stations on foot, covering a distance of about sixty-four kilometres per day. Camels, mules, ponies and porters were used to transport polling parties and their equipment in several terrains.[29]

Apart from Chini in Himachal Pradesh, the rest of India went to the polls in January and February 1952. The highest turnout recorded was 80.5 per cent in Kottayam in Kerala while the lowest was 18 per cent in Shahdol in Madhya Pradesh. Overall, 60 per cent of registered voters voted in the first general elections. The voter turnout has not changed much between 1951 and 2024 and continues to average between 60 and 70 per cent.

Even today the ECI ensures that no family or house misses the opportunity to vote during the elections. In the 2024 Lok Sabha elections, the ECI set up a polling booth for just one family of five members in a location that is about 20 kilometres from the Siachen glacier in Warshi, accessible only by road. The place still lacks basic amenities such as electricity, healthcare and internet. The polling officers had to seek help from the Border Roads

Organisation (BRO) for electricity when the generator they carried failed in the 2024 Lok Sabha elections.[30]

*Leap of Faith*, published by the ECI, mentions that in 2007 a special polling station was set up in Banej, deep in the forests of Sasan Gir, for just one voter – Mahant Haridasji Udasin, a priest of a nearby Shiva temple. No political party had campaigned in the area since it is teeming with wild animals. For every election since 2007, a polling team travelled 25 kilometres to set up a polling booth for a single voter till Mahant passed away in November 2019.[31]

## Voting Rights of Indian Women

From as early as 1832, attempts were made in the UK to introduce legislation to give women the vote. 'It was not until the Equal Franchise Act was passed in 1928 that women won the same voting rights as men.' From 1832 to 1928, the UK took almost a century. Indian women got the right to vote the day India became independent. It took 144 years for the US, from 1776 to 1920. In 1776, only the women of New Jersey had the right to vote. The rest of the country did not allow women to vote.[32]

Post-Independence, when voters were being registered, many women refused to share their names and identified themselves in relation to the names of the male members in the house, for instance, as A's mother or B's daughter or C's wife. Therefore, due to the lack of a clear identification, Sen had to strike down names of 2.8 million women, and these women were not allowed to vote in the first general elections.[33]

British officials were not in favour of universal adult suffrage. In fact, in the beginning even Mahatma Gandhi did not support giving voting rights to women, and rather urged women to assist men in the fight for freedom. According to many historians, Indian women gained voting rights because of Western influence. Writing on Indian women suffrage, the historian Geraldine Forbes says, 'The firm insistence of organised women – that they be treated as equals of men on the franchise issue – emerged not from the perceptions of the needs of the women in India, but as the result of the influence of certain British women.'[34] In her book *Women in Modern India*, Forbes says that the British House of Commons ignored the demands of many Indian and British women's organisations fighting for voting rights for women. Nothing has ever come easy to a woman; they have been suppressed and discriminated against time and again in patriarchal society.

There were multiple arguments for depriving women the right to vote. Forbes writes, 'Obviously, the British promise to safeguard the rights of minorities meant only male minorities. In the case of women, the majority were denied rights because the minority lived in seclusion.' She adds that both Indian and British resisted giving voting rights to women as they 'talked of women's inferiority and incompetence in public affairs'.[35]

As mentioned earlier, men with property won the right to vote during British rule. This was also true in the case of women. In 1918, British women above the age of thirty who owned property had the right to vote. Women gained equal rights to vote in 1928. The struggle for achieving voting rights for women in India was closely linked with the freedom fight against British rule.

Princess Sophia Alexandrovna Duleep Singh is one of the prominent names who fought for women's suffrage primarily in the UK, but she supported the cause in numerous countries including India. She was born in 1876 in London. Her father was Maharaja Sir Duleep Singh who lost his Sikh empire to the Punjab province of British India and was later exiled to England. Sophia's mother, Bamba Müller, was half-German and half-Ethiopian.

Sophia joined the Women's Social and Political Union (WSPU) in 1909 and was an active part of the Women's Tax Resistance League. By 1909, Sophia was a leading member of the movement for women's right to vote and funded various suffragette groups. In 1910, she was part of a delegation of 300 suffragettes who marched towards Parliament in London demanding a meeting with the then prime minister H.H. Asquith, which was turned down. Demonstrations outside Parliament turned violent and police officers charged against them – Sophia, among 119 other women, got arrested. The historian Elizabeth Baker, in her book *The British Women's Suffrage Campaign*, called Sophia 'an important bridge between Indian activists and white British activists for female suffrage'.[36]

In 1919, Sophia accompanied political activists Sarojini Naidu and Annie Besant to the India Office (a department of the British government) in London to put forth their arguments in favour of granting the right to vote to Indian women before the secretary of state. The secretary of state expressed his sympathies to them but declared himself unable to make any promises.[37]

In 1911, while on holiday in Srinagar, Sophia met Herabai and her daughter Mithan Tata. Herabai was a theosophist but Sophia's determination and dedication to the cause of women's right to vote influenced Herabai and she took up the fight against the prevailing system. Herabai was intrigued when she saw the badge with the words 'Votes for women' Sophia always wore. Later, Herabai became honorary secretary of the Women's Indian Association and played a prominent role in promoting women's rights in the Montagu–Chelmsford Reforms in India.[38] This story of Sophia and Herabai breaks the stereotypical image of women as the weaker gender and is symbolic of fighting for the rights of women, irrespective of the country one belonged to.

Lolita Roy, another prominent figure, played an important role in the journey of the women suffragette movement. She was the president of the London Indian Union and a founding member of the Indian Women's Education Association. She petitioned the British government to give Indian women the right to vote after she moved to London in 1900.

On 17 June 1911 the Women's Coronation Procession, a suffragette march through London, was organised in which Sophia and Lolita participated. However, Dr Sumita Mukherjee, a historian who conducted research on the British suffrage movement, pointed out that the Coronation Procession did not reflect a broader inclusion of minority ethnic women by the British suffragettes. She said, 'These women were objectified by British women who wanted to throw in a bit of colour to the campaign and draw attention to tokenistic attempts of being diverse.'[39] On the same day *The Vote*, a women's newspaper, described Roy as 'one of the most emancipated of Indian women'.[40]

Section 6 of the Government of India Act, 1935, qualified electors on the indexes of property, taxation and literacy. After the Act of 1935, the proportion became one woman to five men in an electorate of 35 million voters. Women over twenty-one years of age who owned property or were literate or were the wives or widows of rich men owning property were allowed to vote.

A few Indian women fought for voting rights, while some contested elections. Kamaladevi Chattopadhyay was the first woman to open the doors for women to contest elections under the Montford Act of 1919. She fought the election in 1926 after securing a ticket from the Congress. She was fully aware of the challenge at hand and in her memoir, *Inner Recesses, Outer Spaces*, she wrote, 'It seemed too late and would need a bulldog's courage for a woman to venture into the fray.'[41]

Though she lost the election by just 55 votes, her historic step acted as an inspiration for many women. Muthulakshmi Reddy became India's first woman legislator in 1927 after winning the elections.

The data also shows that Indian women's representation in Parliament has increased since Independence, but it is not on a par with other countries globally.

Women MPs in the Lok Sabha had been between 5 and 10 per cent between 1952 and 2004. In the 2024 elections, 74 women were elected to the Lok Sabha along with 469 men. Women representation in Parliament stood at 13.6 per cent in 2024, which was lower than the 14.4 per cent representation in the 2019 Lok Sabha elections.[42]

In the 2024 general elections in the UK, 263 women (40 per cent) were elected to the House of Commons. The US House of Representatives has 29 per cent women representation and South Africa has 45 per cent.[43]

## Introduction of Panchayat and Municipality Elections

After Independence, Article 326 of the Indian Constitution permitted elections to the Lok Sabha and state legislative assemblies on the basis of universal adult suffrage, giving registered voters the right to 'one vote'.

Mahatma Gandhi did not support panchayat elections in the Constituent Assembly, though he promoted village swaraj in his speeches.

Post-Independence, panchayats were incorporated under Article 40 which provided that 'the State shall take steps to organise village panchayats and endow them with such powers and authority as may be necessary to enable them to function as units of self-government'.[44] As a result, the state had complete control over panchayats or the rural local government.

Since elections to the third tier, which includes panchayats or the rural local governments and municipalities, were dependent on the state, they faced multiple challenges: underrepresentation of women and those belonging to Scheduled Castes and Scheduled Tribes, irregular elections, inadequate devolution of powers and lack of financial resources.

The 73rd Constitutional Amendment Act was passed in 1992 and came into effect on 24 April 1993. This day is also celebrated as National Panchayati Raj Day. The Constitutional Amendment Act added Part IX, 'The Panchayats', to the Constitution which contained provisions from Articles 243 to 43O. On 27 August 2009, the Union Cabinet approved the proposal for an amendment to Article 243D of the Constitution of India to increase reservation for women from one-third (33 per cent) to 50 per cent in Panchayati Raj institutions.[45]

The State Election Commission (SEC) got the power to superintend, direct and control the preparation of the electoral rolls and conduct panchayat elections.[46] Article 243K(1) states that 'the superintendence, direction and control of the preparation of electoral rolls for and the conduct of all elections to the panchayats (municipalities under Article 243ZA) shall be vested in a State Election Commission consisting of a State Election Commissioner to be appointed by the Governor'.[47]

The delimitation of assembly and parliamentary constituencies takes place after 15–20 years, while panchayat and municipal council wards' delimitation is done almost after every census. The ECI and SEC prepare electoral rolls – the former prepares electoral rolls for the Lok Sabha and assembly elections while the latter prepares electoral rolls for panchayat and municipal elections.

## Political Funding

Over the years we have witnessed that the amount of money spent on election campaigns has been growing monumentally. In the 2024 Lok Sabha elections political parties used social media to connect with the public, not completely doing away with physical rallies. Money spent by political parties and their candidates on campaigns is the only visible expenditure, but there are other expenses incurred by political parties such as on inter-election maintenance of their organisations, political activities and support of research and information infrastructure for the parties.

Political donations received from big corporates and businesspeople are still a major source of funding for political parties. The second source of funding is giving election tickets to rich candidates who agree to spend crores in their constituency to win elections, without depending on the political party to fund them. In the process of giving tickets to rich candidates, political parties often ignore the criminal records of the candidate. As a result, in every election we have observed many political candidates undergoing trial for heinous criminal charges like rape, murder and extortion find means to contest elections.

Traditionally, political parties in India were financed through private donations; company donations were also considered legal provided the company declared the donation amount in their accounts. The need for election funding reforms stemmed from three primary reasons: penetration of black money, rising campaign costs and enhanced transparency in political donations for equal participation of the public in the election processes.

E. Sridharan in his paper 'Reforming Political Finance' wrote, 'The introduction of public funding in Germany by the Christian Democratic Adenauer government in 1959 was partly due to politicians' need for autonomy from financial supporters as well as the desire to reduce costs.'[48]

In the 1960s, concerns were raised by policymakers on the infiltration of 'black money' – money on which taxes have not been paid – in the election funding process. Two prominent reports – the Santhanam Committee on Prevention of Corruption (1964) and the Direct Taxes Enquiry Committee (1971), chaired by K.N. Wanchoo – drew attention to the problem of black money entering the political funding system.[49] Black money is generated when people and companies evade taxes. In the 1950s, policymakers levied high taxes, and as a result, big businesses started generating black money and a part of this was donated to political parties in return for favours, or quid pro quo.[50] This is true even today.

There was a limit on election expenditure since the Representation of the People Act, 1951. Interestingly, the then prime minister Indira Gandhi banned private company donations to political parties in 1968. Some said the reason behind this measure was to curb large business groups' influence on political parties, while some believed this measure was primarily to choke right-wing political parties' funding.[51] Since the corporate funding ban was not compensated with state funding, political parties' dependence on black money for election campaigns increased as there was no other legal or legitimate source of election funding.

In 1979 political parties were exempted from income and wealth taxes on the condition of filing annual returns including listing donations of ₹10,000 and above as well as sharing the identities of the donors.[52]

Section 239A of the Companies Act, 1956, as amended by the Companies (Amendment) Act of 1985, once again allowed company donations to political parties and individuals under certain conditions: a ceiling of 5 per cent of average net profit over the previous three years, approval of the board of directors of the company and disclosure of the political donations in the profit and loss statement submitted to the Income Tax Department.[53]

The Goswami Committee on Electoral Reforms was set up by the government in 1990 to analyse election funding. The report submitted did not support state funding, but allowed support in kind like vehicle fuel, rent charges for microphones, issue of voter identity slips and additional copies of the electoral rolls. However, it called for a ban on company donations to political parties, raising significant questions about how political parties would fund their expenses. The bill was introduced in Parliament on 30 May 1990 but lapsed.

In 1996 a public interest litigation (PIL) was filed by Common Cause, an NGO. In response the SC, through its judgement, issued notices to political parties to file returns by 20 February 1996 as per the Income Tax Act and Wealth Tax Act.[54] This brought in transparency in the political funding system because it compelled political parties to disclose their income and expenditures.

In the same year, based on the Goswami Committee's recommendations, the United Front government passed the Representation of People Act (Amendment Bill) that reduced the campaigning period from twenty-one days to fourteen.

The NDA made some significant amendments in the law in September 2003 that made political donations 100 per cent tax-deductible under Section 80GGB and 80GGC of the Income Tax Act. It also became mandatory for political parties to submit a list of political donors to the ECI under Section 28C of the Representation of the People Act, 1951. Section 13A of the Income Tax Act was amended; political parties had to now share the list of donors donating above ₹20,000 instead of above ₹10,000 as per the previous law.[55]

The election funding process has evolved in free India. The fear of black money in the political funding system, influence of big businesses on the ruling government, quid pro quo and misuse of political donations by political parties to pass on favours to big corporates existed then and exists even today. Hence, a lot of deliberations were made by think tanks over the decades to curtail the influx of black money, bring transparency in political funding and save democracy by holding free and fair elections.

# 2

# Bills to Be Paid

## The Costs of Running the 'Mother of Democracy'

### The Shiny Electoral Bonds: Scheme with a Leaky Cover

The thought of contesting elections must have crossed the minds of some honest people in India. It did cross mine during the Anna Hazare movement in 2011, but I did not for two reasons: first, I didn't want to be associated with any political party, and second, I could've contested elections as an independent candidate, but I didn't have the money or any other resources needed for it. As we all know, fighting an election requires loads of money and muscle power. These two requirements have probably stopped many honest and good citizens and good Samaritans of our country from contesting elections.

Our Parliament requires educated, young and visionary representatives; however, what we often get is criminals and wealthy millionaires governing our nation. Politicians need muscle and money power to bribe or threaten voters. Unfortunately, the ECI has no rules that stops candidates with ongoing criminal cases from contesting elections. As per Section 8 of the Representation of People Act, 1951, a person cannot contest election if he/she is convicted of 'certain offences' mentioned in the section.[1]

After analysing the self-sworn affidavits of 8,337 candidates out of 8,360 that contested in the 2024 Lok

Sabha elections, the Association for Democratic Reform (ADR) and National Election Watch (NEW) released some revealing data. Of the 8,337 candidates examined, 1,643 (20 per cent) had declared criminal cases against them. In the 2019 Lok Sabha elections, 1,500 candidates (19 per cent) out of 7,928 had declared criminal cases against them. ADR did a deeper analysis of the data and found that 1,191 (14 per cent) candidates contesting in the 2024 Lok Sabha elections had declared serious criminal cases including charges related to rape, murder, attempt to murder, kidnapping and crimes against women.[2]

Let's analyse the data on candidates with assets worth millions. Out of the 8,337 candidates of the 2024 Lok Sabha elections, 2,572 (31 per cent) were millionaires. The number of millionaire candidates contesting the Lok Sabha elections has steadily gone up since the 2009 elections. Clearly stated, the richer you are, the higher your chances of getting a ticket to contest in elections. Being rich has become an important qualification to be a politician.

India is in election mode almost every year. Pre-2014, Lok Sabha elections were a matter of national importance and Vidhan Sabha or state assembly elections were driven by local, ethnic and regional concerns. But ever since the BJP government has come to power, we have seen extensive involvement of Prime Minister Narendra Modi in all state assembly elections. Since PM Modi conducts rallies and campaigns for every state assembly election, it becomes national news and grabs everyone's attention.

What is a political party's source of income? The primary source of income is donations. This leads to two major questions: Who donates to political parties? Why does a corporate or an individual make political donations?

Anybody can donate to political parties – individuals, businessmen and big companies. People donate to a political party for two reasons: first, because an individual or a company adheres to a political party's ideology and wants to support it financially. Second, because the individual or the company stands to get some favour from the political party in return for donations. Sometimes, it could be for both the reasons.

In the first instance, an individual or a company shouldn't have any problem if their names come into the public domain. As we all know, giving donations to a political party is not an illegal or a criminal activity.

But in the second case, an individual or a company would not want anyone to know that they had donated to a particular party if they received a favour in return. Legally speaking, when a company or an individual engages in such an act, then they could face criminal charges for quid pro quo under the Prevention of Corruption Act, 1988.

Not all political parties can provide favours against donations. Only the ruling political parties at the Centre and in the states can pass on favours to companies that have made donations to them. Companies making substantial donations to political parties generally expect a government project, relief in an ongoing criminal case or changes in existing government policies that will lead to an increase in their profitability. All these favours can be granted to a company only by the ruling party.

What happens to those parties that are not in power at the Centre or in the state? Do they not get any donations? How do they fight elections? These political parties also receive donations, but the amount received by them could be a pittance compared to national or state political parties.

Why should political funding be transparent? Why do I, as a citizen, have the right to know who donated to what capacity and to which political party?

As per Section 29C of the Representation of the People Act, 1951, any donation above ₹20,000 received by a political party has to be declared to the ECI.

The party must disclose the donor's identity, amount received and other details in its report to the ECI every financial year.[3] These reports are uploaded on the ECI's websites to maintain transparency in the process of funding.

As a taxpayer and a voter of this country, we have the right to know how our tax money is utilised by the government – whether the amount is utilised in public welfare and building infrastructure or if it is misused by awarding government projects to ineligible and incompetent companies because they have donated to the government or because the owner is a relative of a powerful politician.

Bribes are often paid in cash. Simply put, it is black money. But the BJP government found a way that allowed political parties to take alleged bribes in white money through a banking channel. To do this, the BJP government made amendments to four acts in the Finance Bill of 2017 to introduce the 'Electoral Bonds Scheme'.

The amendments were made in the Reserve Bank of India Act, 1934, the Income Tax Act, 1961, the Representation of the People Act, 1951 and the Companies Act, 2013. Then finance minister Arun Jaitley said the main purpose of the government in bringing this scheme was to keep donors' identity anonymous and to channelise money through the banking system, thus preventing the penetration of black money into political funding. The government also stated that many donors have expressed concerns about being pressured by political parties for donations made to rival parties.

By keeping the names of the donors anonymous the scheme infringed upon the citizens' fundamental right to know and made the political funding system opaque. The unreasonable and irrational restriction on the right of the citizens to know about the donors of the bonds was a severe blow to the very fundamentals of transparency and accountability. It not only strengthened the political class but also made them more unanswerable and unaccountable, and that goes against democracy and the rule of law.

The flaws in the scheme along with the threat it posed to democracy did not go unnoticed by some government institutions like the Reserve Bank of India (RBI), the ECI and the Ministry of Law and Justice (MoLJ), and they raised objections to the scheme even before the electoral bonds were first sold in 2018.

These objections were made in strongly worded letters to the finance ministry warning about the potential threats of money laundering and penetration of black money into political funding if the bonds were to be sold.

But the finance ministry did not address the issue. These correspondences and the file notings on the scheme were accessed through several Right to Information (RTI) applications filed by transparency activists Commodore Lokesh Batra (retd) and Anjali Bhardwaj. Transparency activists file RTIs on various issues and demand transparency in governance and public policy. The information from the RTI documents on bonds was extensively reported by digital news platforms like The Quint and HuffPost. Though these correspondences were between the finance ministry and other entities in 2017, they were accessed through RTIs much later, in 2018.

A petition was filed by the ADR in the SC in September 2017 raising concerns about the amendments to various acts to introduce the electoral bonds scheme. Four amendments were introduced:

1. Section 31 of the Reserve Bank of India Act, 1934 through Part III, Section 135 of the Finance Act, 2017;
2. Section 29C of the Representation of the People Act, 1951 through Part IV, Section 137 of the Finance Act, 2017;

3. Section 13A of the Income Tax Act, 1961 through Chapter III, Section 11 of the Finance Act, 2017;
4. Section 182 of the Companies Act, 2013 through Part XII, Section 154, the Finance Act, 2017

The petition said:

> The amendments introduced through the new Finance Act, 2017, by the Ministry of Finance, passed as a money bill thereby bypassing the Rajya Sabha, are unconstitutional and violate doctrines of separation of powers and citizens' fundamental right to information which are parts of the basic structure of the Constitution. The amendments are also patently arbitrary, capricious and discriminatory as they attempt to keep from the citizens crucial information regarding electoral funding.[4]

The petitioner prayed for a stay on the operation of the scheme. But this petition did not make much of a buzz in the media.

More on this in Chapter 4, but before that let me tell you how I discovered the unique hidden alphanumeric code embedded in the bonds.

## Revelation of a Unique Hidden Alphanumeric Code

Not many were aware about the electoral bonds scheme as there was little media coverage on it in 2017 and 2018.

I heard about the scheme for the first time in early 2018 from my editor-in-chief Raghav Bahl. I was working as an investigations editor with The Quint. During a meeting at the office, Bahl mentioned the scheme and told me to find out how the names of the donors were being kept anonymous.

Before getting into the workings of the scheme I would like to give my readers a sense of how the BJP government was gradually curbing press freedom in its first term from 2014 to 2019, especially after the BJP's massive victory in the 2017 state assembly elections in Uttar Pradesh.

The Paris-based Reporters Without Borders (RWB) an international non-profit and non-governmental organisation (NGO), in its 2018 annual World Press Freedom Index ranked India at 138 out of 180 countries: down two positions since 2017 – lower than Zimbabwe, Afghanistan and Myanmar. The report said, 'At least three of the journalists murdered in 2017 were targeted in connection with their work.' Gauri Lankesh, editor and publisher and critic of right-wing political ideology, was one of them.[5]

In June 2017, the NDTV news channel's offices and promoters' residences were raided after the Central Bureau of Investigation (CBI) registered a criminal case against NDTV founders Prannoy Roy and Radhika Roy in an alleged financial fraud case. In an interview, Prannoy Roy told the media, 'They're trying to tell us we can suppress you even if you have done nothing wrong … and to be clear, that is a signal for the entire free press of India.'[6] The raid at NDTV was probably the beginning of several raids on media organisations that followed in the coming years. Chapter 5 deals with curbing press freedom in India by the ruling BJP government.

Many news channels had more or less become the government's mouthpiece in the BJP's first term. While the godi (biased) media was gradually blacking out anti-government news and deflecting people from serious issues; digital news platforms were on the ascent and were becoming a bigger threat to the government. As the 2019 Lok Sabha elections neared, the government's control on media was increasing every day.

Despite fearing for their lives, many journalists were doing their jobs honestly but cautiously. Speaking about myself: earlier I would check and confirm any news with at least two sources before reporting them – it's a basic principle followed by all journalists. But in the BJP era, I started checking with at least five different sources to confirm any information before writing an article.

When Bahl assigned me this story, the electoral bonds scheme looked like any other financial scheme to me. The questions I was seeking an answer to were: Is the scheme really going to keep the donors' names anonymous? Would the bank not know who donated how much, and to which political party?

Any form of bank transaction can be tracked only if it has a unique transaction number: cheque numbers, bank account numbers and demand draft numbers, all are unique numbers to track any banking transaction.

I spoke to different sources in the SBI and the finance ministry to gather information on the bonds. All of them confirmed that there was no serial number on them. Just the date of the issuance was mentioned on the bonds since it was valid for only fifteen days. Hence purchasers of the bonds could not be tracked.

If no government institution, including the bank, was tracking the donor, it increased the danger of black money penetrating into the political funding system since it would be impossible to track who was donating the money, what the source of the money was and if the money circulating was laundered through a foreign company.

To get answers to these questions, I spoke to a few finance experts and officials at the Directorate of Enforcement (ED). Based on all the input and feedback, I filed my first story on the electoral bonds on 24 March 2018, titled 'Will Non-Serialised Electoral Bonds Enable Corruption?'[7]

According to the financial experts and ED officials, if the bonds did not carry a serial number it could lead to 'a potential misuse of these bonds to channelise black money and further corruption'.[8]

In March 2018 the government had sold the first tranche of electoral bonds and the second tranche was to be sold in April 2018. I had no clue about the unique hidden alphanumeric codes in the bonds and the intent of the government to use it as a tool to keep donors' names secret from the knowledge of the opposition political parties and from the public.

After writing my first article on the bonds I wanted to know more about the scheme. I asked my editor if I could buy a bond worth ₹1,000 as the SBI was going to sell it in the first week of April. After getting his approval, I went to the Shastri Bhawan branch of SBI in Delhi hoping to purchase a bond there. I chose this branch because many politicians and bureaucrats had their bank accounts here due to its proximity to most of the ministries and Parliament.

But surprisingly, the bank officials had never even heard about the electoral bonds scheme. I still remember their reactions: it was as if I was talking in a language alien to them.

I again contacted my SBI sources who had told me about the bonds initially. They told me that they were sold only at the Parliament Street branch of the SBI. At the bank, an employee instructed me to go to the fifth floor of the building to enquire about the bonds because even he was not aware of it.

When I reached the fifth floor, a bank official escorted me to the cabin of a senior official. I told the official that I wanted to purchase an electoral bond. He looked surprised and asked me who had told me about the scheme. I told him that I had read about it in news articles and found it to be an interesting mode of making political donations.

To convince him further I told him that I worked for a corporate entity and my bosses would like to make some donations through electoral bonds but only if it was confirmed that nobody could track the donor and the amount donated by him to a political party. Hence, my seniors had instructed me to buy a bond worth ₹1,000 in my name. The bank official asked me to fill a form with my name, address and some other personal information. I was asked for my original Aadhaar card and Permanent Account Number (PAN) card, and they made photocopies of the same. I gave a ₹1,000 cheque to pay for the bond. While the paperwork was going on, I checked with a bank official whether there was a serial number on the bond that could be tracked by the SBI or the government. I said that my boss wanted to donate some money to the opposition political party but didn't want the ruling government to know about it. Hence, he wanted to be very sure that he would not be tracked if he donated through the electoral bonds. I also added that my boss didn't want to make cash donations because of the risk involved. The official said that's why this scheme was launched: to protect the identity of the donor and to channelise donations via banks.

After I completed the paperwork, the banker told me to wait in the waiting area. Half an hour later, a lady came and handed me an envelope saying that the bond and a receipt for ₹1,000 were inside it. I couldn't wait to see the bond, so I pulled it out from the envelope right in front of her. I saw that the date of issuance, 5 April 2018, was written in red ink (see Appendix 1). I asked her if there was a serial number on the bond, and she said no. She reconfirmed that only the issuance date was written on the bond due to its fifteen-day validity.

I looked at the bond minutely and I found nothing unusual nor a serial number on it. It was 5 p.m. by then so I headed home. I showed the bond to my editor the next day and told him that there was no serial number on it, and it seemed to me that the scheme was fulfilling its purpose.

I looked at the bond under a tube light and under the sun – just the way we look at a currency note – but I could see no serial number on it.

I was disappointed because there was no story to write, but at the same time something did not seem right. The overcautious behaviour of the bank employees, who looked suspiciously at me, didn't sit well with me. I slept over the matter. The next day was a Saturday, and I was at home when suddenly the thought of getting a forensic test done of the bond crossed my mind. Just a few weeks ago I had visited a forensic test lab in Delhi, Truth Labs, the first independent forensic science laboratory, set up in 2007 in Hyderabad, in connection with a different story.

Excited about pursuing this thought, I immediately texted Raghav Bahl and sought permission to get a forensic test of the bond just to rule out that there wasn't anything hidden in the bond that was not visible to the naked eye. He gave me the go-ahead and I quickly contacted the forensic test lab and briefed them about my requirements.

When I showed the electoral bonds to the manager of the lab, she looked a bit worried. She had not heard about this scheme, but she understood that it had something to do with the Central government. When I told her that I just wanted to check whether there was any hidden serial number in the bond, she asked me why I wanted to check it and what difference it would make. I told her that this bond was meant for political donations and the government said that the identity of the donors would remain anonymous.

The manager knew me as an investigative journalist working with The Quint. She told me that she had to check with her boss whether she could do a forensic test on the bond. Upon asking why she required permission to conduct the test, she said that it was because it was related to a government scheme and that their report could be cited on different legal platforms and might reach the courts, if the situation demanded.

After a brief pause I asked if she could just check whether there was any hidden number in the bond. If there wasn't any serial number, then I would not need an official forensic test report, and she wouldn't need to talk to her boss. But if there was a hidden number then I would definitely need a report from the lab. Since she knew me, she agreed to check the bond.

I impatiently waited at the lab's reception while the manager went inside to check the bond. She came back fifteen minutes later and said a unique hidden alphanumeric code was embedded in the bond. I requested the manager to speak to her boss and get approval to carry out a forensic test.

I had never called my editor during a weekend. And whenever I had called him in the past I had always texted him first with the request to call him. But that day was an exception. I called him and informed him about the unique hidden alphanumeric code on the bond. I informed him about the lab manager's concerns on giving me an official forensic report on it, although she had unofficially confirmed that there was a number.

Now it was clear that there was a hidden number in the bond, but to prove that it was a unique number I would need to buy another bond. I informed my editor that I was going to buy another bond to prove beyond doubt that these hidden alphanumeric codes embedded in the bonds were unique.

The lab manager came back with a positive response. Her boss had given the permission to provide a forensic test report on the bonds. She checked with me the purpose of the forensic test. I told her that I would write a news piece on The Quint news portal and I wouldn't write this article without a forensic report as evidence. She asked me again if it would be submitted in court in the future. I told her that I didn't know and neither could I give a hypothetical answer.

I knew that Truth Labs would not refuse to give me a forensic report on the bonds (see Appendix 2). I had heard high praise about the chairman of the lab, former Inspector General of Police (IGP) Dr Gandhi P.C. Kaza, who was known for his stellar work and integrity.

Before leaving the lab, I informed the manager that I would buy one more bond on Monday and give it to her for the forensic test.

On Monday, 9 April I reached the SBI at 10.30 a.m. to purchase another bond. The officer was surprised to see me again so soon at the bank. He asked me whether I had donated the bond to the political party and whether my boss liked the scheme. I said that the boss loved the scheme and wanted me to buy one more bond worth ₹1,000. He asked me why only ₹1,000 and not more. I told him I didn't know. He didn't ask any further questions and started the process of issuing another bond to me. I was thrilled to buy another bond as I was very sure that the numbers would be unique.

From the bank I went straight to the lab and handed over the second bond for the test. I collected the forensic reports of both the bonds on Tuesday, 10 April. I saw that apart from the unique alphanumeric code on the bonds, there were other security features in the form of designs embedded in the bond which were visible only under ultraviolet rays.

I wrote to the finance ministry asking them about the hidden alphanumeric code embedded in the electoral bonds and its purpose. Was this number recorded by the SBI before issuing the bond to the purchaser? Did the

SBI secretly track the electoral bonds' donors' donations to political parties? I waited for the response for about twenty-four hours but didn't get one. I then published an article explaining how the government had misled the public by saying that the bonds would keep the identities of the donors anonymous and that the government was doing secret policing on them. My article's headline was 'Secret Policing? The Quint Exposed Electoral Bonds Carry Hidden Numbers'.[9]

The finance ministry did not reply to my questions by email, but instead issued a press release admitting that there was a unique hidden code embedded in the bonds which was just a security feature and 'not noted by the State Bank of India in any record associated with a buyer or a political party depositing a particular electoral bond'.[10] I wrote another piece rebutting the finance ministry's statement with the headline 'Mr Jaitley, Your Ministry's Statement on Electoral Bond Is Flawed', where I raised the following points:[11]

1. If the hidden number is a security feature, then why is it unique? The government could've hidden a common number, or a common pattern, in all bonds to achieve the aim of preventing forgery. To prevent forgery, where was the need for these hidden numbers to be unique?
2. Why do you need to add a unique hidden alphanumeric serial number as a security feature? There are already several other watermarks present on the bonds that serve as security features. What is the use of another hidden one?
3. If the RBI has not embedded hidden serial numbers in our currency, why are they required on electoral bonds? Like the bonds, Indian currency already carries several watermarks which are visible to naked eye if looked at against the light. Is the government trying to

> say that the electoral bonds (which expire in 15 days) are more valuable than Indian currency?

I also wrote that if the unique hidden alphanumeric codes were not noted by the SBI, then why did the number exist on the bonds? If the SBI was not recording the unique hidden alphanumeric codes, then how would it be used as a security feature because the genuineness of the bonds could be confirmed only if the numbers were recorded.

As expected, the finance ministry did not react to my article. But this was just the beginning of a long battle.

# 3

# The Spectre of Democratic Backsliding

'Freedom of the press is not just important to democracy, it is democracy,' said American journalist and news broadcaster Walter Cronkite[1] who in 1981 was awarded the Presidential Medal of Freedom by President Jimmy Carter.

The press is seen as the fourth pillar of democracy. It is the duty of the press to serve the governed and not those governing. Similarly, it is the responsibility of the journalist to work in public interest and highlight issues that require corrective measures for the betterment of society at large. Media then acts as a guardian and a mouthpiece of the public, keeping a check on the workings of the government.

I have spent over twenty years in journalism, but never have I felt as suffocated as I have been feeling for the past few years. Earlier, when I pitched an investigative story to my editor, the risk assessment would largely circle around factors like physical harm by the wrongdoer, defamation case and harm to the victim's family. If the story happened to be against a minister or a politician, then the editor had to ensure that all the right questions were sent to the minister or the politician and enough time was given for a reply. No editor would discourage a journalist from pursuing a story against the government because of the fear of facing a criminal charge, being raided by the Income Tax Department or getting trolled on the social media platform X (formerly Twitter).

Often, the journalist in the field faces the wrath and the rage of the public; for instance, in the 2020 farmers' protest; a few journalists were stopped from reporting by the farmers because their channels were allegedly favouring the government and portraying the protest negatively. Field journalists gather facts correctly and report them back to their editors who are working from the office.

Since the news on TV is aired in real time, the editor of the newsroom has the power to present facts in a raw manner or to dilute them with biases. Sometimes, field reporters confront their bosses but mostly they choose to remain quiet because it might cost them the job.

When I started my journalistic career, the United Progressive Alliance (UPA) government, led by the Indian National Congress (INC), was in power. I have spent the first ten years of my career in a highly competitive atmosphere. Journalists seemed to be eager for a scoop or a beat and would be under constant pressure from their editors for an exclusive story. During the UPA years, journalists had their biases and favoured some politicians and bureaucrats, but it was not overt. Now, in the BJP regime, almost all journalists are labelled pro-fascist or pro-liberal, pro-BJP or pro-Congress, pro-Modi or anti-Modi.

The so-called mainstream media like TV news channels and some newspapers are termed 'godi media' – a phrase coined by the Magsaysay award-winning journalist Ravish Kumar in 2014.[2] The word 'godi' means 'lap', referring to the media that had become a mouthpiece of the government.

Let's take a look at some published statistics on press freedom in India over the past two decades. In the World Press Freedom Index, India stood at the 80th position out of 139 countries in 2002. According to the report released by the global media overseer Reporters Without Borders,[3] it slipped to 128th position out of 167 countries in 2023.[4]

During the UPA government's tenure between 2004 and 2009, the position improved to 105th out of 180 countries in 2009. However, in the second UPA government tenure, the index saw a major slip from 105th to 122nd position in 2010 'mainly due to extreme violence in Kashmir', as per the report.[5]

In 2011–12, the index further slipped to 131st position because: journalists were exposed to violence stemming from the persistent conflicts in the states of Chhattisgarh and Jammu and Kashmir. The threat from mafia groups operating in the main cities of the country also contributed to self-censorship. However, the authorities were no better. In May, they unveiled the 'Information Technology Rules 2011,' which have dangerous implications for online freedom of expression. Foreign reporters saw their visa requests turned down or were pressured to provide positive coverage,' mentioned the report.[6]

In 2013, India's position slipped further to 140th. This was attributed to Indian authorities' insistence on 'censoring the Web and imposing more and more taboos, while violence against journalists goes unpunished and the regions of Kashmir and Chhattisgarh become increasingly isolated'.[7]

During the first tenure of the BJP-led government the index stayed at 140th position till 2019, but it slipped to 159th position out of 180 countries in 2024. In fact, Pakistan stands above India at 152nd position.

The RWB stated, 'With violence against journalists, highly concentrated media ownership, and political alignment, press freedom is in crisis in "the world's largest democracy", ruled since 2014 by Prime Minister Narendra Modi, leader of the Bharatiya Janata Party (BJP) and embodiment of the Hindu nationalist right.'[8]

Commenting on the ownership of the media by big business tycoons, the report said, 'India's media has fallen into an "unofficial state of emergency" since Narendra Modi came to power in 2014 and engineered a spectacular rapprochement between his party, the BJP, and the big families dominating the media. Reliance Industries group's magnate Mukesh Ambani, a personal friend of the prime minister, owns more than 70 media outlets that are followed by at least 800 million Indians. The NDTV channel's acquisition at the end of 2022 by Gautam Adani, a tycoon who is also close to Modi, signalled the end of pluralism in the mainstream media.'

The RWB's report said: 'Indian journalists who are very critical of the government are subjected to harassment campaigns by BJP-backed trolls.'[9] It is very true. I have been trolled on X and I know many journalists who are trolled on a regular basis. Most journalists who were victims of harassment by the alleged trolls of the BJP IT Cell did not know how to deal with the situation in the early days when they were subjected to abuses, threats and warnings. Many would end up responding to abusive and humiliating messages on X, which would lead to further harassment. This was the biggest mistake. We eventually learnt that the best way to deal with trolls was not to respond to them. Things changed after a while. Not only did trolls harass and discredit the journalist in public by circulating fake news but pro-BJP digital news media and a few other YouTube channels took to publishing articles and videos disgracing journalists who raised their voices to speak the truth. Some trolls even filed online police complaints against journalists on baseless charges just to traumatise and intimidate them.

In July 2024, the Delhi High Court ordered the Kerala-based news channels Karma News and Janam TV and the newspaper *Janambhumi*, to remove nine YouTube videos and news articles containing statements that amounted to defamation against Dhanya Rajendran, senior journalist and founder of the news web portal The News Minute. The interim injunction order was issued following a petition filed by Rajendran in the Delhi High Court. Additionally, the web portal Newslaundry had filed a separate petition in the high court in 2023 regarding a similar matter. In both petitions the petitioners argued that these digital outlets published reports, both in print and online, claiming that the intent of the petitioners was to separate the country and divide India into North and South, thereby creating a 'United States of India' or 'South India.' The digital platforms also alleged that the petitioners were funded by the American billionaire and philanthropist George Soros.[10]

In recent years, India's ranking has been declining on global indices in reports prepared by international think tanks that focus on subjects like democracy, press freedom, civil liberties and fundamental rights. These global indices cannot be ignored as their inputs are incorporated into the World Bank's World Governance Indicators[11] that, in turn, have 18–20 per cent weightage in sovereign ratings.[12] Let us look into four such indices.

The World Justice Project (WJP), an independent international civil society organisation that works, among others, to 'stimulate action to advance the rule of law worldwide', released its first report in 2015.

One of the factors for its survey was 'Open Government', which measured the openness of a government defined by the extent to which a government shares information (with the public), empowers people with tools to hold the government accountable and encourages participation of citizens in public policy deliberations.[13] In 2015, India stood at 37th position out of 102 countries on this factor. In 2023, India slipped to 42nd position out of 142 countries.

The Economist Intelligence Unit (EIU) is the research and analysis division of The Economist group. It has been publishing a Democracy Index since 2006. The index provides a picture of the state of democracy in 165 independent states and two territories. The index is based on five categories – electoral process and pluralism, functioning of government, political participation, political culture and civil liberties.

India has been falling in the 'flawed democracy' category since 2006. India's rank deteriorated from 27th in 2014 to 53rd in 2020. It improved slightly to 46th in 2021.[14] The overall score that stood at 7.68 in 2006 fell drastically to 6.91 in 2021 but saw an improvement in 2023, when the score was 7.18.[15]

'Improvements are not always what they seem,'[16] said the EIU report. It further elaborated that 'India's scores for functioning of government and political culture improved, but its civil liberties score declined'. It pointed out that the decline in the civil liberties score was due to the Manipur violence and the government's failure in protecting minority rights. The report added, 'Media blackouts are also common in regions with secessionist movements, including Kashmir, and regional governments increasingly justify curbs on freedom of speech on the grounds of challenging disinformation and safeguarding national security.'[17]

The Varieties of Democracy (V-DEM) rankings are published by the Varieties of Democracy Institute, an independent research institute, at the University of Gothenburg in Sweden.

According to the V-DEM 2023 report, India's rank has fallen under all six measures of the index since 2017. Under the 'Liberal Democracy Index' India stood at 70th position in 2017 and fell to 104th in 2023. The 'Electoral Democracy Index' fell steeply from the 73rd rank in 2017 to 110th in 2023 , the 'Participatory Component Index' declined from the 62nd position in 2017 to 103rd in 2023, the 'Liberal Component Index' that was at 76th position in 2017 came down to 92nd in 2023, the 'Deliberative Component Index' tumbled from the 76th rank in 2017 to 101st in 2023, and the 'Egalitarian Component Index' which was at 118th in 2017 was at 137th in 2023.[18]

The report pointed out that:

> India's process of autocratization begins in earnest from 2008 and characteristically proceeded in the incremental, slow-moving fashion of the 'third wave'. Over the years, India's autocratization process has been well documented, including gradual but substantial deterioration of freedom of expression, compromising independence of the media, crackdowns on social media, harassments of journalists critical of the government, as well as attacks on civil society and intimidation of the opposition. The ruling anti-pluralist, Hindu-nationalist Bharatiya Janata Party (BJP) with Prime Minister Modi at the helm has for example used laws of sedition, defamation and counterterrorism to silence critics. The BJP government undermined the constitution's commitment to secularism by amending the Unlawful Activities (Prevention) Act (UAPA) in 2019. The Modi-led government also continues to suppress the freedom of religion rights. Intimidation of political opponents and people protesting government policies, as well as silencing of dissent in academia, are now prevalent. India dropped down to electoral autocracy in 2018 and remains in this category by the end of 2023.[19]

India's score on the 'Freedom in the World' report has declined from 77 in 2018 to 66 in 2024.[20] If we analyse the graph closely, then a steep decline is observed in the score of civil liberties. It stood at 42 in 2018 and slipped to 33 in 2023. The political rights score fell from 35 out of 60 in 2018 to 33 out of 60 in 2023. India was considered a 'free' state in 2021 but has been degraded to 'partially free' status in the 2023 report.[21]

Some of the key elements that led to this decline as observed by Freedom House in the 'Freedom in the World' report in 2023 are:[22]

1. In January 2023 the central government used emergency powers to restrict access to a BBC documentary that examined whether Prime Minister Narendra Modi sufficiently endeavoured to stop interreligious conflicts in Gujarat in 2002 when he was the chief minister. In February, tax officials raided two of the BBC's India offices and questioned staff members
2. In March 2023 opposition leader Rahul Gandhi was disqualified from his seat in Parliament and received a two-year prison term for defaming Prime Minister Narendra Modi and others with the same last name. The SC suspended that conviction in August, allowing Gandhi to return to his seat
3. Hindu and Christian residents of the state of Manipur engaged in clashes beginning in May after [Kuki-Zo] Christians protested [the Meitei] Hindu ethnic group gaining scheduled tribe status. By late June, as many as 40,000 people had been displaced, with 160 deaths reported by mid-August
4. In September 2023 the landmark Women's Reservation Bill, which will reserve one–third of seats in the Lower House of Parliament and state assemblies for women was passed. The bill also mandates gender quotas for seats reserved for scheduled castes. However, its implementation, which relies on a census and redistricting cycle, is likely years away.[23]

The 2023 report gave a score of 2 out of 4 on the question 'Are there free and independent media?' It said:

> Attacks on press freedom have escalated dramatically under the Modi government, and reporting has become significantly less ambitious in recent years. Hindu nationalist campaigns aimed at discouraging forms of expression deemed 'antinational' have exacerbated self-censorship. Online disinformation from inauthentic sources is ubiquitous ahead of elections. Separately, revelations of close relationships between politicians, business executives, and lobbyists on one hand, and leading media personalities and owners of media outlets on the other, have dented public confidence in the press. Journalists risk harassment, death threats, and physical violence in the course of their work. Authorities have used security, defamation, sedition, hate-speech laws, and contempt-of-court charges to quiet critical voices in the media.[24]

The report gave a score of 3 out of 4 to India on the question 'Does the government operate with openness and transparency?' Making an observation on the RTI Act, the 'Freedom in the World' says:

> Millions of requests are made annually under the 2005 Right to Information (RTI) Act, and responses have been used to improve transparency and expose corrupt activities. However, most requesters do not receive the information sought, including those seeking information about core government policies, and noncompliant officials generally go unpunished. Dozens of right-to-information users and activists have been murdered since the RTI Act's introduction, and hundreds have been assaulted or harassed. National and state-level information commissions are hampered by staff vacancies.
>
> The government has used the RTI Act for political purposes or has otherwise weakened the legislation in

> recent years. In 2019, Parliament amended the RTI Act to place the salaries and tenures of the central and state-level information commissioners under the control of the central government.'

Indeed, the RTI Act has seen a setback over the years. Accessing information under the RTI is extremely difficult, but this didn't stop some RTI and transparency activists from filing RTI applications with the authorities.

I sometimes wonder how the transparency activists managed to access crucial information and documents on the electoral bonds under the RTI from 2018, even after facing significant resistance from every government authority. Those bureaucrats perhaps failed to grasp the importance of the file notings they shared under the RTI. These documents and information obtained under the RTI became crucial evidence in court, leading to the SC declaring electoral bonds 'unconstitutional'.

## Objections Raised on the Electoral Bonds Schemes

The electoral bonds scheme was a perfect example of 'saam daam dand bhed' (getting the task done at any cost) adopted by the team of bureaucrats tasked with implementing the scheme, regardless of objections raised by major government bodies.

The ECI and the RBI raised major concerns about the issuance of the bonds. But the finance ministry's bureaucrats, under the supervision of the then finance minister Arun Jaitley, navigated their way around these concerns, finally introducing the scheme in 2017 and selling the first tranche of bonds in March 2018 as a means to facilitate donations to political parties.

Can we say the ruling party, the BJP, was desperate to implement the bonds scheme? I leave this to my readers to decide after they have finished reading the chapter.

The ECI is a constitutional body, and its primary task is to conduct elections in a free, fair and transparent manner across the country. As we know, a huge sum of money is spent on elections, both in parliamentary and assembly elections. It is the responsibility of the ECI to monitor the flow of funds to political parties.

'The use of black funds in elections reinforces illegality in society and thereby undermines representation and democracy,' said retired Prof. Arun Kumar of Jawaharlal Nehru University, Delhi, in an article in *The Leaflet*.[25]

There are no free lunches in this world – the business houses funding political parties in crores, through black money or otherwise, certainly expect favours in return if the party is ruling the country or a state. In legal language, this is termed 'quid pro quo'. In exchange for these donations to political parties, the donors expect lucrative government contracts for their companies.

Black money has become an intrinsic part of our election process. No matter how much political parties promise to curb it when they come to power, in reality, no political party is willing to remove black money from our system. Unfortunately, contesting elections in the world's largest democracy requires huge amounts of money, making it difficult for capable candidates to participate. Instead, we see candidates with criminal records contesting elections. As a result, voters are sometimes left with no choice but to vote for the political party of their liking, rather than for a candidate who may have a long list of criminal cases against them.

Additionally, the ECI is supposed to be closely monitoring the election processes by maintaining transparency in the political funding system. But the electoral bonds scheme took this power away from it.

The BJP government amended Section 29C of the Representation of the People Act, 1951, to keep the identities of electoral bonds' donors hidden. With this amendment, the political parties were under no compulsion to share the details of their bond donors with the ECI. Parties were only required to mention the total amount they received through bonds in their annual report to the ECI, without any further information about the donor or the amount. This made the entire process of political funding opaque and crippled the ECI's powers, permitting political donations through bonds between corporates and political parties.

Criticising the government's step to amend the Act, the ECI wrote a three-page letter on 26 May 2017 to the MoLJ stating, 'This is a retrograde step as far as transparency of donations is concerned and this proviso needs to be withdrawn ...'[26]

A few other amendments were made in the 2017 Finance Bill, in anticipation of the launch of the electoral bonds scheme. The amendment to Section 182 of the Companies Act, 2013, removed the limit of 7.5 per cent of a company's net profit over the preceding three financial years for donations to political parties. The amendment also abolished the requirement for firms to declare their 'political contributions' in their profit and loss statements. Under the amended Act, the company was only required to declare the 'total amount' donated. The ECI strongly objected to this amendment saying, 'This [amendment] opens up the possibility of shell companies being set up for the sole purpose of making donations to political parties, with no other business of consequence having disbursable profits ... [and that it] would lead to increased use of black money for political funding through shell companies.'

The amendment to Section 182 of the Companies Act, 2013, was not just flawed but also rushed. A file noting dated 16 March 2017 accessed under the RTI Act revealed that the Ministry of Corporate Affairs (MoCA) held a meeting on 8 March 2017. According to the agenda of the meeting, issues like the role of independent directors in companies were to be discussed, but instead Section 182, which was not on the agenda, was amended. During this time, Finance Minister Arun Jaitley was also the minister of corporate affairs. Political donations or the electoral bonds scheme was not listed on the agenda for the meeting. Yet the file noting disclosed that 'informal discussions' about amending Section 182 had taken place between officers of the finance ministry's revenue department and the department of corporate affairs.[27]

According to an October 2013 ruling of the SC, any informal discussion among civil servants leading to serious decisions would be considered illegal and void. 'We are of the view that the civil servants cannot function on the basis of verbal or oral instructions, orders, suggestions, proposals, etc. and they must also be protected against wrongful and arbitrary pressure exerted by the administrative superiors, political executive, business and other vested interests,' the Court said in its judgement in *T.S.R. Subramanian* v. *Union of India*.[28]

In addition, the Central Secretariat Manual of Office Procedure issued by the Ministry of Personnel, Public Grievances and Pensions states that all discussions, including telephonic conversations, between two or more government officials from the same or different departments, and the conclusions they reach, must be recorded accurately on files.[29]

The BJP government faced no challenges when amending yet another Act to implement the electoral bonds scheme. The amendment to Section 13A of the Income Tax Act, 1961, allowed political parties to receive a maximum donation of up to ₹2,000 in cash. This amendment had nothing to do with the bonds; rather the ruling party sought to present these changes as efforts to enable more transparency within the political funding system.

However, the officers overlooked Section 29C of the Representation of the People Act, 1951, which directs political parties to declare to the ECI all cash donations exceeding ₹20,000. The ECI requested in its letter to bring the Income Tax Act and the Representation of the People Act, 1951, in alignment.

While the ECI's letter highlighted major flaws in the scheme, internal file notings of the RBI revealed even more issues.

In a letter to Finance Minister Arun Jaitley, RBI governor Urjit Patel said, 'Issue of EBs [electoral bonds] in scrip [physical] form is fraught with serious risk of money laundering ... If RBI agrees to issue EBs in scrip form, it will be accused of acquiescing in the process in spite of the risk that it would almost inevitably result in money laundering.'[30]

Many letters were exchanged between the finance ministry and the RBI governor, who insisted on issuing bonds in digital form instead of a physical one. But the government proceeded with the scheme and issued the bonds in physical form.

Patel wrote another letter on 14 September 2017 to the ministry and demanded to give the RBI the exclusive rights to sell the electoral bonds in a digital form. Patel's letter said:

> We wish to stress that RBI has to be the exclusive authorised entity to issue EBs (electoral bonds) and we strongly believe that the digital form of EBs will mitigate risks and help to put the reform agenda of the government on a firm footing ... The major objective of the electoral bonds scheme is to provide anonymity to persons making a contribution to political parties,

> we believe that this can be better achieved if electoral bonds are issued in electronic form with RBI as the depository.[31]

The RBI never challenged the scheme on grounds of opacity in the political funding system or its dangers to democracy. It focused on two main points: first, that bonds should be sold in digital form to mitigate the risk of money laundering, and second, to entrust the RBI with the right to sell the bonds.

However, the BJP government did not concede to the governor's demands. In response, the finance ministry explained, 'RBI's suggestion on issuance of electoral bonds in electronic (demat) format only with the bond holders sharing unique identifier with the political party may take away a key feature of the Scheme to protect the identity of the donor from the political parties.'[32]

Patel was not ready to give up. On 27 September 2017 he wrote another letter, once again emphasising that the bonds should be issued digitally. He addressed the ministry's concern about protecting the identity of the donors, suggesting that this could be achieved by making the RBI the sole custodian of both donors' and receivers' information. Patel strongly argued that selling the bonds in a physical form could result in them exchanging hands several times before being donated to a political party, which would 'leave no trail of the transactions and in the process of providing anonymity to the contributor and to the political party, anonymity will be provided to several others in the chain of transfer of the electoral bonds. This can render the scheme open to abuse by unscrupulous elements.'

The truth in his argument was evident after the data on electoral bonds was shared by the SBI at the SC's order. I will discuss the electoral bonds data, along with the names of the donors and the recipients, in Chapter 6.

Instead of focusing on the seriousness of the RBI governor's argument, the BJP government pushed him to the margins. In a letter dated 5 October 2017 Subhash Chandra Garg, secretary of the Department of Economic Affairs, informed Patel that the government's stand remained unchanged, and the bonds would be issued in scrip form.

Patel ultimately relented and in an internal meeting on 18 October 2017 the RBI said, 'If the government decides to issue electoral bonds in a scrip form through SBI, the Bank should let it be.'[33]

The letter depicted the frustration of the RBI governor, but Garg understood the 'let it be' as the RBI's approval and went ahead to inform the finance ministry to approve the issuance.

The line of objections did not end with the RBI and the ECI – the MoLJ took up the issue on legal grounds, arguing that the bonds did not qualify as a 'promissory note'.[34]

Like the RBI, the MoLJ too expressed concerns about the bonds being sold in physical form. The ministry feared that it could be used as currency and potentially change hands several times before being donated to a political party. For instance, X might purchase a bond and hand it over to Y, telling him to donate it to political party A because X wanted to remain anonymous.

The bond scheme proposed that 'only political parties which obtained at least 1 per cent share of the electoral votes cast in the Lok Sabha elections or Vidhan Sabha elections'[35] would be eligible to receive electoral bonds. To implement this, the BJP government amended Section 29B of the Representation of the People Act, 1951, allowing every political party to accept any amount of contribution voluntarily offered by any person or company, other than a government company.

The BJP government spent taxpayers' money to print these bonds. The MoLJ objected, arguing that the money should be recovered from the purchasers of the bond, but it was a futile effort.

The SBI was the bank authorised to sell the bonds and was an important stakeholder in the entire scheme. An exchange between the SBI and the budget division under the finance ministry, received through RTI response, revealed that the bank demanded a unique serial number for primarily three reasons:[36]

1. Without serial numbers on the electoral bonds, there will be no audit trail available for internal control and reconciliation.
2. Branch cannot identify the genuineness of the electoral bonds. Any number of forged electoral bonds can be paid if the serial number is not captured in the system.
3. In case forged electoral bonds are paid and Law Enforcement Agencies or a Competent Court ask for details in this regard ... the Bank will not be able to provide any details about to whom it was issued and in which account it was encashed.

The budget division of the finance ministry agreed to the SBI's demands, stating:

> The issues raised by SBI are valid and a bond not having any unique serial number will create a lots [sic] of operational difficulties for the bank and will also bring a lots [sic] of risks the [sic] on bank. Forgery is a real concern which is available even in high security currency notes and this risk is more so in case of these bonds where value can be as high as Rs 1 crore. Bank may be allowed to put a serial number on the bonds to avoid these complication [sic] for the banks and also for the scheme. However, Bank [sic] may be advised to keep

> information highly confidential to prevent its leaking in any way.[37]

The SBI requested to 'capture' the serial number 'in the system' to which the finance ministry agreed in the notings on the condition that it would 'keep information highly confidential to prevent its leaking in any way'.

Two things are very clear: first, the finance ministry knew that the bonds contained unique serial numbers. Second, the SBI was recording the unique numbers before selling the bonds to audit the sale of bonds.

The BJP government admitted the existence of a unique hidden alphanumeric code embedded in the bonds after my exposé in The Quint in April 2018, but it continued to deny that the numbers were recorded or used to track donors. Senior BJP leader and Union minister Piyush Goyal, while speaking on the electoral bonds scheme at a press conference in November 2019, said, 'A serial number is put on the bond through an invisible ink so that there is no harassment to donors. This invisible number ensures that there will be an audit trail available for internal control and reconciliation.'[38]

An invisible ink is used to prevent donors' harassment – what does that mean? As Pluto once said, 'Those who are too smart to engage in politics are punished by being governed by those who are dumber.' It was not surprising to hear an unconvincing, or perhaps illogical, statement from a seasoned politician while defending his government's actions. It is a tragedy for our country that journalists, who are supposed to be the mouthpiece of the public, do not challenge such statements with counter-questions.

Lok Sabha elections were conducted in 2019 and many companies made donations to political parties through electoral bonds. The elections were to be held from April 2019 and on 5 March 2019 the ADR and Common Cause, an NGO, filed an application for a stay on the electoral bonds scheme. The SC heard the matter urgently and passed an interim order on 12 April 2019.[39] The SC did not impose a stay on the sale and purchase of the bonds but directed all political parties to submit the details of the donors to the ECI in a sealed envelope before 30 May 2019. Any sealed document can be opened only by the Court's order. The SC judgement was a small but important win which filled the petitioners and civil society with hope.

By May 2019 the BJP had come back in power with a sweeping majority. The godi media was more brazen than ever now.

# 4

# Electoral Bonds

## A Dummy's Guide

THE SC'S INTERIM ORDER[1] in April 2019 regarding the electoral bonds scheme gave some hope that, if not immediately, eventually the general public would learn the names of the donors of the electoral bonds. But who could have anticipated that the wait would be so long.

A three-judge bench, headed by the Chief Justice of India (CJI) Ranjan Gogoi, ordered political parties to submit the details of their electoral bonds donors in a sealed cover to the ECI by 30 My 2019. The order said:

> All the political parties who have received donations through Electoral Bonds to submit to the Election Commission of India in sealed cover, detailed particulars of the donors as against each Bond; the amount of each such bond and the full particulars of the credit received against each bond, namely, the particulars of the bank account to which the amount has been credited and the date of each such credit.[2]

The SC instructed that these sealed covers be held in the custody of the ECI until further orders. This was a victory for those advocating for transparency in political funding as a means to strengthen democracy. Securing this order from the SC required considerable patience and persistence.

While the opposition political parties were reluctant to take action, members of civil society and NGOs took initiative, filing petitions in the SC against the scheme. Below is a brief history of the series of petitions filed in an effort to protect democracy and demand transparency in political funding system.

The first Public Interest Litigation (PIL) concerning the electoral bonds scheme was filed by the ADR on 4 September 2017 in the SC.[3] The PIL argued that the four amendments introduced by the Finance Act, 2017, 'are patently arbitrary, capricious and discriminatory as they attempt to keep from the citizens crucial information regarding electoral funding'.

The petition contended that the new provisions of the Finance Act, 2017, – presented by the MoF and passed as a money bill bypassing the Rajya Sabha – 'are unconstitutional and in violation of doctrines of separation of powers and citizens' fundamental right to information which are parts of the basic structure of the Constitution'.

## What Is the Money Bill?

Article 110(1)(a)–(f) of the Constitution of India defines a money bill as a bill that only contains provisions dealing with one or more of six specific matters. These are taxation; borrowing by the government; custody of the consolidated fund or contingency fund, payment or withdrawal of money from such funds; appropriation from the consolidated fund; expenditure charged on the consolidated fund; and receipt on account of the consolidated fund or the public account and the audit of accounts of Union or the states.

Under Article 109, a money bill may only be introduced in the Lok Sabha. The Rajya Sabha is required to provide recommendations within fourteen days of the bill's passage in the Lok Sabha. The Lok Sabha may accept, partially accept, or reject the recommendations. Money bills deal 'only' with financial matters essential for the administration of the country.[4] This procedure requires only the approval of the Lok Sabha, where the ruling BJP government enjoyed a majority.[5]

By this definition, the electoral bonds scheme did not fit into the category of a money bill, as it pertained to the political funding system rather than the administration of the country. Nevertheless, the Finance Act, 2017, which introduced the electoral bonds system, was enacted as a money bill, bypassing the Rajya Sabha.

The ADR's petition stated that many 'Members of Parliament (MPs) of the Rajya Sabha showed their condescension in regard to the new Money Bill. The minutes of the Rajya Sabha proceedings were self-explanatory and attest the very fact that the aforesaid amendments [to implement the scheme] would bring turmoil and generate an insurmountable amount of black money in the electoral funding by making it more opaque and impervious.'[6]

The ADR's petition in September 2017 marked the beginning of the legal battle against the electoral bonds scheme in the SC which resulted in the court's judgement in February 2024. The main prayer of the petition was to strike down the Finance Act, 2017, that is, the electoral bonds scheme itself.

Based on the ADR's petition, the SC issued notices to various ministries and government bodies like the RBI and the ECI for their response. However, the ADR's petition received limited coverage in newspapers and digital news portals. It failed to create a public stir, and while the general public may not have fully understood the implications of the scheme, one would have expected the opposition parties to voice their concerns.

Only one political party spoke against the scheme: the Communist Party of India (Marxist) (CPI[M]). Late Sitaram Yechury, who was then general secretary of the CPI(M), filed a separate petition in the SC on 19 January 2018, calling for a striking down of the electoral bonds scheme. The CPI(M) was the only party that refused to accept donations through the bonds, and it took a strong stance against the scheme by filing a petition in the SC. The petition emphasised that the amendments made in the Finance Act, 2017, would 'jeopardise the very foundation of Indian Democracy'.[7] The CPI(M) petition warned of the inevitable consequences of these amendments, stating that they would lead to 'the destruction of the principle underlying Article 19(1)(a) and the concept of democratic institutions functioning for the interests of the people. Quid pro quo arrangements, not unknown to Indian polity, will only be strengthened.'[8]

The SBI started selling the electoral bonds at various branches located in cities across the country from March 2018. The BJP government ignored the pending petition and implemented the scheme as planned.

No one was aware of the unique hidden alphanumeric code embedded in the electoral bonds until March 2018. Unfortunately, even after my article on the unique hidden alphanumeric code published in April 2018, many political parties either couldn't understand the importance of the embedded code or were simply not bothered that their donors were being tracked by the ruling party.

A politician from the opposition party reached out to me after reading my article and requested that I show him the hidden aphanumeric code in the bonds. He informed me over a phone conversation that senior leaders of his party wished to highlight the issues related to electoral bonds. I was pleased that the opposition party was interested in this matter. Voices of concern raised in the public domain would help in expediting the hearing process in the SC, I hoped. Unfortunately, the opposition was neither strong nor active in 2018, but I went to meet him at his Delhi office with a lot of hope.

It was a forty-five-minute meeting where I explained how the ruling BJP was secretly tracking the donors of the electoral bonds through unique hidden alphanumeric codes, but the general public had no right to know about them. He acknowledged the seriousness of the matter, adding that political parties should boycott the scheme by not accepting donations through bonds. He assured me that he would speak with senior party leaders about the tracking done through the numbers on the bonds and would raise the matter in the Parliament. But this did not happen.

It was only civil society members, vigilant citizens and politicians like Sitaram Yechury and his party members who worried about the electoral bonds scheme, fully understanding the ulterior motives of the ruling BJP government leaders. Petitions filed by Yechury mentioned the dangers of quid pro quo and the formation of shell companies to route black money. Only in 2024 did we get to know for sure that those fears were real.

Even after my exposé the SBI continued to sell bonds and donors continued to purchase them despite fully understanding that there was a possibility of them being tracked by the government. This further proved that no political party was worried about the scheme or its flaws and all they were concerned about was the money they were receiving through the bonds.

After reviewing my articles and multiple petitions filed in the SC, two transparency activists, Commodore Lokesh Batra (retd) and Anjali Bhardwaj, filed RTI requests with ministries and bodies like the RBI, the SBI and the MoF to collect more information about the bonds. The ECI too raised objections to the scheme. Batra's and Bhardwaj's labour, patience and persistence in chasing RTI responses of ministries and government institutions exposed that almost every bureaucrat involved in the execution of the scheme had objected to it as I discussed in the previous chapter. Batra filed several RTIs every month to uncover other details related to the electoral bonds like the number and denomination of bonds sold in different tranches since March 2018. One RTI response revealed that 99.9 per cent of the bonds sold were denominations of ₹10 lakh and ₹1 crore,[9] indicating that most donors were big companies and not the general public.

Another RTI filed by Batra revealed that the printing of the electoral bonds was done with taxpayer's money. The Union government had incurred a bill of almost ₹14 crore that was to be paid with taxpayers' money.[10] The cost of printing one bond was ₹25 plus GST charges of 12 per cent levied by the Centre and the state governments, as reported by The Wire.[11]

Apart from me, a few other news organisations published multiple stories highlighting the bond issues, but they never gained the desired traction. I often wondered if it was because the scheme was difficult to follow and did not affect the general public directly or if there was a lack of awareness about the scheme because mainstream media did not focus enough on it.

The ADR filed more applications on the pending bonds petition in the SC to provide information on the issue. The first application was filed on 5 March 2019[12] in the SC, just a few weeks before the 2019 Lok Sabha elections began. It was filed by the senior advocate Prashant Bhushan's team on behalf of the ADR in continuation of the demand to impose a stay on the sale of the electoral bonds. This application cited various news articles and RTIs highlighting issues such as the BJP receiving almost 95 per cent of donations through electoral bonds in financial year 2017–18. The scheme permitted only quarterly sale of the bonds, but the SBI was selling it more frequently since the Lok Sabha elections were approaching. The application demanded an immediate stay on the scheme. This application, however, did not mention the existence of the unique hidden alphanumeric code.

The SC asked the political parties to submit the details of the electoral bonds donations in a sealed cover to the ECI by 30 May 2019. Complying with the SC's orders, political parties submitted information related to the electoral bonds with the ECI.

Batra filed an RTI application with the ECI, seeking information about the number of political parties that had submitted information on the bonds' donors. The ECI's response revealed that as many as 105 political parties had submitted a report to the ECI. But the RTI response raised further concerns and questions.

According to the electoral bonds scheme, only political parties which obtained at least 1 per cent share of the electoral votes cast in the Lok Sabha elections or Vidhan Sabha elections would be eligible to receive electoral bonds. The ECI in its RTI response revealed that 105 political parties had submitted responses on electoral bonds.

I carried out an investigation into these names in collaboration with the Reporters' Collective,[13] along with journalists Shreegireesh Jalihal and Somesh Jha. To our astonishment, after interviewing fifty-four registered but unrecognised parties, reviewing the correspondence they sent to the ECI and examining the annual audit reports of the political parties, we found only 17 political parties of the 105 had received funds through electoral bonds.

Advocate Baburam, founder of the Labour Samaj Party, one of the 105 political parties, said, 'I don't know what electoral bonds are. We haven't got any donations. I can show you our bank passbook. We have around seven hundred rupees in our bank account.'[14]

Rahul Mehta, founder and president of the Gujarat-based Right to Recall Party, also one of the 105 political parties, offered an interesting account. He claimed that when he checked with the State Election Commission about letter concerning electoral bonds donations, he was told that filing a reply to the ECI's letter was mandatory. He wrote to the ECI stating that his party had received 'nil', in other words no donations, through electoral bonds. It always amuses me to see how the bureaucracy operates, especially when it comes to logic and governance.

The ECI's letter to all political parties clearly instructed that those who had 'received donations through electoral bonds [were to] furnish the details of such donation along with detailed particulars of the donors against each bond'. Nowhere did the letter state that parties must submit a 'nil report' if they had not received any donations. Like Rahul Mehta, other small political parties too were not informed properly by SEC or ECI officials.

FIGURE 4.1 Submission of donations received through electoral bonds

**By Special Messenger/Camp Bag/Speed Post/e-mail**

# ELECTION COMMISSION OF INDIA

Nirvachan Sadan Ashoka Road, New Delhi-110001

| SANTOSH KUMAR | Phone-01123052102 |
|---|---|
| UNDER SECRETARY | E-mail-santosh.kumar77@eci.gov.in |

No.76/Transparency/2017/PPEMS/Vol.II Dated: 21st May, 2019

To

The General Secretary/Treasurer,
All Political Parties

**Subject: Submission of details in respect of electoral bonds-Regarding**

Sir/Madam,

Your attention is invited to the interim order passed by the Hon'ble Supreme Court in Association for Democratic Reforms Vs. Union of India, (Writ Petition (Civil) No.333) of 2015, dated 12.04.2019. As you may be aware, the Hon'ble Court has directed all the political parties which have received donations through Electoral Bonds, to furnish the details of such donation along with detailed particulars of the donors against each bond, the amount of each such bond and the full particulars of the credit received against each bond, namely, the particulars of the bank account to which the amount has been credited and the date of each such credit. The details of receipts through the scheme of Electoral Bonds till date are to be furnished to the Election Commission of India by 30.05.2019.

In view of the same, it is requested that the above-mentioned details may be submitted in a sealed cover on or before 30.05.2019 to the office of Election Commission of India, positively.

Your faithfully.

(SANTOSH KUMAR)
UNDER SECRETARY

**Post Script:-** The Information, as sought above, may be filed with/addressed to Sh. Santosh Kumar, Under Secretary, Room No. 508C, Election Commission of India, Nirvachan Sadan, Ashoka Road, New Delhi-110001 and should be clearly marked as "Confidential-Electoral Bond".

(SANTOSH KUMAR)
UNDER SECRETARY

*Source*: The Quint

The year 2019 was eventful in every sense of the word. While the electoral bonds case temporarily took a pause following the SC's interim order, another controversy emerged with the announcement of the 2019 general elections.

A wise man once told me, 'I trust you until you give me a reason to not trust you.' This is how generally most human beings function. The ECI has garnered the trust of voters and every stakeholder involved in the election process since its inception. However, lately, due to a lack of communication and clarity on pertinent issues, voters have begun to question the ECI's actions.

I, like many others, trusted the ECI. But my trust in the institution began to erode when I discovered a significant data mismatch in the 2018 Madhya Pradesh assembly elections that took place in November 2018.[15] I reported on it in February 2019. I may have been one of the first journalists to record a detailed analysis of the election data. I must mention my source, a young college student who reached out to me via social media, whom I will call Sameer to protect his identity. He urged me to examine the discrepancies in the numbers of EVM votes polled and EVM votes counted in the 2018 Madhya Pradesh assembly elections.

Initially, I dismissed his plea, possibly not fully comprehending the gravity of the story or simply not believing it. But Sameer later shared an Excel sheet, revealing a mismatch between the EVM votes polled and counted in the 2018 Madhya Pradesh assembly election. I assured him that I would analyse the EVM votes data and, if warranted, publish an article with the ECI's response. After reviewing the data I found there was indeed a mismatch in the vote totals across 204 of the 230 constituencies in Madhya Pradesh. What shocked me further was that in some constituencies the votes counted were in surplus, while in others they were in deficit.

The discrepancies ranged from a maximum of +2,605 votes to a deficit of −1,831 votes.[16] This data was derived by comparing two sets of figures: first, the total number of votes polled, and second, the total number of votes counted. This data was available on the ECI's website.

TABLE 4.1 Constituency-wise voter turnout report for Madhya Pradesh assembly elections 2018

| ASSEMBLY ELECTION 2018 – CONSTITUENCY WISE VOTER TURNOUT REPORT | | | | | | | | | | | | |
|---|---|---|---|---|---|---|---|---|---|---|---|---|
| AC No & Name | Electors | MALE | | | FEMALE | | | THIRD GENDER | | | TOTAL | |
| | | Voted | Turnout in (%) | Electors | Voted | Turnout in (%) | Electors | Voted | Turnout in (%) | Electors | Voted | Turnout in (%) |
| 1 – SHEOPUR | 117889 | 94177 | 79.89% | 106765 | 83112 | 77.85% | 1 | 0 | 0.00% | 224655 | 177289 | 78.92% |
| 2 – VIJAYPUR | 117528 | 91250 | 77.64% | 103300 | 81328 | 78.73% | 5 | 0 | 0.00% | 220833 | 172578 | 78.15% |
| 3 – SABALAGADH | 109497 | 81779 | 74.69% | 92656 | 69947 | 75.49% | 3 | 1 | 33.33% | 202156 | 151727 | 75.05% |
| 4 – JAURA | 123512 | 87756 | 71.05% | 101809 | 73026 | 71.73% | 16 | 3 | 18.75% | 225337 | 160785 | 71.35% |
| 5 – SUMAOLI | 123095 | 89751 | 72.91% | 98463 | 68461 | 69.53% | 12 | 1 | 8.33% | 221570 | 158213 | 71.41% |
| 6 – MORENA | 131472 | 83766 | 63.71% | 105128 | 65250 | 62.07% | 10 | 0 | 0.00% | 236610 | 149016 | 62.98% |
| 7 – DIMANI | 111075 | 79197 | 71.30% | 89228 | 61300 | 68.70% | 4 | 1 | 25.00% | 200307 | 140498 | 70.14% |
| 8 – AMBAH | 112927 | 69391 | 61.45% | 94625 | 54515 | 57.61% | 5 | 2 | 40.00% | 207557 | 123908 | 59.70% |
| 9 – ATER | 120114 | 74450 | 61.99% | 96131 | 60252 | 62.67% | 3 | 0 | 0.00% | 216248 | 134702 | 62.29% |
| 10 – BHIND | 138144 | 80443 | 58.23% | 111652 | 65840 | 58.98% | 4 | 1 | 25.00% | 249800 | 146284 | 58.56% |

*Source:* https://ceomadhyapradesh.nic.in/Election2018/ACReport.pdf

As shown in Table 4.1,[17] the ECI uploaded detailed data on the votes polled, breaking down the number of votes polled by voters identifying as male and female separately, along with the total number of votes polled.[18]

When I wrote to the ECI seeking a response regarding the discrepancies in the vote counts, I received the following reply:

> For a quick estimate of turnout, provisional data of votes casted collected within 24 hours of poll day 28 Nov & placed on CEO website. The votes polled are votes counted in EVMs on 11 Dec. There is only one figure of votes polled, i.e., votes counted in EVM. Hence there is no discrepancy.

I responded with a second set of questions. First, the data showed that the numbers were divided into three sections – male, female and third gender – which indicated that time and effort were devoted to preparing it. How is it possible that in some constituencies the discrepancy exceeds 2,500 votes, while in others there is no discrepancy at all? Second, why did the CEC upload incorrect or provisional data on its website? What was the urgency?

The ECI did not reply to these questions. I spoke with a few former CECs about the discrepancies, and they expressed surprise, suggesting that the ECI must conduct an internal enquiry into this matter.

This article was the beginning of my complex (and at times fraught) relationship with the ECI. Interestingly, we have yet to part ways.

As mentioned in the previous chapter, the ECI is required to follow the Representation of the People Act, 1951, to conduct parliamentary and assembly elections in the country. To understand how votes data is prepared and who are the election commission officers involved in the process, one has to deep dive into this Act. It is an Act to 'Provide for the conduct of elections to the Houses of Parliament and to the House or Houses of the Legislature of each State, the qualifications and disqualifications for membership of those Houses, the corrupt practices and other offences.'[19]

Here, I will primarily refer to Part IV – 'Administrative Machinery for the Conduct of Elections' and Part V – (Chapter 2) 'Candidates and Their Agents' of the Representation of the People Act, 1951.[20] These two parts focus on the election processes and the roles of the presiding officer, returning officers and polling agents.

## Who Is a Returning Officer?

The returning officer has a very important role in the management of the election process.[21] He oversees the election process in one constituency, or occasionally in two, as directed by the ECI. Under Sections 21 and 22 of the Representation of the People Act, 1951, the ECI appoints the returning officer and assistant returning officer for a constituency in consultation with the state governments or union territories, as applicable.

## Who Is a Presiding Officer?

A presiding officer is the most important officer at a polling station.[22] He has full legal authority to control the proceedings at the polling station and is responsible for all activities that take place there. It is his/her primary duty and responsibility to ensure a free and fair poll at his/her polling station.

## Who Is a Polling Agent?

A contesting candidate or their election agent may appoint, in the prescribed manner, a specified number of agents and relief agents to act as polling agents for the candidate at each polling station.[23] A polling agent represents the party candidate at the polling booth of a particular constituency. It is their responsibility to ensure that the polling process is conducted in a fair manner from start to finish. The polling agent is supposed to remain at the polling station until the polling is complete and collect all necessary information and documents from the presiding officer before leaving the booth.

The ECI follows the Conduct of Election Rules, 1961 to conduct elections in India. The rules outline the key terms used in elections, such as electoral roll, ballot box, polling station, VVPAT slips and the nomination process.

The Conduct of Election Rules, 1961 became the primary reference for many of my articles related to the ECI, EVM-VVPAT and the elections. Citing these election rules in my articles made them solid and indisputable, while also enhancing my understanding of the election process.

In addition to the Conduct of Election Rules, 1961, I frequently referred to other important sources for my articles, including the Handbook for Returning Officers, the Dos and Don'ts for Returning Officers, the Checklist for Returning Officers, the Handbook for Presiding Officers, the Dos and Don'ts for Presiding Officers, the Checklist for Presiding Officers, and several documents and journals related to EVM-VVPAT available on the ECI's website.

The 2019 Lok Sabha elections deepened my understanding of the Indian election process. The Madhya Pradesh assembly elections had already raised doubts for me about the polling and counting procedure followed by the ECI. I was closely monitoring the votes polled data from the start of the Lok Sabha elections. Little did I know that my investigation into the votes polled and counted data would have such a ripple effect – its impact was strongly felt in the 2024 Lok Sabha elections.

The 2019 Lok Sabha elections began on 11 April 2019. During the first phase of polling, the ECI declared the estimated voter turnout in percentages. I was disappointed to see the figures in percentages because I needed the figures in absolute numbers to compare the votes polled and counted data. Since I was covering the election process for the first time, I had no idea that the ECI would upload the votes polled data later. My source, Sameer, was also waiting for the votes polled data out of personal interest.

After the 2018 Madhya Pradesh assembly elections story, Sameer and I reconnected during the 2019 Lok Sabha elections. He called on 27 April 2019 to inform me that the ECI had uploaded the votes polled for the first two phases of the Lok Sabha elections on its website. Upon checking the ECI website, I found a moving ticker at the top stating 'Final Voter Turnout of Phase 1 and 2 of the 2019 Lok Sabha Elections'. I last downloaded the data on 25 May 2019, and it has been since removed from the ECI's website.

FIGURE 4.3 2019 Lok Sabha elections votes polled data for phases 1 and 2

SUVIDHA

**SECRETARIAT OF THE**
**ELECTION COMMISSION OF INDIA**
**Nirvachan Sadan, Ashoka Road, New Delhi-110001**

**User: ECI** **Date of Print: 27-Apr-2019 05:46 pm**

**Voter Turn Out - 69.50%**

**End of Poll Comparision- Phase: 1**

| State | PC No & Name | 2014 Elections | | | 2019 Elections | | | Change from 2014 |
|---|---|---|---|---|---|---|---|---|
| | | Total Elector | Total Voter | 2014 TURNOUT (in %) | Total Elector | Total Voter | 2019 TURNOUT (in %) | |
| Andaman & Nicobar Islands | 1 - Andaman & Nicobar Islands | 268940 | 190175 | 70.71 | 317878 | 207208 | 65.18 | -5.53 |
| Sub-Total | - | 268940 | 190175 | 70.71 | 317878 | 207208 | 65.18 | -5.53 |
| Andhra Pradesh | 1 - Aruku | 1383411 | 1046628 | 75.66 | 1449334 | 1067052 | 73.62 | -2.04 |
| Andhra Pradesh | 2 - Srikakulam | 1317586 | 975867 | 74.06 | 1540170 | 1140787 | 74.07 | 0.01 |
| Andhra Pradesh | 3 - Vizianagaram | 1519629 | 1056055 | 69.49 | 1499300 | 1207944 | 80.57 | 11.08 |
| Andhra Pradesh | 4 - Visakhapatnam | 1473969 | 1064268 | 72.20 | 1825769 | 1228070 | 67.26 | -4.94 |
| Andhra Pradesh | 5 - Anakapalli | 1555678 | 1137257 | 73.10 | 1517497 | 1228541 | 80.96 | 7.86 |
| Andhra Pradesh | 6 - Kakinada | 1857908 | 1299089 | 69.92 | 1563226 | 1225308 | 78.38 | 8.46 |
| Andhra Pradesh | 7 - Amalapuram | 2868094 | 1621505 | 56.54 | 1458788 | 1223856 | 83.90 | 27.36 |
| Andhra Pradesh | 8 - Rajahmundry | 2218189 | 1293240 | 58.30 | 1436010 | 1242742 | 86.54 | 28.24 |
| Andhra Pradesh | 9 - Narsapuram | 1825179 | 989164 | 54.20 | 1438922 | 1167811 | 81.16 | 26.96 |
| Andhra Pradesh | 10 - Eluru | 1838837 | 1008942 | 54.87 | 1594366 | 1321658 | 82.90 | 28.03 |
| Andhra Pradesh | 11 - Machilipatnam | 1511447 | 1010300 | 66.84 | 1472844 | 1234891 | 83.84 | 17 |
| Andhra Pradesh | 12 - Vijayawada | 1468813 | 1079044 | 73.46 | 1652662 | 1274904 | 77.14 | 3.68 |
| Andhra Pradesh | 13 - Guntur | 1459944 | 1166852 | 79.92 | 1704431 | 1338840 | 78.55 | -1.37 |
| Andhra Pradesh | 14 - Narasaraopet | 1468088 | 1191418 | 81.15 | 1669308 | 1427643 | 85.52 | 4.37 |
| Andhra Pradesh | 15 - Bapatla | 1527948 | 1150315 | 75.28 | 1464192 | 1252891 | 85.57 | 10.29 |
| Andhra Pradesh | 16 - Ongole | 1480712 | 1187326 | 80.19 | 1550067 | 1321109 | 85.23 | 5.04 |

SUVIDHA

**SECRETARIAT OF THE**
**ELECTION COMMISSION OF INDIA**
**Nirvachan Sadan, Ashoka Road, New Delhi-110001**

**User: ECI** **Date of Print: 27-Apr-2019 05:47 pm**

**Voter Turn Out - 69.44%**

**End of Poll Comparision- Phase: 2**

| State | PC No & Name | 2014 Elections | | | 2019 Elections | | | Change from 2014 |
|---|---|---|---|---|---|---|---|---|
| | | Total Elector | Total Voter | 2014 TURNOUT (in %) | Total Elector | Total Voter | 2019 TURNOUT (in %) | |
| Assam | 1 - Karimganj | 1164231 | 885823 | 76.09 | 1338005 | 1058086 | 79.08 | 2.99 |
| Assam | 2 - Silchar | 1056273 | 799540 | 75.69 | 1191289 | 945834 | 79.40 | 3.71 |
| Assam | 3 - Autonomous District | 701245 | 543408 | 77.49 | 795085 | 615944 | 77.47 | -0.02 |
| Assam | 8 - Mangaldoi | 1513151 | 1233145 | 81.50 | 1795529 | 1501008 | 83.60 | 2.1 |
| Assam | 10 - Nowgong | 1520615 | 1230000 | 80.89 | 1790683 | 1490560 | 83.24 | 2.35 |
| Sub-Total | - | 5955515 | 4691916 | 78.78 | 6910591 | 5611434 | 81.20 | 2.42 |
| Bihar | 10 - Kishanganj | 1438927 | 928202 | 64.51 | 1659461 | 1100843 | 66.34 | 1.83 |
| Bihar | 11 - Katihar | 1445491 | 975017 | 67.45 | 1652061 | 1116964 | 67.61 | 0.16 |
| Bihar | 12 - Purnia | 1582545 | 1016730 | 64.25 | 1763991 | 1153250 | 65.38 | 1.13 |
| Bihar | 26 - Bhagalpur | 1681880 | 973485 | 57.88 | 1819243 | 1039648 | 57.15 | -0.73 |
| Bihar | 27 - Banka | 1547702 | 899556 | 58.12 | 1696533 | 995274 | 58.67 | 0.55 |
| Sub-Total | - | 7696545 | 4792990 | 62.27 | 8591289 | 5405979 | 62.92 | 0.65 |
| Chhattisgarh | 6 - RAJNANDGAON | 1588647 | 1178345 | 74.17 | 1715492 | 1304324 | 76.03 | 1.86 |
| Chhattisgarh | 9 - MAHASAMUND | 1515460 | 1130800 | 74.62 | 1637002 | 1219725 | 74.51 | -0.11 |
| Chhattisgarh | 11 - KANKER | 1446490 | 1016630 | 70.28 | 1554995 | 1154259 | 74.23 | 3.95 |
| Sub-Total | - | 4550597 | 3325775 | 73.08 | 4907489 | 3678308 | 74.95 | 1.87 |
| Jammu & Kashmir | 2 - Srinagar | 1204958 | 309696 | 25.70 | 1293957 | 182190 | 14.08 | -11.62 |
| Jammu & Kashmir | 5 - Udhampur | 1476913 | 1055741 | 71.48 | 1665511 | 1169263 | 70.20 | -1.28 |
| Sub-Total | - | 2681871 | 1365437 | 50.91 | 2959468 | 1351453 | 45.67 | -5.24 |
| Karnataka | 15 - Udupi Chikmagalur | 1386516 | 1032871 | 74.49 | 1513231 | 1148700 | 75.91 | 1.42 |
| Karnataka | 16 - Hassan | 1559655 | 1146354 | 73.50 | 1650816 | 1272947 | 77.11 | 3.61 |
| Karnataka | 17 - Dakshina Kannada | 1564114 | 1207120 | 77.18 | 1724458 | 1343439 | 77.90 | 0.72 |
| Karnataka | 18 - Chitradurga | 1660917 | 1097380 | 66.07 | 1760111 | 1243502 | 70.65 | 4.58 |
| Karnataka | 19 - Tumkur | 1518144 | 1100874 | 72.51 | 1607991 | 1241578 | 77.21 | 4.7 |
| Karnataka | 20 - Mandya | 1668685 | 1191708 | 71.42 | 1711307 | 1372907 | 80.23 | 8.81 |
| Karnataka | 21 - Mysore | 1721197 | 1156799 | 67.21 | 1894379 | 1312844 | 69.30 | 2.09 |

*Source:* https://www.thequint.com/news/india/lok-sabha-election-results-2019-mismatch-in-votes-polled-and-counted-in-evm-on-multiple-seats#read-more

The data was uploaded sixteen days after the Phase 1 polling and nine days after the Phase 2 polling. The data provided a comparative analysis between 2014 and 2019 voter turnout, suggesting that a significant amount of time was spent by the ECI officials in preparing the data. As a result, it took several days to upload it. Similarly, the votes polled data for Phases 3 and 4 was uploaded on 4 May 2019, while the polling for these two phases took place on 23 and 29 April 2019 respectively. For some reason, the ECI did not upload the votes polled data of the remaining phases.

On 23 May 2019, the results of the Lok Sabha were announced, and once again, the Modi-led BJP secured a majority and formed the government for the second time.

My work of data analysis started after the release of the votes counted data on the ECI website. Sameer and I tallied the EVM votes polled and counted data of the four phases and found discrepancies in at least 373 parliamentary constituencies. Since the ECI did not upload the votes polled data for Phases 5, 6 and 7, we were unable to cross-check them with the votes counted data.

Of the 373 constituencies, more than 220 showed a surplus of votes counted and the remaining constituencies reflected a deficit.[24] The maximum surplus was 18,331 votes, while the maximum deficit was 19,776 votes. I found it hard to believe the data. How could it be possible that the numbers were not matching in any of the constituencies? I went through the data multiple times. I consulted a few experts who had worked with the ECI in the past to understand the reason. Their responses were uniform: it is not possible for the numbers not to match. One of them explained that the EVM operates like a metal handheld tally counter – if you punch it ten times, it will show the number ten. Similarly, if 1,000 votes were punched in one EVM, it should show exactly 1,000 votes polled and counted.

I pitched the story to Raghav Bahl at The Quint. His initial reaction in the editorial meeting was that the ECI had likely not counted a few EVM machines due to technical reasons, which could explain the deficit. I countered that it could be possible, but it did not account for the instances where the ECI counted more votes than were cast in constituencies. After discussing a few more details, he gave me the go-ahead to follow the story.

As journalists, we are skilled salespeople: we first sell our story ideas to our editors and then present the final article to our readers, packaging the news article in an engaging way.

While writing the article, I emailed a set of questions to the ECI for their response, within a specified time frame, and also attached the link from where I had accessed the votes polled and counted data. I also texted the ECI's public relations officer to inform my queries and requested a prompt response.

In an era where the audience's attention span is just six seconds, the way of storytelling has become important for engaging readers. Since this story was heavily focused on data analysis, I invested considerable effort into making the writing clear and the graphics accessible for easy understanding. One day I discovered that the votes polled data had been removed from the ECI website. Why had the ECI taken down the data? I sent a follow-up email to the ECI but received no response.

My article was published on The Quint website on Friday, 31 May 2019 with the headline 'EVM Vote Count Mismatch in 370+ Seats and EC Refuses to Explain'.[25] After publishing the article, I quickly packed my backpack and left for Triund in Himachal Pradesh with a small group of my gym friends. While travelling, I began receiving messages and calls from colleagues who informed me that the article was gaining traction; people were reading it and tweeting about it. I was happy – until I checked my X handle. The trolls on X were calling my article fake and accusing me of propaganda. Some right-wing digital platforms even published news pieces attempting to discredit my article.

I did not pay heed because my data was solid, and I had facts to back my claims. As I got further away from Delhi my mobile network got poorer. By the time I reached Dharamshala the next morning, I started receiving calls from several journalists asking about the data. I explained the source of the data and how I had tallied the votes polled and counted. A fact-checking website also reached out and I provided them with all the details, suggesting they analyse it independently.

The calls and enquiry about the article distracted me from trekking, but as I climbed up, my mobile phone lost network. I spent the night camping on the mountain and almost forgot about the article. But the transition from that blissful state to reality happened quickly. As I descended from the hills, my phone began buzzing with messages as soon as I reached a serviceable area.

I had to take calls from journalists and civil society members who were keen to understand the matter in more detail. Feeling responsible, I answered questions like: Does this mean EVMs were manipulated? Is my article only based on EVM votes or does it also include postal ballot votes? Why didn't I tally the votes for the remaining three phases?

While I was finishing my calls with the journalists, one of my colleagues texted to inform me that the ECI had issued a press release. I quickly called him, curious to learn what the ECI had to say about the vote discrepancies.

The release was a statement from the ECI on how it compiles EVM vote data during elections, but it did not address my article about vote discrepancies. The two main points in the release were, first, ECI claimed that in the 2014 Lok Sabha elections, it took them two-to-three months after the declaration of results to collect and collate the votes polled data in an authenticated form. Second, ECI had used 'innovative IT initiatives' in the 2019 Lok Sabha elections.

I did not rush into writing another article about the ECI's release. I decided to cut short my stay in Dharamshala and return to Delhi. The following day, I had a brief discussion with my seniors about the press release and I decided to check the 2014 Lok Sabha votes polled and counted data.

I published a follow-up article titled 'Is EC Misleading Public on How EVM Votes Polled Data Is Compiled?'[26] We found the ECI's claims were incorrect. While the ECI had claimed that it took it two-to-three months to upload the 2014 votes polled data, we found that the data had been uploaded on its website on 25 May 2014, nine days after the Lok Sabha elections results were announced on 16 May 2014.

The article also asked why the ECI was unable to upload accurate votes polled data within a shorter time frame if it had used 'innovative IT initiatives' in the 2019 Lok Sabha elections. Why did the ECI upload provisional votes polled data in the first place?

There has always been a great deal of controversy surrounding the EVMs. Given that I have written extensively on the EVM-VVPAT issue, people often ask me: Are EVMs hackable? Can EVMs be tampered with?

There is no one answer to these questions. I would like to ask my readers: Have you encountered any technology that cannot be tampered with? The answer is no. There is no device that cannot be tampered with. No one is claiming that EVM-VVPAT cannot be trusted, but it cannot be denied that it is vulnerable to manipulation.

# 5

# Once Bitten Twice Shy

## Public Institutions That Enabled It

I EMBARKED ON MY journalism career in 2004, driven by idealism and a deep desire to serve society by exposing systemic wrongdoings. My enthusiasm was fuelled by senior journalists in the field, photojournalists who would risk their life in war like situations. My initial passion was to study law; however, I reconsidered when learnt from my friends and family that courtroom arguments in Kolkata happened in Bengali. To pursue a legal career there, I would need to be fluent in the language. Little did I know at the time that my career would lead me to Delhi. Kolkata is my janmabhoomi (birthplace), but Delhi is my karmabhoomi (workplace).

When I started my career, journalism was a respected profession, unlike today, when journalists are looked at with suspicion and frequently labelled as either pro-government or anti-government. The term 'godi media' was non-existent then. There was considerable competition among journalists to uncover stories with meaningful impact. Most media outlets, whether newspapers or television channels, had a special investigative team (SIT) dedicated to delving deeper into stories exposing wrongdoings with caution and editorial checks and oversight.

I joined NDTV in October 2005 as a reporter responsible for covering a range of topics. Within a year I earned a position in NDTV's SIT after exposing corruption in the Indian judicial system. Some of you may remember the infamous 1999 BMW hit-and-run case, in which the prime accused was Sanjiv Nanda, the grandson of the former navy chief late Admiral S.M. Nanda Sanjiv. Sanjiv was convicted of mowing down six people with his car.

In 2007, I exposed senior advocate and former member of Rajya Sabha R.K. Anand for attempting to influence the prime witness in the BMW case. Anand, the defence lawyer of Sanjiv Nanda, was a very influential person both in the political and the legal spectrum. NDTV aired the story after thorough editorial and legal scrutiny of the facts. A few days later, Anand filed a defamation case in the SC against me and several senior management at NDTV like Prannoy Roy, Radhika Roy, Barkha Dutt and Sonia Singh. This was the first legal case against me. I was scared and nervous, but I also knew I had the support of one of India's largest news organisations. NDTV fought the case in SC which lasted for almost two years. We won the case and the SC stripped Anand of his designation of senior counsel. The SC said, '... NDTV rendered valuable service to the important public cause to protect and salvage the purity of the course of justice. We appreciate the professional initiative and courage shown by the young reporter Poonam Agarwal ...'[1]

This judgement came as a big relief to all of us. This story was a milestone achievement of my career. After this, I continued my journey as an investigative journalist. I switched to Times Now in 2009. Here I extensively reported many alleged scams, including the 2G spectrum scam, the coal scam and the Adarsh scam. During this period, there was a fearlessness among journalists reporting these issues, even though the scams involved politicians from the ruling government. The editors were cautious about publishing stories against the government, but they did not fear that the Income Tax Department officials might come knocking at their doors for criticising the government or exposing the ruling party politicians.

It might not be true for all media outlets, but in some organisations, it was an unsaid instruction from the editor that no story against the finance minister would be entertained. Why? Running a news media outlet is a business, and many businessmen have skeletons to hide.

That said, I enjoyed considerable freedom in reporting against the government until 2014. Journalists or media organisations were not openly labelled pro- or anti-government. Probably, no one thought that a change in the power at the Centre would also lead to a significant curb on press freedom. Soon, journalists would find themselves operating in an atmosphere of fear and hostility. The division among journalists would lead to the weakening of the nation's fourth pillar, and those who dared to report the truth would face dire consequences.

Since 2014, there has been a sharp rise in criminal cases lodged against journalists and media houses for their work. An analysis conducted by the Free Speech Collective shows that between 2010 and 2020, 154 journalists were arrested, detained, summoned and interrogated for their work in India.[2] Additionally, nine foreign journalists faced deportation, arrest, interrogations, or were denied entry into India. The COVID-19 pandemic turned out to be dire for journalists. They, like many others, faced illness, deaths, salary cuts and job losses. Criminal cases were registered against sixty-seven journalists in 2020 alone.

Among the states in India, Uttar Pradesh has excelled in curbing freedom of speech, making it the second most dangerous place in India for journalists, surpassed only by Kashmir.[3] A report published by the Committee Against Assault on Journalists (CAAJ)[4] on 10 February 2022 highlighted the situation in Uttar Pradesh: between 2017 and January 2022, twelve journalists were killed, forty-eight journalists were physically attacked, sixty-six faced FIRs and twelve were threatened or taken into custody.

Criminal charges and legal expenses affect a journalist's potential to report robustly and hinder the ability of the media to hold power accountable, threatening the foundation of democracy. Journalism is an underpaid profession for ground reporters. While the salaried journalists are protected and financially supported by the organisation if they are charged with a criminal case, independent journalists are vulnerable as they have neither financial nor organisational support.

I often tell my fellow journalists that you can write stories only if you are free and not behind bars. It then becomes essential to keep exposing and criticising the government, but always with calculated risks. And let's not forget that no one suffers alone; family and close friends also face the repercussions. I recall a very personal conversation with a veteran journalist who is currently facing multiple criminal litigations. He remarked, 'No one wants a freedom fighter like Bhagat Singh to be born in their house, but that doesn't mean they don't want Bhagat Singh in our society. The only condition is that he should be born in someone else's home, because no family wants to endure the agony of loss or harassment on their loved ones.' With a deep sense of guilt, he expressed that what troubles him the most is not the criminal case itself, but the pain his family experiences because of him. This conversation has stayed with me.

Many journalists, despite financial insecurity and other challenges, have opted for independent journalism in the past few years. There are two reasons for this: first, it gives them freedom to work on projects or stories of their choosing. If Indian media channels turn down a story pitch on the grounds that it is anti-government or they lack funds to commission the story, an independent journalist can pitch their pieces to international media organisations.

This provides a platform for voices that are silenced. Second, many journalists have begun to feel claustrophobic working within the godi media organisations, along with godi media editors and godi media anchors. This has led some journalists to quit journalism and opt for other professions, instead of compromising their values and principles. The curbing of freedom of the press and the pressure to abide by a certain pushed narrative introduced a troubling trend in media culture.

India is one of the largest media markets in the world, with thousands of registered newspapers and periodicals, over 900 private television channels and more than 1,000 radio stations operating in multiple languages. The country's media and entertainment industry was valued at over a trillion Indian rupees and is projected to grow because of a significant consumption of news, according to an article published by Statista,[5] a global data and business intelligence platform established in Germany in 2007.

The hostile takeover of NDTV by billionaire Gautam Adani in 2022 left many in the media community shocked and speechless. This acquisition marked the end of an era for NDTV, which was founded by Dr Prannoy Roy who is often regarded as the father of Indian television journalism. The Adani Group's acquirement of NDTV came just before the 2024 general elections, and current and former employees have reported that it instantly changed into a government mouthpiece. NDTV was known for its reputation of fearless independent journalism and was home to some of the finest anchors and journalists in the country. This shift raises concerns for those who valued press freedom and good journalism and casts a shadow on the future of independent journalism in the country.

After the Adani Group took over the management of NDTV, more than a dozen journalists left the news channel.[6] Some senior anchors, like Ravish Kumar, started their own YouTube channels after resigning from NDTV. In an interview to *Bloomberg* Kumar stated, 'Journalism is dead,'[7] reflecting the disillusionment felt by many in the field. Dr Prannoy Roy started deKoder one of India's first AI-powered digital content platforms, aimed to provide alternative media perspectives.

The Adani Group didn't stop with the purchase of NDTV. It launched two new regional channels, with plans for many more in the pipeline. In December 2023 the group purchased Indo-Asian News Service (IANS), one of India's oldest news agencies, raising even more concerns about the future of journalism.

Adani is not the only Indian billionaire to own big media operations. Mukesh Ambani, another prominent billionaire, entered the media industry earlier by acquiring the Network 18 Group in 2014. This gave him access to almost seventy media outlets across the country. While there are other business tycoons who own media outlets in India, what sets Adani and Ambani apart is their close association with Prime Minister Narendra Modi. Media reports indicate that Prime Minister Modi's government played a role in facilitating Adani's global business expansion. In January 2023, the US-based short-selling firm Hindenburg Research released a damning report alleging that the Adani Group was 'the largest con in corporate history'.[8] The Adani Group dismissed the Hindenburg report as 'baseless' and 'malicious'. Opposition political leaders raised questions about the relationship between Adani and Modi. Despite the damaging report, the Adani Group made a comeback and successfully attracted billions from foreign investors, including the US private equity firm GQG Partners.[9]

Many successful news channels, like Rajat Sharma's India TV, Arnab Goswami's Republic TV and Times Now owned by the Times Group, enjoy a huge following and are widely recognised as pro-Modi government news channels. Journalists working at these channels or wishing to join them often are in the position where they must accept that reporting anything condemning the current Modi government – even if it is factually correct – may not be published.

Aaj Tak and India Today, owned by Aroon Purie, have frequently lauded Narendra Modi. Purie expressed in one of his tweets, 'PM is a very farsighted person. Somebody who works with him told me that while his team is still collecting the dots, the Prime Minister has already CONNECTED the dots.'[10]

In addition to traditional news channels, the advent of smartphones and cheap mobile internet data has transformed the media outlook in recent years. Not only urban populations but also those in tier-3 and rural areas are consuming news through digital platforms like YouTube, Instagram and Facebook. The younger population that prefers to read and watch news online has become one of the largest consumers of digital news and videos.

Viewers increasingly choose their favourite digital news sources or YouTube journalists/influencers for news and opinions. A notable pattern has emerged on social media platforms, particularly YouTube, where the audience is sharply divided between pro-government/Modi and anti-government/Modi sentiments. A neutral audience is becoming increasingly rare. Digital spaces allow readers and viewers to consume news that aligns with their preferences, enabling them to filter out content that does not resonate with their views.

Since 2014–15, India has seen the emergence of almost a dozen digital news platforms including The Wire, The Quint, The News Minute, Newslaundry, ThePrint, NewsClick, Scroll, Article14 and The Reporters' Collective. These media outlets have established themselves as a major source of news consumption over the past decade. These subscription-based digital platforms provided impactful information as compared to many pro-government channels. Many audiences have shifted their attention from mainstream news channels to these digital platforms for more balanced news articles. However, the rise of these digital platforms has not gone unnoticed by the government, and it started relying on bodies like the CBI, ED and Income Tax Department to target and silence these digital media outlets by lodging criminal cases against many of them.

One such incident occurred on 11 October 2018 when the IT department conducted searches at The Quint's office and the residence of its owner and editor-in-chief Raghav Bahl. Parallel searches and surveys were conducted at the Bengaluru office of The News Minute as The Quint held stakes in the organisation. The IT officials allegedly investigated documents and other evidence related to cases of bogus long-term capital gains (LTCG) received by various beneficiaries.[11] The investigation timing of these news channels led to speculations about political motives against independent journalism. This additionally raised concerns over the future of dissenting voices in media and the country.

Raghav Bahl stated,

> All these and other gains/losses were fully detailed/declared in the appropriate year of tax filings; and more importantly, were accepted and assessed to tax, under this very government! So, the attempt to 'colour' our tax returns, now, as 'bogus', is clearly a frame-up, and we shall take every legal recourse to protect our fair name and reputation in this case.[12]

The Editors Guild of India issued a statement in support of The Quint asserting that 'the Guild believes that motivated income tax searches and surveys will seriously undermine media freedom and the government should desist from such attempts'.[13]

The digital media did not stop from being critical of the government even after the BJP government came back to power with full majority for the second time in 2019. Though there appeared to be considerable control over certain TV news channels and newspaper organisations, digital media platforms continued to enjoy freedom of speech. This situation did not sit well with the Modi-led government.

On 10 September 2021 the Income Tax Department conducted 'survey operations' at the premises of two digital platforms, NewsClick and Newslaundry.[14] The purpose of this was to verify certain tax payment details and other transactions made by these media outlets.

In a statement,[15] the Newslaundry editor-in-chief Abhinandan Sekhri said:

> A team from the Income Tax Department came to the registered office of Newslaundry at approximately 12.15 in the afternoon on the 10th of September and conducted a 'survey' under section 133 A as per the document shown to me. They left the premises at around 12.40 am on the 11th of September. I was told I cannot speak to my lawyer and have to hand over my phone. The team consisting of six or seven people was courteous and professional. I was told the law requires me to comply without seeking legal advice. They searched and looked through all computer devices at the premises. My personal mobile phone, laptop and a couple of office machines were taken control of and all the data on them downloaded by the IT team. In my understanding this (taking all data from my personal laptop and mobile phone) violates my fundamental right to privacy. No signed hash value of the data copied

was provided to me. Even so, we will deal with that later. This is the second visit by an IT team to my office, the first being in June.

Abhinandan Sekhri filed a petition against the 'survey operations', seeking for a direction to prevent the leakage of any material data, including private chats or communication obtained from personal mobile phones and laptops. Upon the seizure of data from Sekhri's phone, his lawyer informed the court that 'this breaches my right to privacy. The data may contain certain investigative stories that I may be doing, may be against the government, may be against other persons. It also contains a lot of my personal information.'[16] The lawyer further expressed concern over the fear of the data being leaked to third parties.

The Delhi High Court asked the Information Technology Department to ensure that Sekhri's personal data was not leaked. The court observed, 'We have seen it on channels, people's data that has been seized is openly being displayed, that should not happen. We don't know who leaks it. You will have to take precaution that it is not leaked. Give an undertaking that it will not be leaked.'[17]

In a statement released on 10 September 2021 the editor-in-chief of NewsClick, Prabir Purkayastha, observed that, like Newslaundry, the Income Tax Department had conducted a 'survey operation' at their office under Section 133A of the Information Technology Act. The officers impounded the editor's phone and took email dumps of senior employees, among other financial documents.

The statement added,

> The offices of NewsClick, as well as the residences of Prabir Purkayastha and other persons associated with us, were also raided earlier this year (2021) by the Enforcement Directorate. NewsClick has cooperated

> with the investigations by the Enforcement Directorate and Economic Offences Wing … These investigations by various agencies, and these selective allegations, are attempts to stifle the independent journalism of media organisations – including NewsClick.[18]

Earlier, in February 2021, the offices and residences of NewsClick editors' had been raided by ED in connection with an alleged money laundering case[19] and funding received by the organisation from supposedly dubious companies abroad.[20]

The DIGIPUB News India Foundation – formed by digital media organisations and freelancers of which Prabir Purkayastha was the vice chairperson – released a statement strongly condemning the ED's raid:

> DIGIPUB News India Foundation believes that the ED raids on NewsClick, its editor and directors, is a clear attempt to suppress journalism critical of the government and its allies. Such use of state agencies to intimidate journalists and suppress adversarial journalism is detrimental to not only the freedom of the press, but also the very idea of democratic accountability.[21]

Senior journalists showed their support for NewsClick by tweeting against the raids and emphasised how the ruling government was completely controlling and using investigating agencies as a means to harass media outlets critical of the government.

NewsClick continued to be the target of the government. After the raids by the ED, the Economic Offences Wing and Income Tax Department raids on 3 October 2023, the Special Cell of the Delhi Police – that investigates terrorism cases – conducted raids at various

NewsClick offices and residences of past and present employees, freelancers and consultants. Anyone who had ever been associated with the organisation was not spared. This time, the investigating agency not only questioned the employees for several hours but also arrested Prabir Purkayastha and administrative officer Amit Chakraborty. NewsClick issued a statement:

> We have not been provided with a copy of the FIR, or informed about the exact particulars of the offences with which we have been charged. Electronic devices were seized from the NewsClick premises and homes of employees, without any adherence to due process such as the provision of seizure memos, hash values of the seized data, or even copies of the data. NewsClick's office has also been sealed in a blatant attempt at preventing us from continuing our reporting. What we have been able to gather is that NewsClick stands accused of offences under the Unlawful Activities Prevention Act (UAPA), for purportedly carrying Chinese propaganda on its website.[22]

Commenting on the previous investigations, the release said:

> In the last two plus years, the Enforcement Directorate has not been able to file a complaint accusing NewsClick of money laundering. The Economic Offences Wing of Delhi Police has not been able to file a charge sheet against NewsClick for offences under the Indian Penal Code. The Income Tax Department has not been able to defend its actions before the courts of law. In the last several months, Prabir Purkayastha has not even been called in for questioning by any of these agencies.[23]

A report in the *New York Times* suggested that NewsClick was part of a Chinese propaganda network led by US businessman Neville Roy Singham. The article titled 'A Global Web of Chinese Propaganda Leads to a U.S. Tech Mogul' said, 'In New Delhi, corporate filings show Mr Singham's network financed a news site, NewsClick, that sprinkled its coverage with Chinese government talking points.'[24]

While seventy-three-year-old Purkayastha was in Tihar jail under the charges of Unlawful Activities (Prevention) Act, his health continued to deteriorate. The deplorable conditions of jails are known to all; for the well-connected politicians, all facilities are available at short notice, while for common folks, a jail is nothing short of torture.

After the Delhi High Court rejected his bail application on October 2023, Purkayastha filed a new bail application on medical grounds in the SC. Senior advocate Kapil Sibal represented Purkayastha and notified the court about the petitioner's deteriorating health ever since imprisonment. Purkayastha was suffering from shortness of breath due to a lung infection, hypertension and diabetes. But the jail report indicated no serious illness. Sibal demanded medical examination by the All India Institute of Medical Sciences (AIIMS). The SC directed a medical board of AIIMS to examine Purkayastha on 27 February 2024.[25]

The stage was set for the Lok Sabha elections by February 2024. The election dates were expected to be announced by the ECI, and the media was brutally suppressed by the government. Many other journalists, like Purkayastha, were imprisoned and treated like criminals.

During the 2024 Lok Sabha elections, the SC granted bail to Purkayastha. The bail order came as an affirmation that not all hope was lost and that truth needs no adornment.

The SC issued a strong bail order, stating that the Delhi Police had failed to inform Purkayastha of the grounds for his arrest before taking him into custody.[26] The SC said that his arrest was 'illegal' because he had not been informed about the case and due process had not been followed by the police.

According to Article 22(1) of the Constitution, 'No person who is arrested shall be detained in custody without being informed, as soon as may be, of the grounds for such arrest nor shall he be denied the right to consult, and to be defended by, a legal practitioner of his choice.'[27]

The SC bench, with Justices B.R. Gavai and Sandeep Mehta, marked Purkayastha's arrest as 'invalid in the eyes of law'.[28] The Bench clarified that none of its 'observations made' in its order 'shall be treated as a comment on the merits of the case'.[29]

Journalists, Indian media and civil society being routinely targeted by the BJP government has weakened the people's trust in the functioning of a democracy. Several freelance journalists, who were critical of the government, started writing for international media houses, including myself. Little did we know that even international media would not be spared if they attempted to be critical of the Modi-led government.

I often visited the BBC office on Kasturba Gandhi Marg for meetings or editing work while working on the documentary 'The Trap: India's Deadliest Scam' with the BBC World Service. On 14 February 2023 I was planning to leave for the BBC office around 10.30 a.m. for some meetings. I received an unplanned call from a colleague that lasted for an hour. The moment I hung up, I saw numerous messages in my BBC office phone chat group, enquiring about my whereabouts and my safety. When I asked what had happened, they informed me that the BBC office had been raided and asked me to not go there.

I was thankful that I had not reached the office before the income tax officials, as I might have been detained for hours like the other BBC employees. The income tax officers seized documents and took away phones and laptops of a few senior BBC employees, cloning all of their data in the process.

The officials said that they were conducting surveys rather than searches, like they had said in several other cases of raids on other media houses in the past. They also stated that they were investigating alleged tax evasion by the BBC.

Members of the opposition parties and civil society argued that the tax officials had targeted the BBC due to the controversial two-part documentary series 'India: The Modi Question', which focused on the role of the Modi government in failing to protect the minorities of the country.

Derek O'Brien of the Trinamool Congress (TMC) party tweeted, 'Censorship ... Twitter India HAS TAKEN DOWN MY TWEET of the #BBCDocumentary, it received lakhs of views. The 1hr BBC docu exposes how PM Narendra Modi HATES MINORITIES. Here's the mail I received. Also see flimsy (a) reason given. Opp will continue to fight the good fight.'[30]

Aakar Patel, the chair of Amnesty International in India, said, 'The Indian authorities are clearly trying to harass and intimidate the BBC over its critical coverage of the ruling Bharatiya Janata Party.'[31] The BBC documentary revealed that a British government document from the time found Modi 'directly responsible' for not preventing the killing of Muslims during the Gujarat riots of 2002 and said the violence had 'all the hallmarks of genocide' according to *The Guardian*.[32]

In January 2023 the Indian government invoked emergency laws to block the BBC documentary on Modi. The first episode of the documentary was only aired in the UK and not in India, but it circulated on social media, eventually reaching Indian audiences. The Ministry of Information and Broadcasting issued directions and banned any clips from the episode from being shared under legislation introduced in 2021 that permitted the 'blocking of information in case of emergency'.

Kanchan Gupta, an adviser to the ministry, tweeted, 'Videos sharing BBC World hostile propaganda and anti-India garbage, disguised as "documentary" on YouTube, and tweets sharing links to the BBC documentary have been blocked under India's sovereign laws and rules.'[33]

Fighting any legal case is expensive and brings immense mental pressure. The criminal cases have not managed to silence the digital media, but the question remains: for how long can they be critical of the government, especially when they are financially weak as compared to other big news channels.

# 6

# The Legal Career of Political Finance or No Free Lunches

MONEY AND POLITICS ARE intricately intertwined in India, making it challenging to contest and win elections without significant financial backing. Regrettably, the practice of offering cash incentives remains prevalent even today. Indian political parties often prioritise securing funds over scrutinising their sources, leading to questionable funding practices. Donors recognise that their financial contributions can yield political influence should their preferred party gain power. This dynamic is mutually beneficial for both the parties and donors, as money and power enter a quid pro quo arrangement.

The electoral bonds scheme became a perfect catalyst to discreetly collect donations, benefiting not only the ruling party, BJP, but also the opposition political parties for two primary reasons. First, the opposition political parties were unconcerned whether the BJP government was monitoring the donors associated with electoral bonds. Second, they felt secure accepting donations through bonds, confident that the ruling government was unlikely to initiate investigations by agencies like the CBI or ED regarding these donations. Initiating a criminal inquiry into any opposition political party's bonds donations would have meant that these agencies were getting access to the bonds data, raising the integral question of how such access was obtained.

After the 2019 Lok Sabha elections got over, public and media attention shifted to the electoral bonds scheme once again. On 29 November 2019 the ADR filed a second application about the bonds. This application, citing multiple news articles and RTI responses, revealed for the first time the existence of a unique hidden alphanumeric code embedded in the bonds, as already referenced in my article published in The Quint.

This comprehensive twenty-one-page application pointed out multiple flaws in the scheme. Here are some relevant issued it raised:

1. The RBI repeatedly opposed the electoral bonds scheme and amendments of the RBI Act through the Finance Bill 2017
2. Prime Minister's Office ordered the special and illegal sale of electoral bonds just before state polls in violation of the scheme
3. Only the government had access to the donors' list. The general public and opposition parties were denied this access
4. The government made the SBI accept expired electoral bonds sold in what was deemed an illegal window i.e. after the expiration of fifteen days
5. 99.7 per cent of the bonds purchased are of ₹1 crore and ₹10 lakh denominations as of October 2019, indicating that regular citizens are not donating through purchase of electoral bonds

The petitioners continued to file several applications in the SC, demanding an urgent hearing regarding the electoral bonds scheme.The SC asked the MoF, the MoLJ and the ECI to file a counter-affidavit addressing the points raised in the said petitions. The MoF and MoLJ expressed full support for the scheme in their counter-affidavits. But the ECI took a stand against the scheme in its counter-affidavit, pressing on the need for transparency in political funding system. The ECI's affidavit stated, 'The answering respondent has time and again voiced the importance of declaration of donation received by the political parties and also about the manner in which those funds are expended by them, for better transparency and accountability in the election process.'

Five years later, a five-judge constitution bench of the SC led by Justice D.Y. Chandrachud, unanimously struck down the Union government's electoral bonds scheme calling it 'unconstitutional'. The other judges were B.R. Gavai, J.B. Pardiwala, Manoj Misra and Sanjiv Khanna. The bench maintained that the scheme violated the voters' right to information as stated under Article 19(1)(a) of the Constitution. The judgement said, 'Information about funding to a political party is essential for a voter to exercise their freedom to vote in an effective manner.' However there was no mention of the unique hidden alphanumeric code in the judgement.

In fact, a close lawyer friend of mine questioned why the SC judges had chosen not to mention the unique hidden alphanumeric codes in their judgement. At the time, I had no answer. He speculated that the SC might have refrained from addressing these codes to avoid exposing the alleged quid pro quo between donors and political parties.

I reflected on this conversation but struggled to find a resolution. Nonetheless, I felt relieved that the SC did not invalidate the scheme; instead, it ordered the SBI to share the electoral bonds data with the ECI, ensuring that this information would be made available on their websites.

The SC's order said that

> the SBI shall submit details of the Electoral Bonds purchased since the interim order of this Court dated 12 April 2019 till date to the ECI. The details shall include

> the date of purchase of each Electoral Bond, the name of the purchaser of the bond and the denomination of the Electoral Bond purchased; SBI shall submit the details of political parties which have received contributions through Electoral Bonds since the interim order of this Court dated 12 April 2019 till date to the ECI. SBI must disclose details of each Electoral Bond encashed by political parties which shall include the date of encashment and the denomination of the Electoral Bond; SBI shall submit the above information to the ECI within three weeks from the date of this judgment, that is, by 6 March 2024.

Since the SC did not specifically instruct the SBI to submit the unique hidden alphanumeric code in its judgement, there were doubts regarding whether the SBI would share this information.

Many civil society members and journalists diligently followed the electoral bonds issue for years. Now that a favourable judgement was secured from the SC, those of us advocating for transparency in the political funding system felt a sense of victory, but the battle was far from over.

This reminds me of a dialogue from *The Walk*, a film produced by TriStar Pictures: 'Most walkers die in the final three steps. They think they've arrived. They get arrogant and die.'

The data revealing who donated how much and to which political party symbolised those 'final three steps' that had yet to be revealed. Simply knowing the names of the donors was not enough for justice. The ultimate aim was to identify the companies that allegedly benefited from their donations through the bonds. Half knowledge in this case was of little use.

The SC judgement's silence regarding the unique numbers raised many questions. WhatsApp groups of civil society members and journalists, which I was a part of, were full of speculations – what if the SBI shared the electoral bonds data without the unique hidden numbers? What if the SBI shared the data without matching the donors' names with the recipient? What if the shared data was not sufficient to prove alleged quid pro quo and the donors weren't exposed?

My independent journalistic video work on YouTube channel ExplainX allowed me the freedom to shed more light on electoral bonds. Through my investigative work, commentary, explainers and analysis, I was able to help raise awareness among viewers and citizens on two critical issues: electoral bonds as well as electoral process.

On 18 January 2024, I published the first welcome post on my channel. On 25 January, I uploaded an EVM-VVPAT video as the 2024 general elections were approaching and the opposition political parties were gaining momentum in their demand for a 100 per cent VVPAT count.

By 9 February, I gradually started publishing more videos related to electoral bonds. The SC had reserved its judgement until the 15th of February. On the morning of 15 February, just before the judgement was pronounced, I uploaded a video on the unique hidden alphanumeric codes in the electoral bonds. I had used archive footage showing the hidden numbers under ultraviolet light, originally captured in my video story published in The Quint in 2018. At that time it didn't occur to me to look for the original electoral bonds and make fresh videos for my viewers.

After the judgement was pronounced, many of us briefly celebrated the success before moving on to covering other stories, awaiting the SBI's compliance for the submission of submit data to the ECI within three weeks' time. This was due by 6 March 2024.

However, just two days before the deadline, the SBI filed an application with the SC seeking an extension until 30 June 2024 to submit the electoral bonds data to the ECI.

They cited the sheer scale and time-consuming nature of the process.

On 7 March 2024, the petitioners filed a contempt petition in the SC against the SBI for failing to comply with the court's order. The petition said, 'The State Bank of India has deliberately filed the said application for direction dated 04.03.2024 at the last moment in order to ensure that the details of donors and the amount of donations are not disclosed to the public before the upcoming Lok Sabha elections.'

The night before filing the contempt petition in the SC, one of the petitioners contacted me, requesting articles to include in the application that revealed the unique hidden alphanumeric codes recorded by the SBI. I shared my article published in November 2019, titled 'SBI Records Hidden Numbers On Electoral Bonds – Govt Misled Public'.

This article cited an RTI response received by Anjali Bhardwaj. The RTI response from the SBI included internal communication that revealed the bank had sought a unique serial number on the electoral bonds to carry out the audit. The RTI further disclosed that the finance ministry had allowed the bank to record the unique hidden alphanumeric codes and had instructed it 'to keep information highly confidential to prevent its leaking in any way'.

The contempt application asserted, '... the electoral bonds are completely traceable which is evident from the fact that SBI maintains a secret number-based record of donors who buy bonds, and the political parties they donate to.'

On 11 March 2024 the SC heard the contempt petition. Senior advocate Harish Salve defended the SBI and expressed difficulty in submitting the electoral bonds data to the ECI because the data was maintained in two separate silos. One silo contained the donors' details, and the other held data about the political parties.

The bench of five judges pointed out that the electoral bonds had numbers which could be viewed under a specific instrument, as cited in the contempt petition. Salve accepted that all electoral bonds did indeed have unique numbers, but he quickly added that those were recorded separately and kept confidential by the SBI. This admission was very crucial, as it confirmed that the hidden numbers were recorded by the bank.

Harish Salve emphasised that the data was stored in different silos and the numbers had no connection with the data of the donors or the political parties. He repeatedly stated that matching the donors' details with the recipient was a tedious exercise. Consequently, the SBI requested three months to compile the data because a minor mistake could lead to wrongful accusations by donors or political parties, or both.

The SBI had stressed on this in its affidavit as well: 'The matching of the information on the purchase and redemption of Electoral Bonds would be a time-consuming process since donor information and redemption information is maintained in two separate silos, independent of each other … A total of 22,217 bonds were purchased between 12 April 2019 to 15 February 2024. This would cumulatively add up to 44,434 data sets since there are two silos of information. In other words, the compilation of this information would be a time-consuming process because of the large number of data-sets.'

The SBI's counsel continued to urge the SC to grant three months to submit the data, but to no avail.

The SC instructed the SBI 'to disclose the details by the close of business hours on 12 March 2024'. It further directed the ECI to compile 'the information and publish the details on its official website no later than by 5 pm on 15 March 2024'.

The SC also mentioned the 'unique identification number' in the order and stated,

> ...ADR has filed a contempt petition in which it submits that the information which was directed to be disclosed by this Court can easily be disclosed by the SBI because of the unique number which is printed on the Electoral Bond. Irrespective of whether the unique identification number which is not discernible to the naked eye will enable the disclosure of details, the submissions of SBI in the application sufficiently indicate that the information which has been directed to be disclosed by this Court is readily available.

In a very strongly worded order, the SC declared:

> We are not inclined to exercise the contempt jurisdiction at this stage bearing in mind the application which was submitted for extension of time. However, we place SBI on notice that this Court will be inclined to proceed against it for wilful disobedience of the judgment if SBI does not comply with the directions of this Court as set out in its judgment dated 15 February 2024 by the timelines indicated in this order.

While this unfolded in the SC on 12 March 2024, I decided to look for the original electoral bonds and make a video showing the unique hidden numbers on them for my YouTube channel.

During the COVID-19 lockdown in 2020, I had brought all the documents from my previous organisation and stored them at home. I had not touched the pile of documents for almost three years, but I suspected that these documents would likely have the original bonds.

I found the original electoral bonds in an envelope atop of a pile of papers. The envelope also contained the forensic test reports from my investigative work from a few years ago. I even found the ultraviolet rays torch in my cupboard drawers, which we had used to reveal the existence of the unique hidden alphanumeric codes embedded in the bond when we broke the story.

In no time, I made a video in Hindi explaining the importance of the unique hidden alphanumeric code and how it is becomes visible under ultraviolet light. I uploaded it on 12 March 2024 and it quickly garnered the attention of several senior digital journalists, who reached out for interviews about the numbers embedded in the bonds.

And the cat was now finally out of the bag. Again.

In the following week, I participated in interviews with various YouTube channels and digital journalists regarding this issue. Shortly thereafter, the unique hidden alphanumeric codes embedded in the bonds became a topic of discussion on X and other social media platforms, as people began to recognise their relevance in linking the names of donors to the recipients.

Complying with the court's order, the SBI submitted the data to the ECI. The ECI uploaded the data on its website on 14 March 2024. The data was uploaded in two silos, Part 1 consisted of the date of purchase, the purchaser's name and the denomination, as shown in figure 6.1. This data is an extract of the full data available on the ECI's website.

FIGURE 6.1 The date of purchase of electoral bonds, along with the Purchaser's name and denomination

| Date of Encashment | Purchaser's Name | Denomination |
|---|---|---|
| 12/Apr/2019 | A B C India Limited | 1,00,000 |
| 12/Apr/2019 | A B C India Limited | 1,00,000 |
| 12/Apr/2019 | A B C India Limited | 10,00,000 |
| 12/Apr/2019 | A B C India Limited | 10,00,000 |
| 12/Apr/2019 | A B C India Limited | 1,00,000 |
| 12/Apr/2019 | A B C India Limited | 1,00,000 |
| 12/Apr/2019 | A B C India Limited | 1,00,000 |

| Date of Encashment | Purchaser's Name | Denomination |
|---|---|---|
| 12/Apr/2019 | A B C India Limited | 10,00,000 |
| 12/Apr/2019 | A B C India Limited | 1,00,000 |
| 12/Apr/2019 | A B C India Limited | 1,00,000 |
| 12/Apr/2019 | A B C India Limited | 1,00,000 |
| 12/Apr/2019 | A B C India Limited | 1,00,000 |
| 12/Apr/2019 | A B C India Limited | 1,00,000 |
| 12/Apr/2019 | Acropolis Maintenance Services Private Limited | 1,00,000 |
| 12/Apr/2019 | Acropolis Maintenance Services Private Limited | 10,00,000 |
| 12/Apr/2019 | Acropolis Maintenance Services Private Limited | 1,00,000 |
| 12/Apr/2019 | Acropolis Maintenance Services Private Limited | 1,00,000 |
| 12/Apr/2019 | Acropolis Maintenance Services Private Limited | 1,00,000 |
| 12/Apr/2019 | Acropolis Maintenance Services Private Limited | 1,00,000 |
| 12/Apr/2019 | Acropolis Maintenance Services Private Limited | 10,00,000 |

*Source:* Election Commission of India

Part 2 data consisted of the date of encashment, the name of the political party and the denomination, as shown in figure 6.2. This data is an extract of the full data available on the ECI's website.

FIGURE 6.2: The date of encashment, the name of the political party and the denomination purchased of the electoral bonds

| Date of Encashment | Name of the Political Party | Denomination |
|---|---|---|
| 12/Apr/2019 | All India Anna Dravida Munnetra Kazhagam | 10,00,000 |
| 12/Apr/2019 | All India Anna Dravida Munnetra Kazhagam | 10,00,000 |
| 12/Apr/2019 | All India Anna Dravida Munnetra Kazhagam | 10,00,000 |
| 12/Apr/2019 | All India Anna Dravida Munnetra Kazhagam | 1,10,00,000 |

| Date of Encashment | Name of the Political Party | Denomination |
|---|---|---|
| 12/Apr/2019 | All India Anna Dravida Munnetra Kazhagam | 10,00,000 |
| 12/Apr/2019 | All India Anna Dravida Munnetra Kazhagam | 10,00,000 |
| 12/Apr/2019 | All India Anna Dravida Munnetra Kazhagam | 10,00,000 |
| 12/Apr/2019 | All India Anna Dravida Munnetra Kazhagam | 10,00,000 |
| 12/Apr/2019 | All India Anna Dravida Munnetra Kazhagam | 10,00,000 |
| 12/Apr/2019 | All India Anna Dravida Munnetra Kazhagam | 10,00,000 |
| 12/Apr/2019 | All India Anna Dravida Munnetra Kazhagam | 10,00,000 |
| 12/Apr/2019 | All India Anna Dravida Munnetra Kazhagam | 10,00,000 |
| 12/Apr/2019 | All India Anna Dravida Munnetra Kazhagam | 10,00,000 |
| 12/Apr/2019 | All India Anna Dravida Munnetra Kazhagam | 1,10,00,000 |
| 12/Apr/2019 | All India Anna Dravida Munnetra Kazhagam | 10,00,000 |
| 12/Apr/2019 | All India Anna Dravida Munnetra Kazhagam | 10,00,000 |

*Source:* Election Commission of India

The SBI data did not explicitly reveal the unique hidden alphanumeric codes, which are the sole identifiers linking donor names to the corresponding political parties. This lack of direct association prevented us from definitively establishing the amount donated by each individual or entity to each specific party. The available data only allowed for the inference that, for example, corporate X contributed a certain sum to political party A.

Many media outlets approached me after the data was released to understand why revealing the unique hidden alphanumeric codes was critical. By refusing to share the codes and related donor data, the SBI was choosing to leave it to the public's imagination and speculation.

My X handle was flooded with congratulatory messages from senior journalists and experts. Some started calling me the 'Bond girl', while others wrote that if I had not exposed the hidden numbers in the bonds, the court and the general public would have remained unaware. Neither the SBI nor the government would have disclosed information regarding the workings of the scheme.

This led to a sudden spike in the engagement with my social media accounts with a huge rise in my followers. My YouTube channel garnered a wide following and subscriptions in a matter of weeks. All this because of a story I broke way back in 2018. I found a steady and sustained audience that began to engage with my work on the electoral bonds and the EVM. Viewers expressed curiosity to know more about bonds and the electoral process.

The demand to disclose the unique hidden numbers corresponding to the electoral bonds intensified following the release of two sets of electoral bond data. People needed to know who donated to whom, when, how much, how frequently and establish the whys of it all soon after. This lack of transparency fuelled calls for greater accountability in political funding.

Despite receiving donations through electoral bonds, opposition parties vocally criticised the scheme while simultaneously refusing to disclose the identities of their own donors. Given the SBI's non-disclosure of the unique hidden alphanumeric codes, the only viable path to expose corporate donors to the ruling party would have been for opposition parties to publicly reveal their own donors. I created a video urging opposition parties to disclose their electoral bond donors. This transparency would have provided a crucial benchmark for estimating the donors to the ruling party. I shared this video with several senior leaders in various opposition parties, hoping to encourage some positive action. At that point, the likelihood of the SBI releasing the hidden codes appeared extremely low.

Some politicians responded by claiming ignorance regarding the identities of their donors, a claim that appeared difficult to substantiate. Others suggested that the opposition sought to protect their donors. This raises several crucial questions: Why would they want to shield their donors, and, more importantly, from whom were they seeking to protect them?

The petitioners' approached the SC on 15 March 2024 informing the judges that the SBI had not shared the unique hidden alphanumeric code, which was needed to match the data of the donors with the political parties. The SC immediately sent notice to the SBI for not sharing complete details of the electoral bonds data with the ECI; including the unique hidden alphanumeric code.

By this time, multiple news articles on companies that had donated to political parties, the names of the biggest donors of the bonds, the top five donors along with their company's profile were published.

On 18 March 2024, the matter of the non-disclosure of the unique hidden alphanumeric code by the SBI was to be heard by the SC. This was the third hearing on the electoral bonds data since the judgement was passed on 15 February 2024. A month later, the SBI was still to share complete data with the ECI for them to then release it on their website for the general public to access.

The SBI's reluctance was noticed by the SC even before the hearing started on 18 March 2024. The lawyer defending the Associated Chambers of Commerce and

Industry of India (ASSOCHAM) and Federation of Indian Chambers of Commerce & Industry (FICCI) requested deferment in the issue of the grant of bond numbers.

The CJI was unwilling to hear him and remarked, 'You have come here after the judgment is delivered, we can't hear you right now. There is no application on record, and we cannot make an exception for you. The whole world knew when the case was being heard.'

The CJI informed the SBI that it could not be selective in disclosing details about the bonds. He contended that SBI's approach of 'You tell us what to disclose, we will disclose' was not fair. The SC emphasised that according to its previous judgement, 'all details' relating to electoral bonds needed to be submitted by the SBI.

The bench further ordered the SBI to disclose the unique hidden alphanumeric code and instructed the SBI chairman to file an affidavit clearly confirming that the SBI was not withholding any information related to the bonds. This was primarily after Harish Salve commented in SC that messages like the SBI was purposely withholding information were circulating on social media.

Solicitor General Tushar Mehta added, 'Now the witch-hunting has started at some other level, not at govt level … Those before the court started giving press interviews deliberately embarrassing the court … A series of, a barrage of social media posts, at least intended to cause embarrassment has started …' The solicitor general was allegedly and indirectly speaking about Prashant Bhushan who often gave media interviews about the electoral bonds proceedings.

In this hearing, the bench clearly demanded for the unique hidden alphanumeric codes stating, 'This, we clarify, will include the alphanumeric number and the serial number, if any, of the bonds redeemed.' The SBI was granted till 5 p.m. by 21 March 2024 to submit complete details about the electoral bonds, especially the unique hidden alphanumeric codes to the ECI.

The court's order initially offered a glimmer of hope, suggesting that the SBI could no longer indefinitely conceal donor data. However, scepticism remained, with many fearing that the SBI would continue to resist disclosure. This apprehension stemmed from the perceived influence of large corporations, who feared exposure and were believed to be exerting pressure on the government to protect their anonymity.

During a dinner conversation with a friend in cybersecurity, I expressed my frustration over the apparent control exercised by the ruling party over government institutions. Despite the court's order, the SBI persistently defied its directives and withheld the crucial data related to electoral bonds and donors. On March 21, 2024, approximately thirty-five days after the court's judgment, the SBI finally released the complete electoral bond data to the ECI. This comprehensive dataset included columns for reference number, journal date, purchase date, expiration date, purchaser name, prefix and bond number, denominations, issuing branch code, issuing teller, and status. The data in figures 6.3 and 6.4 is an extract of the full data available on the ECI's website.

FIGURE 6.3 Data of the purchasers of the bonds

| Sr No. | Reference No (URN) | Journal Date | Date of Purchase | Date of Expiry | Name of the Purchaser | Prefix | Bond Number | Denominat-ions | Issue Branch Code | Issue Teller | Status |
|---|---|---|---|---|---|---|---|---|---|---|---|
| 1 | 00001201904120000001166 | 12/Apr/2019 | 12/Apr/2019 | 26/Apr/2019 | A B C INDIA LIMITED | TL | 11448 | 10,00,000 | 00001 | 5899230 | Paid |
| 2 | 00001201904120000001166 | 12/Apr/2019 | 12/Apr/2019 | 26/Apr/2019 | A B C INDIA LIMITED | TL | 11447 | 10,00,000 | 00001 | 5899230 | Paid |
| 3 | 00001201904120000001166 | 12/Apr/2019 | 12/Apr/2019 | 26/Apr/2019 | A B C INDIA LIMITED | TL | 11441 | 10,00,000 | 00001 | 5899230 | Paid |
| 4 | 00001201904120000001166 | 12/Apr/2019 | 12/Apr/2019 | 26/Apr/2019 | A B C INDIA LIMITED | OL | 1113 | 1,00,000 | 00001 | 5899230 | Paid |
| 5 | 00001201904120000001166 | 12/Apr/2019 | 12/Apr/2019 | 26/Apr/2019 | A B C INDIA LIMITED | OL | 1118 | 1,00,000 | 00001 | 5899230 | Paid |
| 6 | 00001201904120000001166 | 12/Apr/2019 | 12/Apr/2019 | 26/Apr/2019 | A B C INDIA LIMITED | OL | 1112 | 1,00,000 | 00001 | 5899230 | Paid |
| 7 | 00001201904120000001166 | 12/Apr/2019 | 12/Apr/2019 | 26/Apr/2019 | A B C INDIA LIMITED | OL | 1115 | 1,00,000 | 00001 | 5899230 | Paid |
| 8 | 00001201904120000001166 | 12/Apr/2019 | 12/Apr/2019 | 26/Apr/2019 | A B C INDIA LIMITED | OL | 1119 | 1,00,000 | 00001 | 5899230 | Paid |
| 9 | 00001201904120000001166 | 12/Apr/2019 | 12/Apr/2019 | 26/Apr/2019 | A B C INDIA LIMITED | OL | 1110 | 1,00,000 | 00001 | 5899230 | Paid |
| 10 | 00001201904120000001166 | 12/Apr/2019 | 12/Apr/2019 | 26/Apr/2019 | A B C INDIA LIMITED | OL | 1111 | 1,00,000 | 00001 | 5899230 | Paid |
| 11 | 00001201904120000001166 | 12/Apr/2019 | 12/Apr/2019 | 26/Apr/2019 | A B C INDIA LIMITED | OL | 1106 | 1,00,000 | 00001 | 5899230 | Paid |
| 12 | 00001201904120000001166 | 12/Apr/2019 | 12/Apr/2019 | 26/Apr/2019 | A B C INDIA LIMITED | OL | 1114 | 1,00,000 | 00001 | 5899230 | Paid |
| 13 | 00001201904120000001166 | 12/Apr/2019 | 12/Apr/2019 | 26/Apr/2019 | A B C INDIA LIMITED | OL | 1117 | 1,00,000 | 00001 | 5899230 | Paid |
| 14 | 00001201904120000001178 | 12/Apr/2019 | 12/Apr/2019 | 26/Apr/2019 | ACROPOLIS MAINTENANCE SERVICES PRIVATE LIMITED | TL | 11556 | 10,00,000 | 00001 | 5899230 | Paid |
| 15 | 00001201904120000001178 | 12/Apr/2019 | 12/Apr/2019 | 26/Apr/2019 | ACROPOLIS MAINTENANCE SERVICES PRIVATE LIMITED | TL | 11555 | 10,00,000 | 00001 | 5899230 | Paid |
| 16 | 00001201904120000001178 | 12/Apr/2019 | 12/Apr/2019 | 26/Apr/2019 | ACROPOLIS MAINTENANCE SERVICES PRIVATE LIMITED | OL | 1125 | 1,00,000 | 00001 | 5899230 | Paid |
| 17 | 00001201904120000001178 | 12/Apr/2019 | 12/Apr/2019 | 26/Apr/2019 | ACROPOLIS MAINTENANCE SERVICES PRIVATE LIMITED | OL | 1129 | 1,00,000 | 00001 | 5899230 | Paid |
| 18 | 00001201904120000001178 | 12/Apr/2019 | 12/Apr/2019 | 26/Apr/2019 | ACROPOLIS MAINTENANCE SERVICES PRIVATE LIMITED | OL | 1124 | 1,00,000 | 00001 | 5899230 | Paid |
| 19 | 00001201904120000001178 | 12/Apr/2019 | 12/Apr/2019 | 26/Apr/2019 | ACROPOLIS MAINTENANCE SERVICES PRIVATE LIMITED | OL | 1128 | 1,00,000 | 00001 | 5899230 | Paid |
| 20 | 00001201904120000001178 | 12/Apr/2019 | 12/Apr/2019 | 26/Apr/2019 | ACROPOLIS MAINTENANCE SERVICES PRIVATE LIMITED | OL | 1126 | 1,00,000 | 00001 | 5899230 | Paid |

*Source:* Disclosure of Electoral Bonds, The Election Commission of India, 14 March, 2024. https://www.eci.gov.in/disclosure-of-electoral-bonds

*Note:* Prefix and Bond Number of each electoral bond were embedded and visible only under ultraviolet rays.

FIGURE 6.4 Data of the recipient of the bonds

| Sr No. | Date of Encashment | Name of the Political Party | Account no. of Political Party | Prefix | Bond Number | Denominat-ions | Pay Branch Code | Pay Teller |
|---|---|---|---|---|---|---|---|---|
| 1 | 12/Apr/2019 | ALL INDIA ANNA DRAVIDA MUNNETRA KAZHAGAM | *******5199 | OC | 775 | 1,00,00,000 | 00800 | 2770121 |
| 2 | 12/Apr/2019 | ALL INDIA ANNA DRAVIDA MUNNETRA KAZHAGAM | *******5199 | OC | 3975 | 1,00,00,000 | 00800 | 2770121 |
| 3 | 12/Apr/2019 | ALL INDIA ANNA DRAVIDA MUNNETRA KAZHAGAM | *******5199 | OC | 3967 | 1,00,00,000 | 00800 | 2770121 |
| 4 | 12/Apr/2019 | ALL INDIA ANNA DRAVIDA MUNNETRA KAZHAGAM | *******5199 | TL | 10418 | 10,00,000 | 00800 | 2770121 |
| 5 | 12/Apr/2019 | ALL INDIA ANNA DRAVIDA MUNNETRA KAZHAGAM | *******5199 | TL | 126 | 10,00,000 | 00800 | 2770121 |
| 6 | 12/Apr/2019 | ALL INDIA ANNA DRAVIDA MUNNETRA KAZHAGAM | *******5199 | TL | 116 | 10,00,000 | 00800 | 2770121 |
| 7 | 12/Apr/2019 | ALL INDIA ANNA DRAVIDA MUNNETRA KAZHAGAM | *******5199 | TL | 10466 | 10,00,000 | 00800 | 2770121 |
| 8 | 12/Apr/2019 | ALL INDIA ANNA DRAVIDA MUNNETRA KAZHAGAM | *******5199 | TL | 122 | 10,00,000 | 00800 | 2770121 |
| 9 | 12/Apr/2019 | ALL INDIA ANNA DRAVIDA MUNNETRA KAZHAGAM | *******5199 | TL | 158 | 10,00,000 | 00800 | 2770121 |
| 10 | 12/Apr/2019 | ALL INDIA ANNA DRAVIDA MUNNETRA KAZHAGAM | *******5199 | TL | 108 | 10,00,000 | 00800 | 2770121 |
| 11 | 12/Apr/2019 | ALL INDIA ANNA DRAVIDA MUNNETRA KAZHAGAM | *******5199 | TL | 10446 | 10,00,000 | 00800 | 2770121 |
| 12 | 12/Apr/2019 | ALL INDIA ANNA DRAVIDA MUNNETRA KAZHAGAM | *******5199 | TL | 10434 | 10,00,000 | 00800 | 2770121 |
| 13 | 12/Apr/2019 | ALL INDIA ANNA DRAVIDA MUNNETRA KAZHAGAM | *******5199 | TL | 162 | 10,00,000 | 00800 | 2770121 |
| 14 | 12/Apr/2019 | ALL INDIA ANNA DRAVIDA MUNNETRA KAZHAGAM | *******5199 | TL | 128 | 10,00,000 | 00800 | 2770121 |
| 15 | 12/Apr/2019 | ALL INDIA ANNA DRAVIDA MUNNETRA KAZHAGAM | *******5199 | TL | 113 | 10,00,000 | 00800 | 2770121 |
| 16 | 12/Apr/2019 | ALL INDIA ANNA DRAVIDA MUNNETRA KAZHAGAM | *******5199 | TL | 10423 | 10,00,000 | 00800 | 2770121 |

*Source:* Disclosure of Electoral Bonds, The Election Commission of India, 14 March, 2024. https://www.eci.gov.in/disclosure-of-electoral-bonds

*Note*: Prefix and Bond Number of each electoral bond were embedded and visible only under ultraviolet rays.

Following the data release, numerous individuals, including journalists, independently matched donor and recipient data within hours – a task the SBI had initially estimated to take three months.

Many of my followers on X and LinkedIn volunteered their assistance, offering to analyse the bond data and share their findings. Subsequently, media outlets published numerous reports exposing alleged quid pro quo arrangements between large corporations and political parties. The NGO Common Cause filed a new petition in the SC on 17 April 2024, following the news articles, demanding a monitored investigation into the allegations along with the formation of an SIT. The petition referred to twenty-two instances of alleged quid pro quo between 2019 and 2024.

The news reports that followed have alleged three primary forms of quid pro quo:

1. Investigative Influence: Private companies may have donated significant sums running in crores via electoral bonds to political parties, as a form of 'protection money' to influence the then ongoing investigations against them or to secure favourable treatment from investigating agencies.
2. Favouritism: The ruling political may have, in some cases, amended policies and laws to benefit specific private promoters, granting them lucrative government contracts. This constitutes misuse of taxpayers' money for the enrichment of political parties.
3. Inflated Donations: Numerous newly established companies, formed after the introduction of the electoral bonds scheme, have reportedly made more donations exceeding their annual profits, raising concerns about the legitimacy of these so-called contributions.

The SC dismissed the petition of quid pro quo allegations as speculative and refused to begin a 'roving and general enquiry'. The SC advised the petitioners to invoke normal remedies available under the law of criminal procedure if they suspected criminality in the donations of electoral bonds. The SC advised the petitioners to file a writ with the state high court under Article 226 of the Constitution if the investigating agencies refused to further probe the matter.

Many people, including myself, were unhappy by the SC order. At this point, I must bring up a critical interview I conducted with the former finance secretary Subhash Garg, who was closely involved with the implementation of the electoral bonds scheme. I interviewed him on 30 March 2024 for my channel where he stated 'we [Finance Ministry] was [sic] not aware that the SBI was clandestinely recording this (alphanumeric code on Bonds). And I think no one was aware of it.' He added that no one was aware of the unique hidden alphanumeric code until my video became viral and led to citizen and judicial action. It appeared as if he was seemingly targeting the SBI with his statement. And yet, the correspondence between the SBI and the finance ministry clearly stated that the codes were recorded by the bank.

A similar account was cited in one of Prime Minister Narendra Modi's interviews with Thanthi TV on 31 March 2024 during the 2024 Lok Sabha election campaign, where he claimed:

> I want to ask these people, before 2014, money was spent during elections. Was there any trail of funds that were given to political parties during elections? Which agency can say where the money was sourced from, who did it go to and who spent it? Because Modi made electoral bonds, we can now search who bought the bonds, where it went, and how it was spent. Otherwise, before this we did not even know. Elections included spending. Today

> there is a trail because of electoral bonds. No system is perfect. There may be shortcomings, which can be fixed. But at least due to electoral bonds you know where the money has gone.

These interviews revealed a significant shift in government rhetoric. Previously silent on the very existence of unique hidden alphanumeric codes within electoral bonds, the government was now openly claiming credit for embedding them in the bonds in the first place. This glaring inconsistency highlights that the public lives in a constant state of surveillance. It raises important concerns about transparency and the integrity of the electoral process. It also exhibits how the ruling party adapts and changes its positions and narratives to best serve its interests, potentially eroding public trust and the Indian democratic spirit.

# 7

# A Biography of the Election Commission

'There have been numerous CECs (Chief Election Commissioner) and T N Seshan happens once in a while. We do not want anyone to bulldoze him. Enormous power has been vested on the fragile shoulders of three men (CEC and two election commissioners). We have to find the best man for the post of CEC.'[1]

Supreme Court of India

No one before or after the former chief election commissioner Tirunellai Narayana Iyer Seshan has been able to reform the ECI as effectively as he did. The SC made this observation while hearing a petition seeking reforms in the appointment of election commissioners. Seshan, the tenth CEC, served a full tenure of six years from 1990 to 1996. The constitution bench also noted that since 2004, no CEC had completed a six-year term. During the UPA rule from 2004 to 2014, there were ten CECs, and eight CECs in the eight years of the NDA government.[2]

T.N. Seshan, in one of his old interviews, explained the meaning of independence for the ECI and the expected conduct of the CEC. He stated:

The Chief Election Commissioner used to go and wait outside the room of the Law Minister, waiting for his convenience to be called in. I said I will never do this.

> I am available at any time but on condition that the office is treated with respect. In all papers they used to write: Chief Election Commissioner, Government of India. I said, 'Sorry, I'm not part of the Government of India. I am part of the structure of this country but I am not part of the Government of India.' Ministers used to send notes between one department and another. In government there is a method of sending a piece of paper called UOO note. It's called an Unofficial Note. I used to get UOO notes from various ministers saying, 'Don't do this. Don't do that.' I used to send them back politely and said, 'Don't send me UOO notes. I am not part of your government.
>
> So it took considerable effort to satisfy or bring home to the government that the Election Commission was of the government, part of the government but not under the government. Certainly, people used to ask 'to whom do you report'. I report to the President, I report to the Prime Minister, I report to the Law Minister. Similarly, Chief Election Commissioner is of course directly answerable to the President of India. But not in the sense of being a subordinate like the rest of the government is. So establishing the independence of the Election Commission was one part of the whole story.[3]

Over the years, the ECI has lost credibility due to lack of communication and action. The ECI is at a stage where it may require another T.N. Seshan for it to regain its lost independence, stature and credibility.

Let's rewind a few decades and talk about the formation of the ECI.

## Establishment of the Election Commission of India

The subject of constituting the ECI was designated as Draft Article 289, discussed on 15 June and 16 June 1949 in the Constituent Assembly. Article 289 proposed separate election commissions for the Centre and the states. Dr B.R. Ambedkar made a change to the draft. He said:

> The original proposal under Article 289 was that there should be one commission to deal with the elections to the central legislature, both the Upper and Lower Houses, and that there be a separate election commission for each province and each State, to be appointed by the governor or Ruler of the State. Comparing that with the present article 289, there is undoubtedly a radical change. This (new Article 324) article proposes to centralise the election machinery in the hands of a single Commission to be assisted by regional Commissioners, not working under the provincial Government, but working under the superintendence and control of the Central Election Commission. As I said, this is undoubtedly a radical change. But, this change has become necessary because today we find that in some of the provinces of India, the population is a mixture. No person who is entitled to be brought into the electoral rolls on the grounds which we have already mentioned in our Constitution, namely, an adult of 21 years of age, should be excluded merely as a result of the prejudice of a local Government, or the whim of an officer. That would cut at the very root of democratic Government. Therefore, this new change has been brought about, namely, that the whole of the election machinery should be in the hands of a Central Election Commission which alone would be entitled to issue directives to returning officers, polling officers and others engaged in the preparation and revision of electoral rolls so that no injustice may be done to any citizen in India, who under this Constitution is entitled to be brought on the electoral rolls. That alone is, if I may say so, a radical and fundamental departure from the existing provisions of the Draft Constitution.[4]

The top body must be free from executive interference to ensure smooth functioning. Dr Ambedkar pressed on the ECI's independence:

> The Chief Election Commission shall not be liable to be removed except in the same manner as a Judge of the Supreme Court. If the object of this House is that all matters relating to Elections should be outside the control of the Executive Government of the day, it is absolutely necessary that the new machinery which we are setting up, namely, the Election Commission should be irremovable by the executive by a mere fiat. We have therefore given the Chief Election Commissioner the same status so far as removability is concerned as we have given to the Judge of the Supreme Court. We, of course, do not propose to give the same status to the other members of the Election Commission. We have left the matter to the President as to the circumstances under which he would deem fit to remove any other member of the Election Commission, subject to one condition that the Chief Election Commissioner must recommend that the removal is just and proper.[5]

Ambedkar's mechanisms of drafting the constitution allotted powers to the ECI and the CEC. He recognised that only free and fair elections could protect democracy. To ensure such elections, the ECI and the CEC must be independent of government interference. Only then could a CEC act with sincerity and conviction. Seshan is perhaps the only CEC who embodied the vision of the framers of the Constitution.

The chairman of the Drafting Committee suggested an amendment to replace draft Article 289 with Article 324, which aimed to centralise the election machinery. However, Ambedkar's amendments faced opposition from the Constituent Assembly during the parliamentary debate. In January 1950, Part XV of Article 324 of the Constitution established the ECI. It stated:

The superintendence, direction and control of the preparation of the electoral rolls for, and the conduct of, all elections to Parliament and to the Legislature of every State and of elections to the offices of President and Vice-President held under this Constitution shall be vested in a Commission (referred to in this Constitution as the Election Commission).[6]

On the removal of the CEC and election commissioners Article 324(5) states,

Provided that the Chief Election Commissioner shall not be removed from his office except in like manner and on the like grounds as a Judge of the Supreme Court and the conditions of service of the Chief Election Commissioner shall not be varied to his disadvantage after his appointment.

Articles 324–329 of Part XV of the Constitution provide a legal constitutional framework for the ECI to conduct free and fair elections in the country. The six clauses in Article 324 ensure the independence of the commission and allow a degree of political oversight by Parliament. This allows the ECI to enact appropriate laws and establish mechanisms to conduct elections and safeguard voters' rights.

## Members of the Election Commission

When the ECI was set up it only had a CEC, despite Article 324 permitting the appointment of both a CEC and election commissioners. For many years, the ECI had only one head – the CEC.

Today, the ECI includes one CEC and two commissioners, a change implemented on 16 October 1989 to strengthen decision-making power by majority vote.[7]

In *T.N. Seshan* v. *Union of India*, the SC ruled that the CEC's status is equal to that of the other two commissioners, despite differences in their services.[8] As of September 2024, the ECI has appointed twenty-five CECs, including the current CEC, Rajiv Kumar, and eight election commissioners. These include the current commissioners Gyanesh Kumar and Dr Sukhbir Singh Sandhu.

Article 324(6) of the Constitution grants the ECI power to request for staff from the central and state governments during elections. The ECI is often short-staffed and relies on government employees (junior officers) to work as poll officers. They are required to undergo formal training or attend workshops organised by the ECI.

The presiding officer heads the polling booth, while the returning officer manages parliamentary or assembly constituencies. To account for the possibility that the same government officer may not be assigned election duty in subsequent years, the ECI has handbooks for returning officers, presiding officers, EVM-VVPAT manuals and the Conduct of Election Rules, 1961. These ensure that newly appointed officers can review the documents before polling day. It is the duty of the returning and presiding officers to ensure that the polling goes smoothly. The commission has the authority to recommend disciplinary action against any government staff who fail to perform their duties.

## Powers Given to the ECI Under Article 324

Article 324 grants powers to the ECI, but the institution can exercise those powers within the limitations set by law.

The ECI announced the Punjab state elections towards the end of June 1991. T.N. Seshan cancelled the elections without consulting the then Punjab governor O.P. Malhotra. According to former chief secretary of Punjab Tejendra Khanna, two factors influenced this: first, the targeted killings of Hindu passengers on two trains headed to Delhi from Amritsar; second, the swearing-in of the former prime minister P.V. Narasimha Rao as the leader of the INC in the Lok Sabha. Due to this situation, Seshan postponed the elections, which took place in February 1992. This incident instilled Seshan's fear in many politicians and showcased the ECI's power to ensure a safe environment for voters.

The ECI has the authority to assign symbols to political parties. Political parties must be registered with the commission, or they may be barred.

All political parties and candidates have to adhere to the ECI's code of conduct. Each candidate is required to submit an affidavit listing their assets and income. The ECI has also set limits on the candidates' expenditure for election campaigning. In January 2022, the ECI revised the expenditure limits from ₹70 lakh to ₹95 lakh in parliamentary elections and from ₹28 lakh to ₹40 lakh in state assembly elections due to rising inflation.[9] If a candidate violates the code of conduct, the ECI has the authority to disqualify them or impose penalties.

## Model Code of Conduct

The MCC is a set of rules and regulations instituted in the 1960s to check the conduct of political parties and candidates during election campaigning, rallies, public speeches and meetings. It aims to keep a watch on actions that could incite communal tensions. Violations of the MCC can lead to barring from contesting elections.

New guidelines were added to keep political parties from making promises that were 'repugnant to the ideals and principles enshrined in the Constitution'.[10] Prohibitions on inciting communal feelings, serving or distributing liquor, belittling and insulting the private life of opponents and engaging in corrupt practices like bribing or impersonating voters are among the main MCC guidelines.

Any violations of the MCC guidelines are classified as electoral offences and corrupt practices under the Bharatiya Nyaya Sanhita (BNS) (formerly known as the Indian Penal Code [IPC]) and the Representation of the People Act, 1951. Sections of the Act refer to hate speech and other incitement methods, with penalties listed. For example, in the Representation of the People Act, 1951, 'corrupt practices' are mentioned in Section 123(3A) and Section 123(4). On hate speeches, Section 125 lists:

> Any person who in connection with an election under this Act promotes or attempts to promote on grounds of religion, race, caste, community or language, feelings of enmity or hatred, between different classes of the citizens of India shall be punishable with imprisonment for a term which may extend to three years, or with fine, or with both.[11]

On the other hand, Section 153A of the BNS can also be invoked for delivering hate speeches. The Section says,

> The purpose of the Section 153A is to punish persons who indulge in wanton vilification or attacks upon the religion, race, place of birth, residence, language etc of any particular group or class or upon the founders and prophets of a religion. The jurisdiction of this Section is widened so as to make promotion of disharmony, enmity or feelings of hatred or ill-will between different religious, racial, language or regional groups or castes or communities punishable. Offence on moral turpitude is also covered in this section. The offence is a cognizable offence and the punishment for the same may extend to three years, or with fine, or with both. However, the

punishment of the offence committed in a place of worship is enhanced up to five years and fine.[12]

Article 329 of the Constitution bars interference by courts in electoral matters, however under Section 80 of the Representation of the People Act, 1951,[13] the high courts have the power to decide election disputes which can later be appealed in the Supreme Court.[14]

The first challenge to the legality of the MCC was in 1997 when the Punjab and Haryana courts declared the ECI's authority to enforce it. But the ECI is also referred to as a 'toothless institution' for its failure to effectively implement law and its structure, despite having the framework for it.

Controversies about MCC violations have been reported during the 2019 and 2024 Lok Sabha elections. Since the BJP government came to power, there has been a rise in hate speeches and communal violence, especially during election campaigns. In 2019, the ECI lodged complaints against Parvesh Verma and former minister of state (finance) Anurag Thakur for their hate remarks.Verma was barred from campaigning for ninety-six hours for his comments about anti-Citizenship Amendment Act (CAA) and National Register of Citizen (NRC) protesters, while Thakur was banned for seventy-two hours for inciting a crowd in an election rally to chant 'Desh ke gaddaron ko (traitors of a country)' and the crowd responded with 'goli maaro saalon ko (shoot these bloody traitors)'.[15] Viewing the ban as insufficient, critics questioned why no formal complaint was filed against them under the BNS.

The ECI was under scrutiny around the same time when senior Election Commissioner (EC) Ashok Lavasa faced strong reaction for dissenting opinion regarding four speeches by Prime Minister Modi (minority-majority speeches in Wardha and his speech appealing to first-time voters by invoking the Balakot airstrike) and one by Home Minister Amit Shah (his Nagpur speech), which he believed violated the MCC. It led to public controversy, and he recused himself from MCC meetings until his opinions were formally recorded. CEC Arora made sharp comments on Lavasa's issue, calling it 'unsavoury and avoidable controversy'. The government also scrutinised Lavasa – his house was raided by the ED and the Income Tax Department on alleged tax evasion grounds. He resigned from the ECI in August 2020 and joined the Asian Development Bank as the vice-president.

The 2024 Lok Sabha elections were marred by controversy surrounding PM Modi's allegedly communal statements. Critics, including prominent figures like Saket Gokhale, accused the ECI of inaction and derisively labelled the Model Code of Conduct as the 'Modi Code of Conduct'.

This speech prompted numerous complaints from organisations like the ADR and the CPI(M), alleging violations of the Broadcast Code of the News Broadcasting Standards Authority (NBSA) and the Representation of the People Act, 1951. In response, the ECI issued a notice to the BJP seeking clarifications regarding PM Modi's speech. Notably, the ECI also addressed complaints against opposition leaders Mallikarjun Kharge and Rahul Gandhi, who were accused by the BJP of making divisive speeches.

The first communal speech by PM Modi that came under MCC violation was delivered in Banswara, Rajasthan, on 21 April 2024. This is an excerpt of the speech as reported by the Citizens for Justice and Peace team:

> Tum use chhinane ki baat kar rahe ho apne manifesto mein. Gold le lenge, aur sabko vitrit kar denge. Aur pehele jab unki sarkar thi to unhone kahah tha ki desh ki sampatti par pehela adhikar Mussalmano ka hai. Iska

> matlab, yeh sampatti ikhatti karke kisko batenge … jinke jyada bacche hain unko batenge … Ghuspaithiyo ko batenge. Kya apki mehenat ki kamayi ka paisa ghuspaithiyo ko diya jayega … Apko manzur hai ye … Ye congress ka manifesto keh raha hai ki woh matao aur beheno ka sone ka hisab karenge, uski jadti karenge, jankari lenge aur phir uss sampatti ko baant denge. Aur unko batenge … jinko Manmohan Singhji ki sarkar ne kaha tha ki sampatti par pehela adhikar musalmano ka hai. Bhaiyo beheno ye urban naxal ki soch mere matao aur beheno ye apka mangal sutra bhi bachne nahi denge [16]
>
> You [Congress] are referring to grabbing that [gold and property] in your manifesto … They will take the gold and distribute it to all. When their [Congress] government was there, they had said that Muslims have the first right over a country's property. Whom they [Congress] will distribute to after accumulating the property? They will give to people who have more children … will your hard-earned money be given to infiltrators … Do you accept it? This is what Congress manifesto says that gold of mothers and sisters will be accounted for, searched and inquired and then it will be distributed to Muslims, whom Manmohan Singh ji had said have the first right over property. Brothers and sisters, this is urban naxal mentality … my mothers and sisters, they [Congress] will not even leave your mangalsutra.

This speech led to multiple complaints by the ADR and the CPI(M), citing violations of the IPC and the Representation of the People Act, 1951.

The ADR demanded action against PM Modi's speech under Sections 123(3), 123(3A) and Section 125 of the Representation of the People Act, 1951 and also under the provisions of Section 153A of the BNS that reads,

'Promoting enmity between different groups on ground of religion, race, place of birth, residence, language, etc., and doing acts prejudicial to maintenance of harmony.'[17]

Apart from writing to the ECI, the CPI(M) leaders sent a complaint to the Delhi police commissioner against PM Modi over his speech in Banswara after the local police refused to accept the complaint. Former general secretary of CPI(M) Sitaram Yechury demanded an FIR against PM Modi for 'inciting communal passions and hatred'.[18]

In response, the ECI issued a notice to the BJP on 25 April 2024 for clarification about Modi's speech.

The ECI also issued a notice to the Congress on a complaint against the party president Mallikarjun Kharge and leader Rahul Gandhi for complaints made by the BJP alleging that while delivering a speech in Kottayam in Kerala, Gandhi falsely accused the BJP of promoting the idea of 'one language' and 'one religion', giving the impression that the BJP was against the people and culture of the state. The BJP flagged Kharge's remark allegedly implying that he was not invited for the Ram Mandir ceremony because of his Scheduled Caste status.[19]

Even more interesting was that the ECI did not name Modi, Kharge and Gandhi in the two separate notes issued to the political parties. This was not usual.[20]

The ECI directed J.P. Nadda, BJP president, that the 'Commission expects BJP, as the ruling party at the Centre, to fully align the campaign methods to the practical aspects of the composite and sensitive fabric of India'. Nadda 'is to convey to all star campaigners to not make speeches and statements which may divide the society'.[21]

In an interview to the digital news platform Scroll, CEC Rajiv Kumar stated that the ECI decided not to reprimand top leaders from either party (Modi and Shah from the BJP and Gandhi and Vadra from the Congress). Rajiv Kumar said, 'We deliberately decided – this is such a huge nation

– that the top two people in both the parties we did not touch. Both party presidents we touched equally…Why did we leave two this side and two that side? The persons in position in this huge country also have responsibility. We reminded them of their responsibility.'[22]

This raised concerns about the ECI's effectiveness and ability to carry out the MCC guidelines. The ECI's inaction forced the general public to seek judicial intervention for violation, which they believed was a failure of the ECI's duty.

Two critical observations arise from the ECI's handling of MCC violations:

1. Impartial Enforcement: The MCC guidelines should be applied equally to all politicians, regardless of their stature or affiliation with any political party. By failing to act decisively against top leaders from both major parties, the ECI set a dangerous precedent that undermines the impartiality of the electoral process.
2. Active Enforcement: The ECI, as a constitutional body empowered by Article 324 of the Constitution, possesses the authority to independently investigate and act upon MCC violations. Instead, the onus has often fallen on citizens, political parties, and civil society organisations to resort to legal recourse, suggesting a lack of proactive enforcement by the ECI.

The RTI response by the ECI on the MCC matter further questioned its credibility. The former secretary in the Government of India E.A.S. Sarma filed an RTI application in June 2024 after the Lok Sabha election results were declared in which he asked three questions:

1. Has the Commission received complaints of Prime Minister Modi having committed Model Code of Conduct (MCC) violations and how many such

violations involved religion being invoked in his election speeches? Details of action taken.

2. How many such complaints were received with reference to his speeches in Tamil Nadu, Assam, Rajasthan and Uttar Pradesh? How many were investigated, how many acted upon, how many rejected? Provide me written orders passed if any. If rejected, provide me reasons, if any.
3. Has the commission ordered action under Representation of the People Act with special reference to Section 123 and under the IPC and its successor legislation? Provide me details. If not, reasons for the same.[23]

The commission refused to answer these questions under the RTI on the ground that the information sought was not available in a compiled format.

The ECI responded:

> 1 and 2: It is informed that information sought by you is not available in compiled form and compilation of the information disproportionately divert the resources of the commission. You may refer to Section 7(9) of the RTI Act, 2005.
>
> 3: Information sought by you is in nature of clarification/opinion which is not covered under the meaning of 'information' as defined under Section 2(1) of the RTI Act, 2005.[24]

This was one of the many RTI responses under which the ECI had dodged or refused to provide correct information to the applicant. Isn't it the duty and the responsibility of the ECI to provide a detailed response to the citizens of the nation?

The effectiveness of the RTI Act has been significantly undermined by the persistent understaffing of the Central Information Commission (CIC), particularly the shortage of information officers. This chronic understaffing has resulted in a substantial backlog of RTI applications, leading to prolonged delays and significant frustration among citizens seeking information.

## The Representation of the People Act, 1951

The ECI was set up as a constitutional body, necessitating legislation to conduct free and fair elections. To ensure this, the Indian Parliament enacted the Representation of the People Act, 1951. This outlined voter qualifications, the preparation and publication of electoral rolls, delimitation of constituencies of both houses of Parliament and the number of seats allocated.

This act provided the legal framework for preparation of elections. The second major legislative measure focused on the actual conducting of elections.

It covered qualifications and disqualifications for membership, notifications for elections, the administrative machinery for conducting elections, election agents, vote counting, election expenses, publication of results, election petitions, electoral offences and bye-elections.

Under both acts, the Union government established certain rules. Handbooks for returning officers and presiding officers are based on the Representation of the People Act, 1951. Chapter 8 will discuss the relevance of the act and its role in assisting the citizens to question the ECI's conduct during the 2024 Lok Sabha elections.

Sukumar Sen, the first election commissioner, prepared a report on the challenges faced during the 1951–52 general elections. He noted:

> Certain piece-meal amendments of the election law are on the legislative anvil but no attempt has yet been made to codify the entire election law in a comprehensive

> manner. It is very desirable, however, that this work should be completed at least a year before the next general elections so that the election machinery, the political parties, the candidates and the individual voter may become fully conversant with the law under which the next elections will take place. [25]

The ECI emerged as an institution to safeguard democracy. The act introduced a new set of challenges regarding electoral rolls. The act established 1 March 1950 as the new cut-off date (previously it was 1 January 1949) for voter registration, removing a significant number of voters from the electoral rolls.[26]

The act provided for the delimitation of constituencies. While the electoral rolls were published constituency-wise, it was impossible without established constituencies. Delays in publishing the electoral rolls could further delay the elections, leading to amendments that allowed preliminary publication of the electoral rolls based on administrative units.

Sen highlighted in his report that:

> The RPA (Preparation of Electoral Rolls) Rules, 1950 empowered the Electoral Registration Officers to file applications before the appropriate Revising Authorities for the inclusion in or the exclusion from the electoral rolls of the names of persons belonging to certain categories, namely Armed Forces of the Union, persons holding any office in India declared by the President to be an office the holder of which would be entitled to such inclusion.[27]

Before holding the first elections, the ECI prepared the electoral rolls. The 1951 census indicates that the adult population (over twenty-one years) was 50–55 per cent of the total population. Of the total adult population of 18,03,07,684, the electoral rolls included 17,32,13,635, leaving 70,34,839 adults unregistered due to a lack of necessary qualifications.[28]

The appointment of electoral registration officers was suggested by the state governments, and the 'ECI's notifications making these appointments were issued under the amended law and published in the Gazette of India, on 1 November 1950'.[29]

Under the provisions of Section 22 of the Representation of the People Act, 1951, the ECI appointed an electoral registration officer for constituency-wise publication of electoral rolls.

The commission then appointed a returning officer and an assistant returning officer for each constituency under Sections 20, 21 and 23 of the act. The appointment of many returning officers required many senior government officers in the states. A more pressing challenge was finding sufficient people to be appointed as presiding and polling officers for every booth. As early as 8 April 1950, the ECI requested the state governments to list their requirements for presiding and polling officers, along with police personnel, to carry out polling duties.

## Appointment of Election Commissioners

It is necessary to maintain the neutrality of the appointments of the CEC and ECs to uphold democracy. On 2 March 2023, the SC's bench of five judges, addressed this in the PIL *Anoop Baranwal* v. *Union of India*, filed in 2015. In 2018, the PIL filed by Advocate Anoop Baranwal was referred to the Constitution Bench to interpret Article 324. It challenged the appointment of the EC members by the executive, stating it would be a hurdle in conducting a free and fair election.

During the hearing, the bench stated: 'There has been a disturbing trend after 2004 of picking people who they know will not be able to complete six years of tenure … The so-called independence that you pay lip service to is completely destroyed by having this kind of term.'[30] The bench further added: 'Since the ECI performs a quasi-judicial function of conducting elections and resolving disputes among parties, the appointment of the Chief Election Commissioner and Election Commissioners by the executive alone may allow the biases of the ruling party to reflect in appointments.'[31]

However, the Central government informed the bench that any alteration in the current appointment process could only be executed by an amendment in Parliament, otherwise it would be a breach of the procedures of appointment of ECI members. The SC held that the ECI should be fearlessly and robustly independent. This can happen only if the selection process is not done by the executive who has a critical stake in the electoral process.

The SC directed that CEC and ECs appointment shall be done by the president on the basis of the advice tendered by a committee consisting of the prime minister, the leader of opposition in the Lok Sabha and, in case of no such leader, the leader of the largest party in the opposition and the CJI.

After the SC judgement, the Parliament passed a legislation – The Chief Election Commissioner and other Election Commissioners (Appointment, Condition of Service and Term of Office) Bill, 2023.

In December 2023, President Droupadi Murmu gave her assent to the bill that brought in the process for the appointment of CEC and other ECs. The new Act has provisions to set up a search committee chaired by the law minister and two other persons not below the rank of secretary to prepare a panel of five persons for consideration by the selections committee for appointment as CEC or ECs.

Section 7 of The Chief Election Commissioner and other Election Commissioner (Appointment, Conditions of Service and Term of Office) Act,2023, stated that the Selection Committee, consisting of the prime minister as Chairperson, the leader of opposition and a Union cabinet minister, is to make recommendations to the president for the appointment of CEC and other ECs.[33]

The new law removed the CJI from the selection committee and introduced cabinet ministers as the third member (to be nominated by the prime minister), thereby increasing the involvement of executives in the appointment process of the CEC and ECs.

The petition pointed out that the act was 'passed in Lok Sabha at a time when the majority of the opposition Members of Parliament were suspended by the speaker of Lok Sabha. Such an important legislation has been passed without any debate or discussion which was the important and critical forum to raise issues about the autonomy of the Election Commission.'[34]

The intent of the Constituent Assembly was that the appointments of the CEC and ECs were not to be made by the executive, but the new Act gave more power to the executive.

The new Act increased the involvement of the executive in the appointment procedures that raised critical questions about the transparency and fairness of the ECI. The petitioner demanded quashing of the new Act on the appointment of CCs and ECs as unconstitutional. The matter remains pending as of February 2025 when this book goes to print.

You will read how the ECI disregarded public and civil society protests about the lack of openness and dialogue during the 2024 Lok Sabha elections in the following chapter.

# 8

# A Can of Worms

## Unpacking Questions Raised about the Election Process

In the early 1980s, EVMs were used in conducting elections in many constituencies. In the 2004 elections, EVMs replaced ballot paper votes in 543 parliamentary constituencies, since the results could be declared much faster. But the transition to EVMs brought up major concerns of machine tampering and machine swapping that continue to this day.

Political parties often raise concerns about the vulnerability of EVM-VVPATs to manipulation during elections, still these claims are frequently made without substantial evidence. One of the primary reasons for the inability to prove the alleged vulnerabilities of EVMs and VVPATs is that only the ECI and the manufacturers have access to the machines. For other stakeholders and the general public, the inner workings of these systems remain a 'black box', making it difficult to verify the integrity of the voting process. This lack of transparency contributes to ongoing debates and suspicions surrounding the reliability of electronic voting in India.

The debate on the voting machines skyrocketed when Kannan Gopinathan, who was a returning officer of the Dadra and Nagar Haveli constituency in the 2019 Lok Sabha elections and an IAS officer, raised questions about the vulnerabilities of EVMs and VVPATs post-elections. On 2 October 2019 he wrote a letter to CEC Sunil Arora highlighting 'Concerns about the vulnerability of Election Process (due to the introduction of VVPATs) and the potential threats to national security'.[1] This letter revealed information about the EVM-VVPAT that was intentionally not disclosed to the general public.

Kannan's letter to the CEC said, 'Post the introduction of VVPATs, the EVM as a whole is now electronically aware of which candidate is at which serial number on the ballot box.'

Before VVPATs, there was no requirement to upload party symbols on the machine. However, after the introduction of the VVPAT machines, the party symbols and names are electronically uploaded on the machines through symbol loading unit (SLU). This ensures that a slip comes out of the machine with the details of the party and the candidate after the vote is cast for the voter to verify. Kannan, also a computer engineer said, 'This is highly undesirable as this opens the EVMs to pre-programmed hacking. A smart program can manipulate EVM behaviour at a large scale using this exposure.'[2]

The ECI marked his letter and informed the media that it had been forwarded to the technical committee for further deliberation, but never shared the committee's findings with Gopinathan, the complainant.

When the issue of EVM-VVPAT was heard in the SC a few weeks before the 2024 Lok Sabha elections, the ECI informed the SC that the SLU was connected with the VVPAT to upload party symbols, confirming the existence of a fourth device used in the election process. However, the ECI keeps updating its FAQ sections on EVM-VVPAT issues. When I checked the FAQ a few days after the SC hearing for writing an article, I found interesting bits on the SLU, although I am not sure whether the ECI updated this section on SLU before or after the SC hearing.

The FAQ section mentions, 'The EVM uses secure controllers which can disable further programming after a step known as one-time programming (OTP). Further, the ECI-EVM is a standalone device without any wired or wireless connectivity outside the EVM systems.' On the SLU, the ECI stated that 'in order to print the VVPAT slips, the VVPAT needs to have the symbol information, and the candidate information loaded as data in graphical format. This can only be done through an authorized EVM-specific device known as the Symbol Loading Unit.'

The SC ordered the ECI to preserve all used SLUs for a minimum of forty-five days after using it and concluded,

> On completion of the symbol loading process in the VVPATs undertaken on or after 01.05.2024, the symbol loading units shall be sealed and secured in a container. The candidates or their representatives shall sign the seal. The sealed containers, containing the symbol loading units, shall be kept in the strong room along with the EVMs at least for a period of 45 days post the declaration of results. They shall be opened, examined and dealt with as in the case of EVMs.[3]

This came after the petition filed by independent lawyers and civil society members demanding 100 per cent counting of the VVPAT slips and granting voters the right to verify the VVPAT slips before depositing them in the ballot box. During this hearing, the SC provided the ECI with an opportunity to explain the functioning of the EVM-VVPAT. It was only then that the ECI informed the SC about the SLU and other relevant facts related to the process followed by the ECI in preparing voting machines for polling.

The petition also cited my article on discrepancies between votes polled and votes counted in the 2019 Lok Sabha elections.[4] When this issue arose in the SC, the

ECI defended itself by stating that 'the report referred to in The Quint is with reference to the live voter turnout data uploaded on the website of the ECI during 2019 Lok Sabha Elections'.[5] When the ECI made this statement about my article, I texted one of the petitioner's lawyers, asking her to inform the SC that I had considered the final voter turnout data, rather than the live data. The ECI, however, maintained that the EVM-VVPAT could not be hacked or tampered with.

In its 26 April 2024 judgement the SC rejected two primary demands: 100 per cent counting of VVPAT slips and allowing voters to drop the VVPAT slip into the ballot box. This came as a disappointment to many, including me. But this was not the first time the demand for VVPAT slips verification had been raised in the SC. To understand this better, we must note that VVPATs came much later than EVMs.

Former BJP law minister Subramanian Swamy played a significant role in adopting VVPATs in the election process. In 2013, he sought a writ of mandamus from the SC to ask the ECI to incorporate a paper trail or paper receipt system in EVMs.

The SC held,

> From the materials placed by both the sides, we are satisfied that the "paper trail" is an indispensable requirement of free and fair elections. The confidence of the voters in the EVMs can be achieved only with the introduction of the "paper trail". EVMs with VVPAT system ensure the accuracy of the voting system. With an intent to have fullest transparency in the system and to restore the confidence of the voters, it is necessary to set up EVMs with VVPAT system because vote is nothing but an act of expression which has immense importance in democratic system.[6]

The SC permitted the ECI to introduce VVPATs 'in a phased manner' and directed the Government of India 'to provide required financial assistance for procurement of units of VVPAT'. This order left a gap by not including the number of VVPAT machines to be counted during the tallying process.

Even before the SC pronounced its judgement in favour of introducing the VVPAT in the election process, the ECI had already been working on the prototype of the VVPAT since 2010. The ECI amended the Conduct of Election Rules, 1961, following the SC's order to introduce VVPAT machines and used them for the first time in all twenty-one polling stations of the Noksen Assembly constituency in Nagaland in 2013. This marked the beginning of the usage of VVPAT machines. After this, the ECI continued to use VVPAT machines in a phased manner. By June 2017, VVPAT machines were used in 100 per cent of polling stations.

In February 2019, a few weeks before the Lok Sabha elections, former Andhra Pradesh chief minister N. Chandrababu Naidu and other opposition parties filed a petition in the SC demanding a verification of 50 per cent of VVPAT slips in each constituency. The ECI had informed the SC that the election results could be delayed as it would take six days to count 50 per cent of the VVPAT slips.[7]

The bench, consisting of former CJI Ranjan Gogoi and Justices Deepak Gupta and Sanjiv Khanna, ordered stating, 'having regard to the need to generate the greatest degree of satisfaction in all with regard to the full accuracy of the election results, it was held that the number of EVMs that would now be subjected to verification so far as VVPAT paper trail is concerned would be 5 per Assembly Constituency or Assembly Segments in a Parliament

Constituency ... it was also held that random selection of the machines that would be subjected to the process of VVPAT paper trail verification'.[8]

In the 26 April 2024 judgement, the SC refused 100 per cent VVPAT slip verification. But the judgement was not a complete letdown for the petitioners. The SC, through its order, allowed the contesting candidates in the second and third positions to check and verify the EVM-VVPAT if they feared any tampering or manipulation.

The SC said,

> Nevertheless, not because we have any doubt, but to only further strengthen the integrity of the election process, we are inclined to issue the following directions:
>
> 1. On completion of the symbol loading process in the VVPATs undertaken on or after 01.05.2024, the symbol loading units shall be sealed and secured in a container.
>
> 2. The burnt memory/microcontroller in 5 per cent of the EVMs, that is, the control unit, ballot unit and the VVPAT, per assembly constituency/assembly segment of a parliamentary constituency shall be checked and verified by a team of engineers from the manufacturers of the EVMs, post the announcement of the results, for any tampering or modification, on a written request made by candidates who are at Sl. No. 2 or Sl. No. 3, behind the highest polled candidate. Such a request should be made within a period of seven days from the date of declaration of the result. The District Election Officer, in consultation with the team of engineers, shall certify the authenticity/intactness of the burnt memory/microcontroller after the verification process is conducted.

Since the 2024 Lok Sabha elections were under way when this judgement was pronounced, it was applicable to the ongoing elections. The ECI released the standard operating procedure (SOP) to check and verify the EVM-VVPAT machines before the Lok Sabha elections results were announced.[9] According to the SOP, the ECI requested ₹40,000 plus GST for the checking and verification of each EVM-VVPAT machine, making the entire process expensive for the contesting candidates. The SC included a condition in the judgement: if the machines were found to be manipulated or tampered with, the ECI would bear the cost.

The ECI announced that it had received requests from eleven candidates for checking and verification of the microcontroller of the EVM-VVPAT after the results of the 2024 Lok Sabha elections were announced. It is interesting to note that three candidates from the BJP, who had been supportive of the EVM-VVPAT, had asked for verification of the machines.[10]

On 16 July 2024, after receiving these requests, the ECI released the technical SOP to check and verify the machines.[11] There was discussion among the experts and candidates regarding the methods the ECI might adopt to conduct these checks. But the ECI's methods simply meant that candidates would be allowed to press the ballot unit buttons a maximum of 1,400 times. They could be pressed in any order; for example, button one could be pressed fifty times, button two could be pressed thirty times, and so on. Candidates could then check whether the votes recorded by the control unit and the VVPAT matched their votes cast. This would determine whether the microcontrollers were working accurately.

This process seemed incomplete for the checking and verification of EVMs. Polling officers would conduct a mock poll of fifty votes before the start of polling at a booth, in the presence of agents from political parties. The ECI suggested the same mock poll process but allowed candidates to cast 1,400 votes on each machine. As a layperson, I found this process inadequate for conducting proper checks. To gain more insight, I spoke with experts about the technical SOP, and they shared my concerns. They argued that a proper check should have included forensic testing of the memory and microcontroller of the EVMs. Simply casting votes on the EVM-VVPAT did not confirm that the machine had never been tampered with.

Subhashis Banerjee, an IIT alumnus and computer science engineer, mentioned in an interview that the SC's decision to allow engineers to conduct checks and verification based on complaints from the candidates was the opposite of what the 'maker-checker' aimed to accomplish.[12] He emphasised that the SC should have instructed the manufacturers to hire independent engineers to check the voting machines as the makers cannot be the checkers of the machines manufactured by them.

He also noted that the court's decision to refuse an independent audit of the source code of the EVM-VVPAT machines was misplaced because any gadget or machine should be handed over to an independent hacker who can assess whether the machine was vulnerable to manipulation. He further added that the SC wanted citizens to accept the ECI's claim that the machines were tamper-proof.

Many people expressed disappointment over the order, which did not permit 100 per cent counting of VVPAT slips and cross verification of EVM-VVPAT votes. Despite the petitioner emphasising that counting VVPAT slips would not take more than a day, I think the longevity of the process – whether a day, or six, or twelve – was not the major concern. What mattered was whether the counting process was accurate, leaving no doubt in the minds of voters.

## EVM-VVPAT versus Paper Ballot Voting

Journalists often ask me if I support paper ballot voting because EVMs cannot be trusted. My response has always been that it shouldn't be one of the two. I support both EVM and VVPAT voting systems, provided the ECI conducts 100 per cent counting of the VVPAT slips and maintains transparency by answering the questions raised by stakeholders.

In our current voting system, we count votes that voters cannot see – EVM votes – while neglecting to count the votes that have been verified by the voters –VVPAT slips. Essentially, once a voter presses the ballot unit (one part of the EVM), they cannot be sure that their vote has been recorded as cast in the control unit. While voters can see and verify the VVPAT slip, the ECI does not count the slips.

The current Indian electoral system utilises both EVMs and VVPATs. While EVMs record votes electronically, VVPATs generate a physical paper slip that displays the candidate or party the voter chose. This paper slip serves as a verifiable record of the vote cast.

To enhance the system's transparency and address concerns about the accuracy of EVM results, the ECI could implement a more robust verification process. This could involve:

1. Randomised VVPAT Slip Counting: Instead of counting all VVPAT slips, a statistically significant random sample could be selected and counted. This would provide a reliable estimate of the overall vote distribution.
2. Public Verification: The counting of VVPAT slips could be conducted in a transparent manner, potentially with representatives from political parties and civil society organisations observing the process.

3. Automated Matching: Advanced technology could be employed to automatically compare the results from the VVPAT slip count with the EVM results, flagging any discrepancies for further investigation.

By implementing these measures, the ECI could significantly enhance the credibility and transparency of the electoral process, thereby strengthening public confidence in the integrity of elections.

The purpose of introducing the VVPAT, as per the SC's order, was to let voters verify their votes. However, in the current system, the voter gets only about seven seconds to verify the VVPAT slip before it falls into the VVPAT box. According to experts, this process cannot be termed as a full verification of VVPAT slips votes. A true check can only occur if the voters have access to the VVPAT slip and have time to inspect it while holding it in their hands before dropping it into the ballot box. This process would strengthen the election process and boost voter confidence.

In the SC, the ECI provided arguments for not counting the slips, stating that the 'VVPAT slip is made of a 9.9 cm x 5.6 cm thermal paper coated with chemical to ensure print retention for about five years. It is very soft and sticky, which makes the counting process tedious and slow.'[13]

Regarding the decision to not hand over the VVPAT slip to the voter, the ECI informed the SC that there was a real risk of voters switching the slip or not dropping it into the box at all. We should not forget that EVMs were used in the 1980s elections in India in a limited capacity. Before that, elections were conducted using paper ballots for a long time. Even then, voters could have run away with or switched ballot papers before dropping them into the box. A VVPAT slip is similar, it is essentially a small ballot paper.

Moreover, a voter who has come to a polling station to vote would not choose to quit the process.

The SC acknowledged the ECI's argument and denied allowing voters physical access to the VVPAT slips, stating misuse, malpractice and disputes. It added that the electoral protocols, with the checks and data, ensured the exercise of the right to fundamental franchise of the citizens.

A key concern regarding VVPATs is their short retention period. As reported in my article 'Why did EC destroy VVPAT slips of 2019 LS polls in Such a Hurry?' published in The Quint on 2 April 2024,[14] I filed an RTI request with the Delhi State Election Commission to inspect the VVPAT slips used in the 2019 Lok Sabha elections. However, the district election officer informed me that the slips had already been destroyed based on an ECI directive. I also received a letter from the ECI instructing both the Delhi State Election Commission and the chief electoral officers of all states and Union Territories to destroy the VVPAT slips. This letter was circulated four months after the 2019 Lok Sabha election results were announced. It also stated that the VVPAT slips for those parliamentary constituencies where an election petition had been filed should be retained.

Rule 94(b) of the Conduct of Elections Rules, 1961 iterates, 'The used or printed VVPAT slips in any election ... shall be retained for one year and shall thereafter be destroyed.' However, the rule also mentions that the used slips can be destroyed prior to one year only with the 'approval' of the ECI. This highlights a critical question: Why did the ECI hurry in disposing of the VVPAT slips? I am yet to receive an answer to this question.

It is important to note that VVPAT slips act as crucial evidence in the electoral process. According to the Conduct of Election Rules, 1961, if there are any discrepancies between the counts of EVM votes and VVPAT votes, the

ECI must consider the VVPAT slip count as the final result. The election rules prioritise the VVPAT slip count over the EVM vote count and it is puzzling why the ECI does not count them in the first place.

## Form 17C Row During the 2024 Lok Sabha Elections

The 2024 general elections brought in changes in the election processes. Form 17C and its relevance in the elections became an important debating point for political parties and digital spaces. Though political parties had been participating in the elections for several years, still many did not know the importance of Form 17C.

## Form 17C

Form 17C is a document which is divided into two parts – Part 1 and Part 2.[15] Part 1, called 'Accounts of Votes Recorded', is filled by the presiding officer at the end of polling day. Two primary pieces of information mentioned in Form 17C are the unique serial numbers of the ballot unit, control unit, VVPAT and 'total number of votes recorded as per voting machine', which refers to the actual number of votes polled in the EVM. According to the election rules, the presiding officer of each polling booth must accurately fill the form, sign it and hand over one copy to each polling agent representing a political party candidate. The returning officer also receives a copy.

Part 2 of Form 17C is titled 'Result of Counting'. This is filled out on the counting day by the returning officers and includes multiple items such as the name of the candidate, number of votes as displayed in the control unit and number of valid votes. The form lists whether the total number of votes counted match the total number of votes polled. If any political party agent points out any discrepancies between the data, they can raise an objection to the returning officer. A copy of Form 17C Part 2 is handed over to the political party agent after the results are announced.

When the 2024 Lok Sabha elections started, I found after multiple interactions that the public, polling agents and candidates contesting the elections were generally unaware of the relevance of Form 17C.

Form 17C became a point of conflict during the 2024 Lok Sabha elections when the ECI refused to share the absolute number of votes polled after phase 1 polling was over. The ECI shared the data of votes polled as percentages for each constituency. Some journalists appreciated the ECI for maintaining transparency by sharing these percentages, oblivious to the fact that it was impossible to tally the percentages of votes polled with the actual figure.

Many people began tweeting my 2019 Lok Sabha election article about discrepancies in votes polled and counted and started questioning the ECI. The demand for the absolute votes polled kept increasing during the election. Opposition political parties raised concerns about a spike in the votes polled data. A spike of 4 to 6 per cent was observed in the phase 1 and phase 2 data when comparing polling day data with the ECI data released almost ten days after phase 1 polling.[16]

The INC president and civil society members wrote separate letters to the ECI asking for an explanation regarding the votes polled percentages and the release of absolute votes polled numbers. The ECI wrote a letter to the INC president stating that the political party agents were given a copy of Form 17C after the polling concluded, allowing candidates to collect the absolute votes polled from these forms.[17]

The ECI's letter gave the impression that the constitutional body had forgotten that voters are equally important stakeholders in the elections, but there was no acknowledgement from the ECI on this.

I filed RTIs with the ECI requesting the absolute votes polled numbers for different phases. The ECI claimed to not have the data and to ask the SEC for the same.

To gain some insight into the situation, I spoke to a polling agent who stated he had never heard about Form 17C. After this encounter, I tried to explain the relevance of Form 17C through my tweets and by posting videos on my YouTube channel ExplainX as it was the only documentary proof that a candidate would have, and it would be admissible in court in the event of a petition regarding discrepancies in votes polled and counted data.

When I interviewed a polling agent, I realised many agents had not undergone proper training about Form 17C. These agents monitored whether voters were able to cast their vote and asked the presiding officer about the number of votes polled at the booth. Many of these agents would not even note the unique serial numbers of the control unit, ballot unit and VVPAT, and would not know if the machines were swapped or changed. My interview with the agent created a lot of awareness among the people. In fact, former Congressman Kapil Sibal also made a video explaining to the polling agents that they should carry Form 17C on counting day, match all the votes polled numbers with the counted numbers and check the serial numbers of the EVM-VVPAT.

Advocate Prashant Bhushan's team asked the SC to release the absolute votes polled numbers by the ECI and to make Form 17C public.[18] The SC accepted the petition and issued a notice to the ECI, but the ECI refused to make Form 17C public citing misuse concerns and a lack of technical resources to upload it. The SC deferred the matter for consideration after the 2024 Lok Sabha elections.

However, on 25 May 2024 – the day of the SC's interim order – while the sixth phase of the Lok Sabha elections was under way, the ECI shared the absolute votes polled numbers of all five phases in a press release. Most of us were shocked. I spoke to my sources in civil society, a lawyer and former CEC about why the ECI had suddenly released this data. No one had a clear answer. I was happy that we finally had access to the absolute votes polled numbers. The ECI also shared the absolute votes polled numbers for the sixth and the seventh phases after the polling was over.

The BJP government once again came to power, but this time they could not secure a majority in Parliament. They formed a coalition NDA government with the parties of Nitish Kumar and Chandrababu Naidu. For the first time in ten years, we had a leader of the opposition in Parliament. This provided some hope for maintaining democracy in the country, keeping a watch on the government's actions and becoming the voice of the people.

Post the elections, I began to analyse the EVM votes polled and counted figures from the 2024 Lok Sabha elections. This time, both sets of data were officially available on the website of the ECI. When the ECI released the absolute votes polled numbers, it stated that 'any alteration in the number of votes polled is not possible'.[19]

I was not expecting the results I found after completing the data analysis of the seven phases – there was a mismatch between the votes polled and the counted data. In some constituencies, the votes counted were in deficit, while in others they were in surplus. I repeatedly tweeted about this issue, made videos and uploaded them on my channel, but the ECI did not respond. A few independent analysts also found discrepancies in the votes polled and counted numbers.

The issue raised on X by Aniket Aga, an academic, about the discrepancy in the number of votes counted in some parliamentary constituencies on twitter was addressed by the Uttar Pradesh CEC. He replied,

> The polling stations whose votes polled are not counted are of two categories.[20]
>
> (1) Where the Presiding Officer by mistake fails to clear the Mock Poll data from the Control Unit before starting the actual poll or he fails to remove Mock Poll slips from the VVPAT before starting the actual poll.
>
> (2) The total votes polled in the Control Unit does not match the record of votes in Form 17C prepared by the Presiding Officer and who records [an] incorrect number by mistake. The votes of above two categories of polling stations are counted towards the end of the counting only in the case if [the] sum total of votes polled in all such polling stations is equal to or greater than the margin between the first and the second candidate. If it is lower than the margin then the votes are not counted at all and therefore there arises a difference between total votes polled by EVMs and votes counted.

The ADR also conducted an independent analysis of the EVM votes polled and counted numbers and found disparity in the data. In its press release, the ADR said that of 543 constituencies, 176 constituencies displayed greater number of votes counted than polled. In 362 constituencies, the number of votes counted was less than the number polled. In four constituencies, the numbers matched accurately and in one constituency – Surat – elections did not take place because no one filled an election nomination except for the BJP candidate.[21]

Such unopposed victories of a candidate are not a new phenomenon, but they are relatively rare. Since the inception of general elections in India, around thirty candidates have secured parliamentary polls and by-elections without facing any opposition.[22] However, the victory of the BJP candidate in Surat marks the first such incident in Gujarat's electoral history.

Winning an election uncontested poses a threat to democracy because the candidate is not chosen by the people. Opposition is a core part of democracy which ceases to be one if a candidate is elected without contesting elections. In Surat, signatories for Congress candidate Nilesh Kumbhani's nomination papers declared on affidavit that their signatures were forged. Suresh Padsala, who was fielded as a dummy candidate by the Congress, also had his nomination papers rejected because one of his proposers declared on affidavit that his signature was forged. Eight other candidates withdrew their nominations, making the BJP candidate, Mukesh Dalal, the sole winner.[23]

The mystery of the discrepancy that began with my article in 2019 continued into the 2024 Lok Sabha elections. This time, even the ECI could not invalidate the claims by arguing that the numbers were provisional. However, it failed to come up with a clarification.

The ECI's slogan 'Every vote matters' is of importance here. Congress minister C.P. Joshi lost the Nathdwara assembly constituency in the 2008 Rajasthan assembly elections by just one vote to BJP's Kalyan Singh Chauhan. In another incident, A.R. Krishnamurthy of the Janata Dal (Secular) lost to R. Dhruvanarayana by a single vote in the 2004 Karnataka assembly elections.[24]

The 2024 Lok Sabha elections have hollowed voters' faith in the electoral process. During the elections, many civil society organisations and active citizens undertook a postcard campaign – 'Grow a Spine or Resign'[25] – against the ECI for its inaction against politicians for violating the MCC and for the delay in sharing the absolute numbers of votes polled. The lack of communication from the ECI adds to the prevalent doubts in the minds of voters. To regain its credibility, the ECI must become more accountable to the public by maintaining transparency.

# 9

# One Nation One Election

## What Will India Choose?

The idea 'One Nation One Election' has been part of the public discourse for over a decade, ever since the BJP government came to power at the Centre. This proposal raises critical questions like whether it will strengthen or weaken democratic principles and its impact on democracy. While potentially reducing logistical costs, will ONOE ensure fair and equitable representation for all states and regions? Even more concerning are matters of execution: – Does the current constitutional framework allow for such a drastic change to the electoral calendar? Is India adequately equipped with the necessary infrastructure, including EVMs and VVPATs, to conduct elections of this magnitude seamlessly?

The proposed scheme of ONOE was first introduced in the BJP's 2014 election manifesto as a promised goal. It said, 'The BJP will seek, through consultation with other parties, to evolve a method of holding assembly and Lok Sabha elections simultaneously. Apart from reducing election expenses for both political parties and government, this will ensure certain stability for state governments. We will also look at revising expenditure limits realistically'[1]

The scheme is not a new concept. It was first mentioned by the ECI in its 1983 annual report prepared by the former CEC R.K. Trivedi.[2] The report mentioned the feasibility of ONOE, stating,

In September 1982 the Commission recommended holding simultaneous elections to the House of the People and the Legislative Assemblies of States for the following reasons:

1. Huge administrative expenses can be avoided if Lok Sabha and State Assembly elections are held together.
2. Simultaneous elections will lessen the administrative workload, as there would be no need to revise electoral rolls separately for the Lok Sabha and State Assembly elections.
3. Conducting elections separately requires the deployment of lakhs of officers and staff, along with a few lakhs of police personnel for each election, which affects their normal course of duties.
4. Government functions and activities slow down during the election phase, whether for the Lok Sabha or the State Assembly elections, resulting in inconvenience for the common man.
5. Simultaneous elections will significantly reduce the campaigning expenses incurred by candidates and political parties.
6. If simultaneous elections are held, states would not have to bear the expense of dismantling or slowing down the administrative setup for infrastructure development twice in five years.

The Law Commission, in its 170th report released in 1999, advocated for simultaneous elections for the Lok Sabha and all assemblies but with conditions. It said,

> This cycle of elections every year, and in the out of season, should be put an end to. We must go back to the situation where the elections to Lok Sabha and all the Legislative Assemblies are held at once. It is true

> that we cannot conceive or provide for all the situations and eventualities that may arise whether on account of the use of article 356 (which of course has come down substantially after the decision of Supreme Court in *S.R. Bommai* v. *Union of India*) or for other reasons, yet the holding of a separate election to a Legislative Assembly should be an exception and not the rule. The rule ought to be one election once in five years for Lok Sabha and all the Legislative Assemblies.[3]

The report emphasised that ONOE is possible only with full support of political parties. The report further added,

> ... adjustments may have to be made in future with a view to achieve the desired goal of one election for Lok Sabha and to all the Legislative Assemblies simultaneously. If all the political parties co-operate, the necessary steps can be taken without hurting the interest of any political party. Maybe, a constitutional amendment can solve the problem. [4]

The two reports – one by the ECI in 1983 and the other by the Law Commission in 1999 – never gained momentum until the Modi-led government came to power.

In December 2015, the first report supporting ONOE was released during the BJP government by the Parliamentary Standing Committee on Personnel, Public Grievances, Law and Justice titled Feasibility of Holding Simultaneous Elections to the House of People (Lok Sabha) and State Legislative Assemblies.[5] The report outlined certain objectives supporting ONOE: massive expenditure incurred in separate elections, slow progress in development programmes due to the implementation of the MCC, disruption of normal public life due to political campaigns and the sizeable deployment of forces in separate elections.

Along with this, it outlined the possible barriers in conducting ONOE. The biggest challenge would be to make a large-scale purchase of EVM-VVPAT machines to carry out simultaneous elections at the Centre and in the states.

Articles 83(2) and 172(1) specify that the tenure of the Lok Sabha and state legislative assemblies cannot exceed five years, except in the case of an emergency. The political parties stated that the people elect the government for a five-year term; however, in coalition governments elections may be necessitated before the end of the stipulated term period.

Political parties that extended their support for ONOE were the All India Anna Dravida Munnetra Kazhagam (AIADMK),Asom Gana Parishad (AGP) and Indian Union Muslim League (IUML). Certain parties, like the Desiya Murpokku Dravida Kazhagam (DMDK) and Shiromani Akali Dal (SAD) had queries and suggestions about the scheme. SAD suggested:

> An important point needs to be considered is that in case if in some State a hung Assembly is formed, as recently happened in Delhi, what mechanism will be available? As President Rule in such a situation cannot be imposed for the remaining full term of the Legislative Assembly. And if there happens to be a re-election due to any factor what should be the term of the Assembly thus constituted? Such solution [sic] needs to be clarified in time so as to implement the new policy.[6]

Parties such as the INC, the CPI, All India Trinamool Congress (AITC), the All India Majlis-e-Ittehadul Muslimeen (AIMIM) and Nationalist Congress Party (NCP) rejected the ONOE scheme.

The INC stated that holding simultaneous elections was 'impractical' and 'unworkable' given the diversity of the country. The AITC argued that postponing elections was anti-democratic and unconstitutional; however, the party supported the idea of simultaneous elections for panchayats and municipal bodies.

The CPI rejected the proposal, labelling it 'unscientific' and 'impracticable'. They argued that it was not feasible to unilaterally abolish all legislative assemblies to conduct simultaneous Lok Sabha and state elections.

The AIMIM in its written submission to the Parliamentary Standing Committee, stated that amending the Constitution could not guarantee the smooth functioning of simultaneous elections. The party also pointed out that early elections could happen due to an unstable government, which would disrupt the process of simultaneous elections.

As many as seven of the sixteen Lok Sabhas were dissolved after the emergence of coalition governments. The Parliamentary Standing Committee report concluded, '... gaining consensus of all political parties may be difficult in certain States of the country…holding simultaneous elections may not be feasible in 2016 or even in a decade but it expresses confidence that a solution will be found to reduce the frequency of elections which relieve people and government machinery …'[7]

## NITI Aayog on ONOE

NITI Aayog published an analysis of simultaneous elections titled 'The "What", "Why", and "How": A Discussion Paper' in 2017. NITI Aayog listed the same points in support of synchronising the Lok Sabha and state legislative assembly elections as the other reports mentioned before.

On the impact of the MCC on governance, the report stated that in the year 2014, 'governance and developmental activities due to imposition of Model Code remained largely suspended for about seven months: three months across the country and about two months in Jharkhand and J and K and another two months in Maharashtra and Haryana'.[8]

An analysis of the costs incurred by the government for Lok Sabha elections showed a significant increase. The cost in the 2009 Lok Sabha elections was approximately ₹1,115 crore, while in the 2014 Lok Sabha elections, it tripled to ₹3,870 crore.[9]

The report noted that as contesting elections became increasingly expensive each year, the winning candidates explored every means to recover the spent money through corruption. This led to the misuse of taxpayers' money. In an interview with a news channel, Prime Minister Narendra Modi remarked, 'Electoral reforms are necessary if the country has to be rid of black money. It is one of the areas for electoral reforms. I believe the Prime Minister cannot take a decision on this, nor should he do that. There should be a broad discussion.'[10] To support the argument of cost-effectiveness, the report stated that holding simultaneous elections would cost ₹4,500 crore.[11]

The issue of black money permeating political funding has been a problem since the first elections conducted by the ECI. The assertion that cost-effective simultaneous elections would reduce the influx of black money is not fully correct, as it might not prevent politicians from corrupt practices.

A substantial number of security forces are deployed during elections, depending on the location of the polling booth. This results in a lock-in of the Central Armed Police Forces and state police, who are on election duty every six months. The report states that this situation is undesirable as the armed forces could be deployed elsewhere in that prolonged election period.

The report highlights that the implications of frequent elections go beyond financial costs and security concerns. It states that the elections contribute to communal, caste or religious issues leading to political instability. The 2024 Lok Sabha elections witnessed communal speeches delivered by top leaders of the BJP with the intent to polarise the nation. This issue raises important questions about the impact of ONOE on governance, security, democracy and the harmony of the country.

But the question remains: In the times we are living in, are politicians solely dependent on elections to spread hatred and polarise people? It is a complex situation, as revealed by the actions of the BJP, which, despite holding 240 seats and forming a coalition government, issued a problematic order to the state police of Uttar Pradesh. This order mandated that all eateries, such as hotels and dhabas, located along the kanwar yatra route display the names and addresses of the operator, proprietor, manager along with other relevant personnel details. For decades, kanwar yatris have taken the same route to their pilgrimage sites during the month of sawan, dining at the same eateries without considering the religious identity of the owners. However, the BJP's order highlighted how political actions can implant societal and communal divisions.

NITI Aayog's report recognised the challenges of synchronising Lok Sabha and state assembly elections. It noted that introducing ONOE might require reducing the tenure of many state assemblies by more than two years, while others might need to be extended by more than two years. NITI Aayog referred the Parliamentary Standing Committee's recommendation: 'The Committee has envisaged holding of elections of same Legislative Assemblies at midterm of Lok Sabha and remaining with the end of tenure of Lok Sabha. Similarly, the second phase of elections can be held in 2019 along with the General Elections to Lok Sabha.'[12]

In 2018, the Law Commission of India published a report on ONOE, which shared the same views. The commission supported the idea of conducting simultaneous elections for the Lok Sabha and the state legislatures, adding that it would prevent the country from being in constant election mode.[13]

Jagdeep Chhokar, founder of ADR, released a paper on ONOE titled 'Simultaneous Elections: Striking at the Roots of Parliamentary Democracy'. Chhokar asked a relevant question: Should the nation strive to create the 'most effective' democracy or the 'least expensive' democracy'?[14] He argued that the combination of Union and state elections is flawed; this exercise would require extensive amendments to the Constitution, upsetting the balance of power between the state and the Centre and would create favourable conditions for the Union government.

About the proposition of shortening the terms of certain state assemblies, Chhokar questioned whether the conduct of elections – intrinsic for the survival of a democracy – can be sacrificed for 'development' or administrative compulsions. He stated that the 'MCC merely prevents the party from attempting to misuse the fact of it being in power to acquire unfair advantage over opposing parties and candidates. To say that the MCC prevents usual development and governance activities is just not true.'[15]

Most reports on ONOE concluded that the imposition of the MCC would put development programmes on a pause at the central and state levels. This was disproved by the former CEC S.Y. Quraishi in his book *The Making of the Great Indian Election*. Quraishi observed that the 'ECI only says, no new announcement will be done, which would seduce the voter' during this period. Quraishi in his article

'Desirability and Feasibility of Simultaneous Election' further adds, 'All that ECI disallows is new policies. What stops the governments from announcing new policies in four years and eleven months? Why all the bright ideas come only on the eve of elections? That is ECI's only objection. Everything ongoing must continue.'[16]

During elections, political parties and politicians are alert and announce schemes and policies in public welfare to woo voters. Politicians in power expedite infrastructure projects before elections so that they can inaugurate them just before the elections and capture newspaper headlines. These are tactics used by politicians, and while voters are aware of them, they still fall for these tricks.

Does governance suffer as a result? Many of us have heard people say, 'Election dates announce ho gaye hain, ab koi afsar kaam nahin karega' (Election dates have been announced, now no bureaucrat will work). This reflects a mindset among government employees: once election dates are announced, they relax until the next government takes over. Chhokar asserts, 'Governance does not suffer because of the MCC but because members of the political executive decide to overlook or forget the "Oath of Office" they take while being sworn-in as Ministers in the Union or state government … the smallest of election anywhere in the country is treated as if it is a referendum on the government and almost all Ministers spend their work time campaigning or doing other things related to election.'[17]

During the 2019 Lok Sabha elections, Prime Minister Narendra Modi attended 145 public engagements. However, he crossed this figure in the 2024 Lok Sabha elections by organising over 200 public rallies and 80 interviews to various media outlets within a few months.[18]

Most experts and think tanks believe that the current electoral process keeps politicians alert during Lok Sabha and state assembly elections. If India adopts ONOE, political parties will likely become active only once every five years.

India's 16th CEC Navin Chawla stated in an interview regarding ONOE, 'The cost of a general election is about Rs 4,500 crore to the exchequer, a small price to pay when the benefit lies in upholding the pillars of the electoral edifice because periodic elections are also reaffirmation of the democratic process.'[19]

Chawla also pointed out that holding simultaneous elections could be more expensive logistically, as 'at least two-thirds more EVM-VVPATs would have to be manufactured because these are not available off the shelf'.[20] The requirement for the number of trained poll staff would increase, which would further add to the cost.

On 17 January 2024, Mallikarjun Kharge wrote a letter to Dr Niten Chandra in which he argued against the ruling government's claim about cost-effectiveness of ONOE, stating, 'Considering elections are held once in 5 years, the expenses make up less than 0.02% of the total Union budget for the preceding 5 years. When elections are held separately to the state assemblies, the cost of the election is fully borne by the respective states. The expenses for assembly elections may also be (a) similar percentage of their state budgets. We feel the people will be willing to consider this small amount as the cost of free and fair elections to uphold democracy.'[21]

Late Sitaram Yechury, former general secretary of the CPI(M), stated in an article that voters 'welcome elections' because they feel empowered to elect their representatives. 'People in rural areas say that they get water, road, power whenever election is announced.'[22]

In his book *India's Experiment with Democracy*, Quraishi asserts that people in India have a strong affinity for elections because politicians disappear after elections and reappear only to seek votes. Quraishi offers suggestions for tackling the cost of elections by proposing a cap on political parties' campaign expenditure. Second, the state should fund the candidates based on their performance in the most recent elections.

Two main reasons to implement ONOE, according to many reputed institutions and their reports, are the expensive election process and the disruption of development activities. However, these have been constantly challenged by former CECs, opposition political party leaders and experts of electoral processes. One major objection raised by the opposition political parties and think tanks is voter behaviour. The critics of ONOE have pointed out the high possibility of voters voting for the same political party during simultaneous Union and state elections. However, NITI Aayog and different arms of the government have discarded this argument. Evidence suggests that voter behaviour may favour a single political party if the ONOE scheme is implemented. According to data from IDFC, an independent think tank focusing on economic development, there is a 77 per cent chance that a voter will support the same party for both the Centre and the state legislature in the case of simultaneous elections.[23]

On 6 March 2018, former SC judge Justice P.B. Sawant voiced a similar concern in an article for *The Indian Express*:

> Voters vote on local issues while voting for the state assemblies and are motivated by national and international concerns while electing their representatives in the Lok Sabha. But simultaneous elections may steamroll them into voting for the same party for both the Houses, although they do not desire to do so. This may distort the true opinion of the people. The purpose of election itself may thus be defeated.[24]

The diversity of issues and the complex social structure in the country have a direct impact on elections. In 2024, simultaneous Lok Sabha and Assembly polls were held in four states: Andhra Pradesh, Odisha, Sikkim and Arunachal Pradesh. During this time, discussions on TV, social media and among friends and family focused only on the Lok Sabha elections, with many voters being unaware of the assembly elections. National political parties campaigned on national issues, suggesting that regional concerns might be sidelined in the ONOE scheme.

Separate elections for the Centre and the states provide a balance between national and regional issues. Political parties are more likely to address local issues when campaigning for state elections. Separate elections provide voters a platform to voice their demands to candidates. A successful democracy should strengthen the voice of the people, no matter the cost.

## Amendments of the Constitution of India

There is consensus on one point among those who are in favour of and against ONOE: it would require amendments to at least five articles of the Constitution. Articles 83, 85, 172 and 174 that mentions the duration and the dissolution of the Lok Sabha and legislative assemblies. It would also require an amendment of Article 356 under which a state legislative assembly can be dissolved by imposing President's Rule.[25] Would these amendments impact the federal structure of the Constitution?

### *What Does the Federal Character of the Indian Constitution Mean?*

Federalism is a form of government in which the sovereign power authority is divided between the Union and the states, allowing both to function within their respective jurisdictions. India is a union of many states and has a unitary element. Although the term 'federal' does not appear in the Constitution, Article 1(1) states that 'India, that is Bharat, shall be a Union of States'.[26] This structure ensures checks on the governance of different ruling parties at the Centre and in the states. In India, multiple strong regional parties govern various states, questioning the actions of the ruling government at the Centre.

After understanding the relevance of India's federal character, the question that arises is would it be appropriate to introduce multiple amendments in the Constitution to implement ONOE. Louise Tillin, a professor of politics at King's College London, said,

> ... simultaneous elections may flatten the diversity of political cultures across India and weaken the connectedness of voters to their state governments – as distinct from the national government. Indian federalism is better seen as an original form of federalism rather than a lesser form. India's unique federal system was designed by constitutional architects to address the challenges the country faced in the mid-20th century. Federalism in practice has evolved in the decades since the Constitution, shaped especially by changes within the party system.[27]

Ever since the Modi government came to power with a full majority, 'federalism has seemed to be under threat from the ability of a nationally dominant party to centralise power', Tillin further expressed.

Additionally, K.C. Tyagi, former Rajya Sabha member, said, 'Simultaneous elections are an attack on the autonomy and independence of state governments. This can not only weaken this federal structure but also increase the conflict of interest between the Centre and states.'[28]

Citing *S.R. Bommai* v. *Union of India* (1994), Manuraj Shanmugasundaram, an advocate and Dravida Munnetra Kazhagam spokesperson, contended that ONOE raises several legal concerns. He stated that the introduction of a simultaneous election process would either increase or cut short the tenure of the state legislatures. This would go against the Indian Constitution and would be a violation of the SC's order in the S.R. Bommai case. Thus, simultaneous elections in the Lok Sabha and state assemblies would naturally be anti-federal and unconstitutional.[29]

Jagdeep Chhokar in *The Hindu* wrote about the validity of the amendments to the Constitution to conduct ONOE saying that the answer to this question lies in 'the Basic Structure Doctrine which was laid down by the Supreme Court in the 1973 landmark case, *Kesavananda Bharati Sripadagalvaru and Others* v. *State of Kerala and Another*'.[30]

*What Does the Basic Structure Doctrine Mean?*

> The basic structure doctrine holds that certain fundamental features of the Constitution, such as the supremacy of the Constitution, the rule of law, and the independence of the judiciary, cannot be amended or abrogated by the Parliament through a constitutional amendment.
>
> This doctrine has served as a check on the power of the Parliament to amend the Constitution and has ensured that the Constitution remains a living document that is responsive to changing times while preserving its fundamental values and principles.[31]

Chhokar quoted a few leading judgements explaining the basic structure of the Indian Constitution. Justice S.M. Sikri in the Kesavananda Bharati case stated that every provision of the Constitution can be amended provided that the basic foundation and structure of the Constitution remains the same.

> The basic structure may be said to consist of the following features:
> 1. Supremacy of the Constitution
> 2. Republican and Democratic form of Government
> 3. Secular character of the Constitution
> 4. Separation of powers between the Legislature, the executive and the judiciary
> 5. Federal character of the Constitution.[32]

Justice Sikri emphasised that the dignity and freedom of the individual are of 'supreme importance' and cannot be amended by any means. Chhokar stated 'that the Basic Structure Doctrine asserts that while Article 368 of the Constitution grants Parliament the power to amend the Constitution through addition, variation, or repeal, it does not allow Parliament to amend the basic structure of the Constitution.'[33]

In addressing if holding simultaneous Union and state elections would transform the Constitution into a 'unitary structure', Chhokar cited former Supreme Court judge P.B. Sawant's article 'Keep the Polls Apart' published in *The Indian Express*.[34] Sawant noted that the constitution of legislative assemblies and the formation of state governments are autonomous functions, and the Union government cannot interfere with the governance of a state except in cases of emergency as outlined in Articles 352, 355 and 356 of the Constitution.

These landmark judgements should serve as a sign for institutions that have supported the ONOE scheme. Amendments to the Constitution would not only disturb the federal structure but may also fail to withstand judicial scrutiny.

A question needs to be answered here: Why has the ruling Modi government been pushing for the ONOE scheme since it came to power in 2014? Not only have Prime Minister Narendra Modi and Home Minister Amit Shah demonstrated their support for ONOE, but former president Ram Nath Kovind also released a statement validating simultaneous Union and state elections.

Shekhar Gupta, editor-in-chief of ThePrint, referred to the ONOE scheme as the BJP's brahmastra. He asserted, 'If your weakness is having only one leader to get you the votes across states, where most of your leaders are nobodies, why not turn it into a strength? What if every vote was sought for Modi, at the Centre or in states? Each election will be Modi versus who?'

Indeed, in all elections in India, be it central or state, BJP has been seeking votes in the name of Prime Minister Narendra Modi. The state elections that had not grabbed much media attention prior to 2014 have now become an event because of multiple public rallies attended by PM Modi.[35]

Most of India's elections have turned into a presidential style 'Modi versus who' dynamic. However, the 2024 Lok Sabha elections displayed a setback in Modi's leadership. Despite the entire election being centred around him, the ruling party failed to secure a majority.

During the 2024 Independence Day speech at the Red Fort, Prime Minister Narendra Modi, in his third term, urged the general public to support simultaneous elections in the country. He said, 'I request everyone to come together to achieve the resolve of "One Nation One Election", which is the need of the hour.' He further added that elections should be held for a shorter period and that 'politics should not be done for all five years'.[36]

An eight-member high-level committee was formed to examine the issue of ONOE and make recommendations.

The committee was chaired by former president Ram Nath Kovind and the other members included Amit Shah, minister of home affairs and minister of cooperation, Adhir Ranjan Chowdhury, leader of opposition in Lok Sabha; Ghulam Nabi Azad, former leader of opposition in the Rajya Sabha; N.K. Singh, former chairman of the 15th Finance Commission; and Subhash C. Kashyap, former secretary general of the Lok Sabha.[37]

As reported in *The Indian Express*,[38] the high-level committee proposed the insertion of a new provision, Article 82 A(1), which states that the president of India will notify the 'appointed date' on the first sitting of the Lok Sabha after a general election. The first sitting of the Lok Sabha will occur only after the 2029 general elections, as the 2024 general elections were completed months ago.

The committee also proposed the insertion of Article 82 A(2), which states that the terms of the state assemblies elected after the 'appointed date' would be curtailed to synchronise with the end of the full term of the Lok Sabha.

A joint parliamentary committee of 39 members was formed by the Lok Sabha to examine The Constitution (One Hundred and Twenty-Ninth Amendment) Bill, 2024 and the amendments to the Government of Union Territories Act, 1963, the twin bills on simultaneous elections at the Centre and the states. The members include leaders from both national and state level political parties. Only after the committee is concluded, will the fate of ONOE be decided.

# Acknowledgements

I WAS ENTERING PUNE airport when I received a WhatsApp message from Chirag Thakkar saying, 'I wanted to ask if you'd like to discuss the possibility of doing a book. When might be a good time to speak with you?' These words excited me. I want to thank him for envisioning the idea of this book and helping me present it in the best way possible.

Thanks to Srishti Khare and the Bloomsbury team for publishing this book. I wish to express my gratitude to Raghav Bahl, the founder of The Quint, for letting me investigate and publish stories about the electoral bonds scheme and EVMs. I would like to express my heartfelt gratitude to Rashi Sarawgi for her invaluable inputs, which have significantly enhanced the impact of several of my articles. I want to thank people who appreciated my work in interviews and social media and encouraged me to work on this book.

I want to thank my family and friends for their support. My friend Indrojit Chaudhuri provided me with the soft copies of many books that I read and cited in this book. My thanks to Vakasha Sachdev for guiding and encouraging me whenever I reached out to him.

It takes a steady regime – specifically, a morning workout routine at the gym – to complete a book project of this scale. I would like to thank my gym buddies, Shradha Singh and Sagar Verma, for their humour which helped me through my writing days. I am also grateful to my domestic worker, Laxmi Haldar, whose incredible cooking and management of the household allowed me to focus on my writing without worrying about daily chores.

# Appendix 1

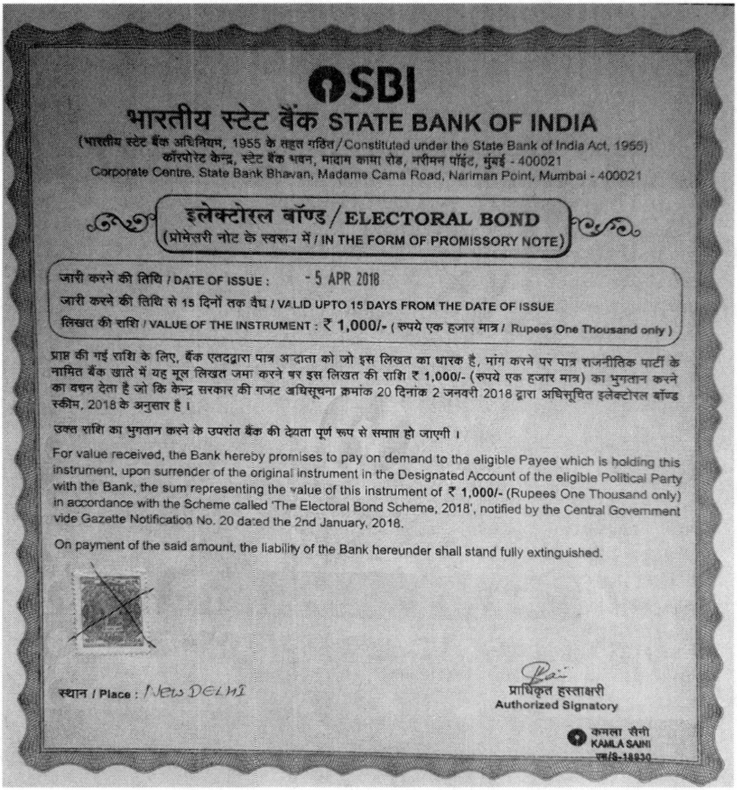

SBI

भारतीय स्टेट बैंक STATE BANK OF INDIA

(भारतीय स्टेट बैंक अधिनियम, 1955 के तहत गठित / Constituted under the State Bank of India Act, 1955)

कॉरपोरेट केन्द्र, स्टेट बैंक भवन, मादाम कामा रोड, नरीमन पॉइंट, मुंबई - 400021

Corporate Centre, State Bank Bhavan, Madame Cama Road, Nariman Point, Mumbai - 400021

**इलेक्टोरल बॉण्ड / ELECTORAL BOND**

(प्रोमेसरी नोट के स्वरूप में / IN THE FORM OF PROMISSORY NOTE)

जारी करने की तिथि / DATE OF ISSUE : - 5 APR 2018

जारी करने की तिथि से 15 दिनों तक वैध / VALID UPTO 15 DAYS FROM THE DATE OF ISSUE

लिखत की राशि / VALUE OF THE INSTRUMENT : ₹ 1,000/- (रुपये एक हजार मात्र / Rupees One Thousand only)

प्राप्त की गई राशि के लिए, बैंक एतदद्वारा पात्र अदाता को जो इस लिखत का धारक है, मांग करने पर पात्र राजनीतिक पार्टी के नामित बैंक खाते में यह मूल लिखत जमा करने पर इस लिखत की राशि ₹ 1,000/- (रुपये एक हजार मात्र) का भुगतान करने का वचन देता है जो कि केन्द्र सरकार की गजट अधिसूचना क्रमांक 20 दिनांक 2 जनवरी 2018 द्वारा अधिसूचित इलेक्टोरल बॉण्ड स्कीम, 2018 के अनुसार है।

उक्त राशि का भुगतान करने के उपरांत बैंक की देयता पूर्ण रूप से समाप्त हो जाएगी।

For value received, the Bank hereby promises to pay on demand to the eligible Payee which is holding this instrument, upon surrender of the original instrument in the Designated Account of the eligible Political Party with the Bank, the sum representing the value of this instrument of ₹ 1,000/- (Rupees One Thousand only) in accordance with the Scheme called 'The Electoral Bond Scheme, 2018', notified by the Central Government vide Gazette Notification No. 20 dated the 2nd January, 2018.

On payment of the said amount, the liability of the Bank hereunder shall stand fully extinguished.

स्थान / Place : NEW DELHI

प्राधिकृत हस्ताक्षरी

Authorized Signatory

कमला सैनी

KAMLA SAINI

एम/S-18930

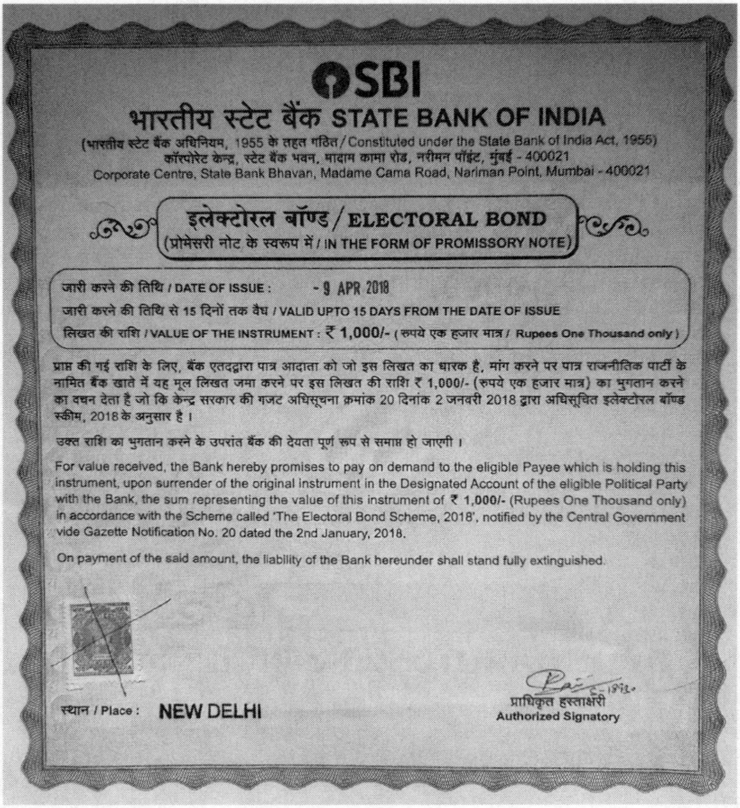

SBI

भारतीय स्टेट बैंक STATE BANK OF INDIA

(भारतीय स्टेट बैंक अधिनियम, 1955 के तहत गठित / Constituted under the State Bank of India Act, 1955)

कॉर्पोरेट केन्द्र, स्टेट बैंक भवन, मादाम कामा रोड, नरीमन पॉइंट, मुंबई - 400021

Corporate Centre, State Bank Bhavan, Madame Cama Road, Nariman Point, Mumbai - 400021

**इलेक्टोरल बॉण्ड / ELECTORAL BOND**

(प्रोमेसरी नोट के स्वरूप में / IN THE FORM OF PROMISSORY NOTE)

जारी करने की तिथि / DATE OF ISSUE : - 9 APR 2018

जारी करने की तिथि से 15 दिनों तक वैध / VALID UPTO 15 DAYS FROM THE DATE OF ISSUE

लिखत की राशि / VALUE OF THE INSTRUMENT : ₹ 1,000/- (रुपये एक हजार मात्र / Rupees One Thousand only)

प्राप्त की गई राशि के लिए, बैंक एतदद्वारा पात्र आदाता को जो इस लिखत का धारक है, मांग करने पर पात्र राजनीतिक पार्टी के नामित बैंक खाते में यह मूल लिखत जमा करने पर इस लिखत की राशि ₹ 1,000/- (रुपये एक हजार मात्र) का भुगतान करने का वचन देता है जो कि केन्द्र सरकार की गजट अधिसूचना क्रमांक 20 दिनांक 2 जनवरी 2018 द्वारा अधिसूचित इलेक्टोरल बॉण्ड स्कीम, 2018 के अनुसार है ।

उक्त राशि का भुगतान करने के उपरांत बैंक की देयता पूर्ण रूप से समाप्त हो जाएगी ।

For value received, the Bank hereby promises to pay on demand to the eligible Payee which is holding this instrument, upon surrender of the original instrument in the Designated Account of the eligible Political Party with the Bank, the sum representing the value of this instrument of ₹ 1,000/- (Rupees One Thousand only) in accordance with the Scheme called 'The Electoral Bond Scheme, 2018', notified by the Central Government vide Gazette Notification No. 20 dated the 2nd January, 2018.

On payment of the said amount, the liability of the Bank hereunder shall stand fully extinguished.

स्थान / Place : NEW DELHI

प्राधिकृत हस्ताक्षरी
Authorized Signatory

# Appendix 2

Dr. Gandhi P.C. Kaza MA (USA), M.E., H.Sc., Ph.D
Founder Chairman, Truth foundation

TRUTH FOUNDATION

TRUTH LABS FORENSIC SERVICES
(An Initiative of Truth Foundation)



**FORWARDING LETTER**

Date: 11.04.2018

Sub: - Examination of documents and report thereof.
Ref:- Request Letter dated 07.04.2018.

Sir.
Please refer to your above said letter forwarding there with documents for examination and opinion thereon.

After careful and thorough examination, opinions along with forensic observations are furnished in the enclosure. Also enclosed are the documents sent along with your above said letter.

For expert testimony, if required, the summons may be got issued in the name of Shri Ami Lal Daksh, Deputy Director, Document Division, Truth Labs, NCR Delhi quoting our File No. TLD/QD/[illegible]/08.

The evidence fees of Rs. 1500/- per day along with TA & DA for performing the journey as per actual expenditure may be paid to the expert concerned.

Please acknowledge receipt.

Yours truly,

For Chairman
Truth Labs

Encl:

1. Report/Opinion No: TLD/QD/055/2018 (07 sheets),
2. All original Electoral Bond bearing date of issue 05.0-1.201, for Rs. 1,000/-. (01 sheet).
3. Photocopy of [illegible] in S. No. 2 [illegible] and marked D1 (01 sheet).

Office: A-1/106, Safdarjung Enclave, New Delhi- 110029. Tel: 011- [illegible]1354431; 9711779779

HEAD OFFICE : 402, Apoorva Towers, Road No. 2, Banjara Hills, Hyderabad - 500 034, Telangana, India.
Tel: +91 40 2339 6999, Fax: +91-40-2335 0888, M: +94906 90222/333, email: info@truthlabs.org, www.truthlabs.org
**BRANCHES** : **Delhi:** +91 - 97117 79779 **Mumbai:** +91-98673 94333 **Chennai:** +91 - 95660 11665 **Bangalore:** +91- 94490 30933

**INDIA'S FIRST INDEPENDENT FORENSIC SCIENCE LABORATORY ISO 9001 CERTIFIED**

File No: **TLD/QD/055/2018**

TRUTH FOUNDATION
(A Non Profit Public Society)

TRUTH LABS FORENSIC SERVICES

**Dated: 11.04.2018**

**Report/Opinion of Truth Labs**

**REFERENCE**

Ms. Poonam Agarwal, Associate Editor, Quintillion Media Pvt. Ltd., 8th Floor, Plot No. 1, Sector 16A, Film City, Noida-201301 referred the following document along with a request letter dated 07.04.2018 to Truth Labs, Delhi for forensic document examination and report thereof. The case was received at Truth Labs on 07.04.2018 and registered vide file no. TLD/QD/055/2018.

The case was assigned to Sh. Ami Lal Daksh, Deputy Director, Documents Division, Truth Labs, Delhi by the Chairman, Truth Labs for forensic examination.

**DESCRIPTION OF DOCUMENTS RECEIVED FOR EXAMINATION**

The following document was received and marked at Truth Labs, Delhi for the purpose of examination.

A. **Questioned Document:-**

An original Electoral Bond bearing date of issue 05.04.2018 for Rs. 1,000/- issued by the State Bank of India, in one sheet which has been marked **D1** on its reproduction copy.

**EXPERT'S PROFILE**

| | |
|---|---|
| Name of the Expert: | **Sh. Ami Lal Daksh** |
| Educational Qualification: | (i) B.Sc<br>(ii) Certificate course in Forensic Science |
| Professional Training: | Training in forensic examination of documents in N.I.C.F.S, MHA, Government of India at Delhi, Govt. Examiners of Questioned Documents and FSL Delhi). |
| Professional Experience: | Over 36 years of experience in Forensic Document Examination. Reported documents cases from 2001 have examined thousands of exhibits in criminal and civil cases and reported about 1400 cases of various types. Working as Deputy Director, Documents in Truth Labs since 2014. |
| Expert Testimony: | Gave evidence in over 250 cases in Courts of Law at Delhi. |

Page 1 of 7

(A.L. Daksh)

Delhi : A-1/106, Ground Floor, Safdarjung Enclave, Behind Ambience Public School, New Delhi - 110 029, India
Tele Fax : +91-11-4135 4431, Mob : +91-97117 79779, email : info@truthlabs.org, www.truthlabs.org
HEAD OFFICE : 402, Apoorva Towers, Road No. 2, Banjara Hills, Hyderabad - 500 034, Telangana, India. Tel: +91-040-2339 0999, Fax: +91-40-2339 0888
BRANCHES : Mumbai: +91-98673 94333 Chennai: +91-95660 11665 Bangalore: +91- 94490 30933

**INDIA'S FIRST INDEPENDENT FORENSIC SCIENCE LABORATORY ISO 9001 CERTIFIED**

File No: **TLD/QD/055/2018**

TRUTH FOUNDATION

TRUTH LABS FORENSIC SERVICES (An Affiliate of Truth Foundation)

**PURPOSE OF EXAMINATION**

To decipher the security features and any other crucial observations for identification of the document, which has been marked **D1,** on its reproduction copy.

**NATURE OF EXAMINATION**

The referred document have been carefully and thoroughly examined in the laboratory with the help of scientific aids like VSC-40FS, stereo microscope (Leica make) coupled with computer imaging system, hand magnifiers, different lighting arrangements viz. direct incident light, oblique light, transmitted light and ultra violet light etc.

**OBSERVATIONS & FINDINGS**

The original document, which has been marked **D1** on its reproduction copy when examined under VSC-40FS, revealed the following:

a) Serial No. reading "0T 015101" visible on the right top corner of the original document showing fluorescence when examined under UV Light, as seen in Figure-1 below.

Figure-1

**Page 2 of 7**

**(A.L. Daksh)**

**Delhi** : A-1/106, Ground Floor, Safdarjung Enclave, Behind Ambience Public School, New Delhi - 110 029, India
Tele Fax : +91-11-4135 4431, Mob : +91-97117 79779, email : info@truthlabs.org, www.truthlabs.org
**HEAD OFFICE** : 402, Apoorva Towers, Road No. 2, Banjara Hills, Hyderabad - 500 034, Telangana, India. Tel: +91-040-2339 0999, Fax: +91-40-2339 0888
**BRANCHES** : **Mumbai:** +91-98673 94333 **Chennai:** +91-95660 11665 **Bangalore:** +91- 94490 30933

**INDIA'S FIRST INDEPENDENT FORENSIC SCIENCE LABORATORY ISO 9001 CERTIFIED**

File No: **TLD/QD/055/2018**

TRUTH FOUNDATION (A Non Profit Public Society)

TRUTH LABS FORENSIC SERVICES (An Affiliate of Truth Foundation)

b) Logo of State Bank of India is visible on the left top corner of the original document showing florescence when examined under UV Light, as seen in Figure-2 below.

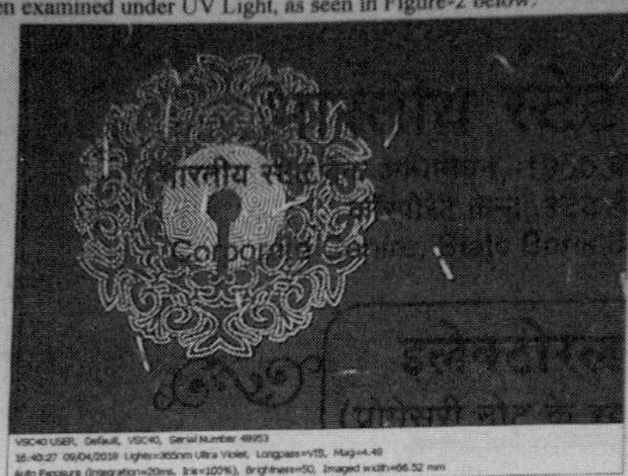


Figure-2

c) Presence of paper fibers showing florescence is visible all over the original document in two sets of color (red-green and blue green) when examined under UV Light, as seen in Figure-3 below.

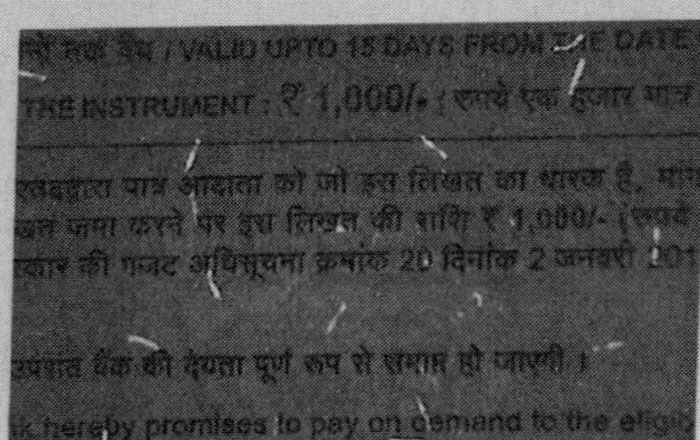


Figure-3

Page 3 of 7

(A.L. Daksh)

**Delhi** : A-1/106, Ground Floor, Safdarjung Enclave, Behind Ambience Public School, New Delhi - 110 029, India
Tele Fax : +91-11-4135 4431, Mob : +91-97117 79779, email : info@truthlabs.org, www.truthlabs.org
**HEAD OFFICE** : 402, Apoorva Towers, Road No. 2, Banjara Hills, Hyderabad - 500 034, Telangana, India. Tel: +91-040-2339 0999, Fax: +91-40-2339 0888
**BRANCHES** : **Mumbai:** +91-98673 94333 **Chennai:** +91-95660 11665 **Bangalore:** +91- 94490 30933

**INDIA'S FIRST INDEPENDENT FORENSIC SCIENCE LABORATORY ISO 9001 CERTIFIED**

File No: **TLD/QD/055/2018**

TRUTH FOUNDATION
(A Non Profit Public Society)

TRUTH LABS FORENSIC SERVICES
(An Affiliate of Truth Foundation)

d) Micro lettering reading as "STATE BANK OF INDIA" is visible all around the border of the page of original document when examined under high magnification, as seen in the Figure-4 below.

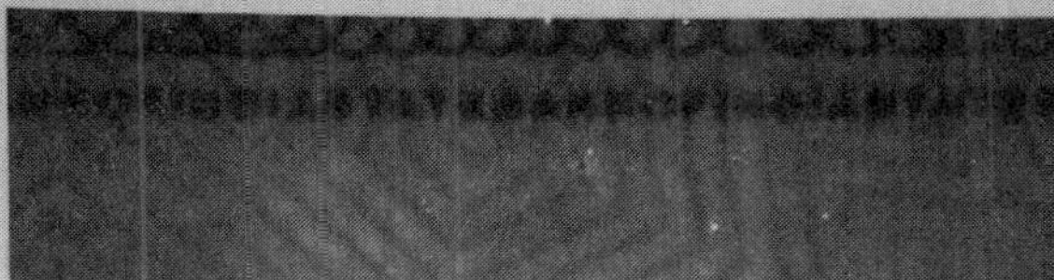

VSC40 USER, Default, VSC40, Serial Number 48953
16:16:23 09/04/2018 Lights=365nm Ultra Violet, Longpass=VIS, Mag=23.46
Auto Exposure (Integration=20ms, Iris=100%), Brightness=50, Imaged width=12.70 mm

Figure-4

e) Watermarks of the pattern of Ashoka Emblem is visible on the original document when examined under transmitted light, as seen in the Figure 5 below.

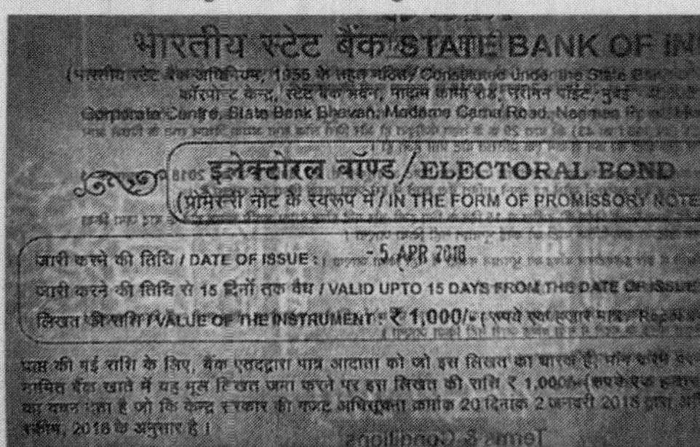


VSC40 USER, Default, VSC40, Serial Number 48953
13:04:11 10/04/2018 Lights=Transmitted, Longpass=VIS, Mag=1.98
Auto Exposure (Integration=20ms, Iris=41%), Brightness=50, Imaged width=150.51 mm

Figure-5

Page **4** of 7

(A.L. Daksh)

Delhi : A-1/106, Ground Floor, Safdarjung Enclave, Behind Ambience Public School, New Delhi - 110 029, India
Tele Fax : +91-11-4135 4431, Mob : +91-97117 79779, email : info@truthlabs.org, www.truthlabs.org
HEAD OFFICE : 402, Apoorva Towers, Road No. 2, Banjara Hills Hyderabad - 500 034, Telangana, India. Tel: +91-040-2339 0999, Fax: +91-40-2339 0888
BRANCHES : Mumbai: +91-98673 94333 Chennai: +91-95660 11665 Bangalore: +91- 94490 30933

INDIA'S FIRST INDEPENDENT FORENSIC SCIENCE LABORATORY ISO 9001 CERTIFIED

File No: **TLD/QD/055/2018**

TRUTH FOUNDATION
(A Non Profit Public Society)

TRUTH LABS FORENSIC SERVICES
(An Affiliate of Truth Foundation)

f) Security Printing reading as SBI, COPY is visible on the horizontal strip on the lower part of the document and STATE BANK OF INDIA is visible all over the document as well as the background security printing on the original document is also visible when examined under infrared rays, as seen in the Figure 6 and 6a to 6c respectively.

Figure-6

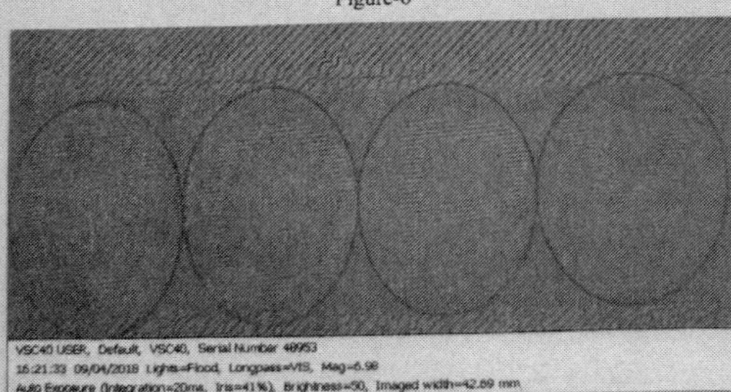


Figure-6a

Page 5 of 7

(A.L. Daksh)

**Delhi** : A-1/106, Ground Floor, Safdarjung Enclave, Behind Ambience Public School, New Delhi - 110 029, India
Tele Fax : +91-11-4135 4431, Mob : +91-97117 79779, email : info@truthlabs.org, www.truthlabs.org
**HEAD OFFICE** : 402, Apoorva Towers, Road No. 2, Banjara Hills, Hyderabad - 500 034, Telangana, India. Tel: +91-040-2339 0999, Fax: +91-40-2339 0888
**BRANCHES : Mumbai:** +91-98673 94333 **Chennai:** +91-95660 11665 **Bangalore:** +91- 94490 30933

**INDIA'S FIRST INDEPENDENT FORENSIC SCIENCE LABORATORY ISO 9001 CERTIFIED**

File No: **TLD/QD/055/2018**

TRUTH FOUNDATION (A Non Profit Public Society)

TRUTH LABS FORENSIC SERVICES (An Affiliate of Truth Foundation)

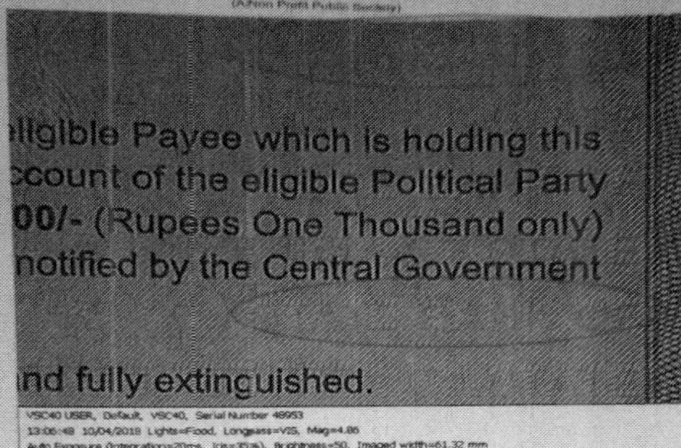


Figure-6b

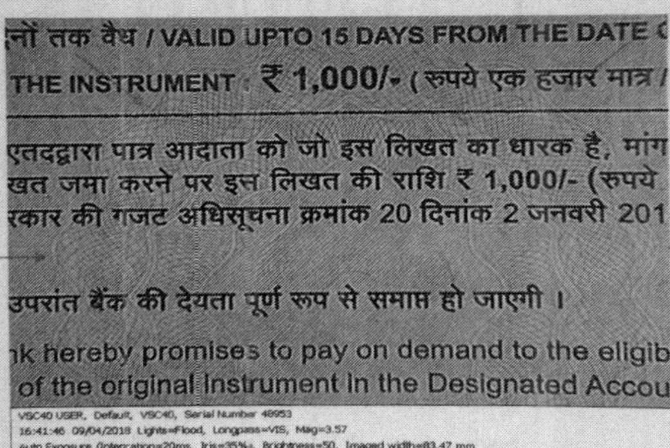


Figure-6c

Page **6** of **7**

**(A.L. Daksh)**

**Delhi** : A-1/106, Ground Floor, Safdarjung Enclave, Behind Ambience Public School, New Delhi - 110 029, India
Tele Fax : +91-11-4135 4431, Mob : +91-97117 79779, email : info@truthlabs.org, www.truthlabs.org
**HEAD OFFICE** : 402, Apoorva Towers, Road No. 2, Banjara Hills, Hyderabad - 500 034, Telangana, India. Tel: +91-040-2339 0999, Fax: +91-40-2339 0888
**BRANCHES** : **Mumbai:** +91-98673 94333 **Chennai:** +91-95660 11665 **Bangalore:** +91- 94490 30933

**INDIA'S FIRST INDEPENDENT FORENSIC SCIENCE LABORATORY ISO 9001 CERTIFIED**

File No: **TLD/QD/055/2018**

TRUTH FOUNDATION
(A Non Profit Public Society)

TRUTH LABS FORENSIC SERVICES
(An Affiliate of Truth Foundation)

**CONCLUSION**

***All these could be deciphered under different arrangements of light and magnifications which rendered visible the invisible to naked eye security features.***

Note: The document was examined and reported based on the request received from Ms. Poonam Agarwal, Associate Editor, Quintillion Media Pvt. Ltd. vide letter dated 07.04.2018.

11/04/2018

**(A.L. Daksh)**

**Deputy Director, Documents Division,**

**Truth Labs, Delhi.**

A. L. DAKSH
Dy. Director (Documents Division)
Truth Labs, New Delhi NCR

**Page 7 of 7**

**Delhi** : A-1/106, Ground Floor, Safdarjung Enclave, Behind Ambience Public School, New Delhi - 110 029, India
Tele Fax : +91-11-4135 4431, Mob : +91-97117 79779, email : info@truthlabs.org, www.truthlabs.org
**HEAD OFFICE** : 402. Apoorva Towers, Road No. 2, Banjara Hills, Hyderabad - 500 034, Telangana, India. Tel: +91-040-2339 0999, Fax: +91-40-2339 0888
**BRANCHES : Mumbai**: +91-98673 94333 **Chennai**: +91-95660 11665 **Bangalore**: +91- 94490 30933

**INDIA'S FIRST INDEPENDENT FORENSIC SCIENCE LABORATORY ISO 9001 CERTIFIED**

# Notes

## Introduction

1 Poonam Agarwal, 'Jankari ki Kami ke Karan Bahot Saare Agents Form 17C Election Officer se Nahi Lete – Polling Agent', posted 16 May 2024, YouTube, https://www.youtube.com/watch?v=GX-_3nxbTdw

2 Shrirag P.S., 'VVPATs Introduce Vulnerability into the Voting Process: Former IAS Officer Kannan Gopinathan', *The Caravan*, 30 September 2019. https://caravanmagazine.in/politics/kannan-gopinathan-vvpat-evm-election-process-vulnerability

3 Kyle Khan-Mullins and John Hyatt, 'The Billions Behind The 2024 Presidential Election', *Forbes*, updated 7 November 2024. https://www.forbes.com/sites/kylemullins/2024/11/04/the-billions-behind-the-2024-presidential-election/

4 Aishwarya Paliwal, 'Most Expensive Polls Ever? Nearly Rs 1.35 Lakh Crore Spent in 2024 Election', *India Today*, 31 May 2024. https://www.indiatoday.in/elections/lok-sabha/story/lok-sabha-election-2024-expenditure-election-commission-2546455-2024-05-31

5 'General Elections – 2024, Schedule of Elections', Election Commission of India, 16 March 2024. https://www.eci.gov.in/eci-backend/public/api/download?url=LMAhAK6sOPBp%2FNFF0iRfXbEB1EVSLT41NNLRjYNJJP1KivrUxbfqkDatmHy12e%2FzBiU51zPFZI5qMtjV1qgjFsK5bO1Fe8raUy8r%2B3VvV90Cjp15bRUMwNJOR%2Fnxz8QuCSv%2B1yJkuMeCkTzY9fhBvw%3D%3D

6 Ibid.

7 'Voting by Tribal Communities Blossoms as ECI's Outreach to Them Bears Fruit, ECI's Efforts Over Last Two Years Bring PVTG Communities and Tribals into Electoral Process in a Big Way', Election Commission of India, 1 May 2024. https://pib.gov.in/PressReleasePage.aspx?PRID=2019294

8 CAN Insider, 'India's War on Fake News: How Disinformation Became India's # 1 Threat | Fact Vs Fiction', posted on 12 April 2024. YouTube, https://www.youtube.com/watch?app=desktop&v=nPHrjxlHx2E
9 Ibid.
10 Simon Lobo, 'AI Not a Significant Threat in 2024 Elections, but Led to Erosion of Trust: Fact-checkers #NAMA', Medianama, 16 July 2024. https://www.medianama.com/2024/07/223-ai-limited-but-noteworthy-impact-2024-elections-fact-checkers/
11 ETV Bharat English Team, 'Lok Sabha Election 2024: Social Media War Rooms Building Image of Candidates', ETV Bharat, 11 April 2024. https://www.etvbharat.com/en/!bharat/ls-polls-social-media-war-rooms-building-image-of-candidates-enn24041106354
12 'Poonam Agarwal to Deliver the 2024 CIJ Gavin MacFadyen Memorial Lecture', The Centre for Investigative Journalism, 3 June 2024, https://tcij.org/summer-conference-announcement/poonam-agarwal-to-deliver-the-2024-cij-gavin-macfadyen-memorial-lecture/

## Chapter 1: The Beast That Is Indian Elections

1 Jesuitresource.org. https://www.xavier.edu/jesuitresource/online-resources/quote-archive1/election-dayvoting
2 V.S. Rama Devi and S.K. Mendiratta, 'How India Votes: History of Elections During the British Rule' Sahapedia. https://www.sahapedia.org/how-india-votes-history-elections-during-british-rule
3 Ibid.
4 Ibid.
5 Chakshu Roy, 'History Headline| 1920: The Start of India's Election Journey', *The Indian Express*, 16 April 2024. https://indianexpress.com/article/opinion/columns/1920-the-start-of-indias-election-journey-9242440/
6 Ibid.
7 Ibid.
8 Suchitra Karthikeyan and Diksha Munjal, 'Elections That Shaped India | The First General Election: A Free Country in Full Bloom', *The Hindu*, 24 May 2024. https://www.thehindu.com/elections/lok-sabha/

first-general-elections-of-india-the-free-country-in-full-bloom/article67702823.ece

9 S.P. Sathe, 'Fundamental Rights and Directive Principles', in *Constitutional Amendments, 1950–1988: Law and Politics*, N.M. Tripathi Pvt Ltd, 1989.

10 S.Y. Quraishi, *India's Experiment with Democracy: The Life of a Nation Through Its Elections*, HarperCollins Publishers, 2023, 33.

11 Prasun Chaudhuri, 'Electorate', The Telegraph Online, 17 March 2024. https://www.telegraphindia.com/culture/electocrat-the-role-of-sukumar-sen-in-the-grand-success-of-indias-election-machinery/cid/2007428

12 Pranab Mukherjee, 'First Sukumar Sen Memorial Lecture', Election Commission of India, 23 January 2020. https://www.ceoandaman.nic.in/election/AnnounceContent/24012020_1.pdf

13 S.Y. Quraishi, *An Undocumented Wonder, The Making of Great Indian Election'*, Rupa Publications, 2014, 44.

14 Pranab Mukherjee, 'First Sukumar Sen Memorial Lecture', Election Commission of India, 23 January 2020. https://www.ceoandaman.nic.in/election/AnnounceContent/24012020_1.pdf

15 Prasun Chaudhuri, 'Electorate', The Telegraph Online, 17 March, 2024. https://www.telegraphindia.com/culture/electocrat-the-role-of-sukumar-sen-in-the-grand-success-of-indias-election-machinery/cid/2007428

16 Desk, 'The Biggest Election in the World: Journey of Indian Election', *The New Indian Express*, 16 March 2024. https://www.newindianexpress.com/nation/2024/Mar/16/the-biggest-election-in-the-world-journey-of-indian-election

17 One Nation One Election, Government of India. https://onoe.gov.in/

18 Sravasti Dasgupta, '"One Nation, One Election", Fourth Committee', The Wire, 2 September 2023. https://thewire.in/government/one-nation-one-election-fourth-committee

19 Justice B.P. Jeevan Reddy, Justice Leila Seth, Dr N.M. Ghatate, Dr Subhash C. Jain, 'Law Commission of India, One Hundred Seventieth Report on Reform of the

Electoral Laws,' 'Chapter II, Measures for Improving the Electoral System', 29 May 1999. https://cdnbbsr.s3waas.gov.in/s3ca0daec69b5adc880fb464895726dbdf/uploads/2022/08/2022082424.pdf

20 170th Report of Law Commission of India, 1999, One Nation One Election, Government of India. https://onoe.gov.in/onoe-reports

21 Sukumar Sen, 'Report on the First General Elections in India 1951–52 Volume - 1 (General)', Election Commission of India, 4 February 1955. https://hindi.eci.gov.in/files/file/11294-report-on-the-first-general-elections-in-india-1951-52-volume-1-general/

22 Ibid.

23 Ibid.

24 Ibid.

25 Ibid.

26 Ibid.

27 Ibid.

28 Anand Bodh, 'At 100, India's 1st Voter to Cast Vote Again', *The Times of India*, 29 October 2017. https://timesofindia.indiatimes.com/city/shimla/at-100-indias-1st-voter-to-cast-vote-again/articleshow/61313607.cms

29 Sukumar Sen, 'Report on the First General Elections in India 1951–52 Volume – 1 (General)', Election Commission of India, 4 February 1955. https://hindi.eci.gov.in/files/file/11294–report–on–the–first–general–elections–in–india–1951–52–volume–1–general/

30 Sharafat Ali, 'Family in Remote Himalayas Gets Own Polling Station for Indian Election', Reuters, 20 May 2024. https://www.reuters.com/world/india/family-remote-himalayas-gets-own-polling-station-indian-election-2024-05-20/

31 Press Trust of India, 'From Gir Forest for Lone Voter to Village on Indo-Bangla Border: How EC Conducts Polls at Remotest Inaccessible Places', *The Economic Times*, 27 March 2024.https://economictimes.indiatimes.com/news/elections/lok-sabha/india/from-gir-forest-for-lone-voter-to-village-on-indo-bangla-border-how-ec-conducts-polls-at-remotest-inaccessible-places/articleshow/108809812.cms?from=mdr

32 'Women's Suffrage: 100th Anniversary of the 19th Amendment', Utah Historical Society. https://history.utah.gov/womens-suffrage-100th-anniversary-of-the-19th-amendment/

33 Prasun Chaudhuri, 'Electorate', The Telegraph Online, 17 March 2024.
https://www.telegraphindia.com/culture/electocrat-the-role-of-sukumar-sen-in-the-grand-success-of-indias-election-machinery/cid/2007428

34 Barbara Southard, 'Colonial Politics and Women's Rights: Woman Suffrage Campaigns in Bengal, British India in the 1920s', *Modern Asian Studies* 27, no. 2 (1993): 397– 439.

35 Soutik Biswas, 'Did the British Empire Resist Women's Suffrage in India?', BBC, 22 February 2018. https://www.bbc.com/news/world-asia-india-43081429

36 Meryl Sebastian, 'Sophia Duleep Singh: Indian Princess Who Fought for Women to Vote in UK', BBC, 24 July 2023. https://www.bbc.com/news/world-asia-india-66220501

37 The Glasgow Herald, 8 August 1919 https://books.google.co.in/books?id=gxY-AAAAIBAJ&pg=PA7&dq=sophia+duleep+singh+india&article_id=1517,3775532&hl=en&sa=X&ved=2ahUKEwj8kKCwoZuAAxUXwzgGHVpQDBQQ6AF6BAgLEAI#v=onepage&q=sophia%20duleep%20singh%20india&f=true

38 Nishah Malik, 'Princess Sophia Duleep Singh and the Important Role of Indian Women in the Suffragette Movement', British Online Archives, 15 October 2021. https://britishonlinearchives.com/posts/category/articles/426/princess-sophia-duleep-singh-and-the-important-role-of-indian-women-in-the-suffragette-movement

39 Dr Sumita Mukherjee, 'The Untold Story of the Indian Suffragettes', University of Bristol. https://bristol.ac.uk/research/impact/stories/indian-suffragettes/

40 Nikhat Hoque, 'Meet 7 Indian Suffragettes of the British Suffrage Movement', Feminism in India, 4 February 2019. https://feminisminindia.com/2019/02/04/7-indian-suffragettes-british/

41 Adrija Roychowdhury, 'Margaret Cousins: The Irish Suffragette Who Fought for Voting Rights of Indian

Women', *The Indian Express*, 16 March, 2024. https://indianexpress.com/article/research/margaret-cousins-the-irish-suffragette-who-fought-for-voting-rights-of-indian-women-9215128/

42 Akshi Chawla, 'Lok Sabha Elections 2024: On Women's Representation, a Step Backwards', *The Indian Express*, 10 June 2024. https://indianexpress.com/article/opinion/columns/lok-sabha-elections-2024-womens-representation-9381396/

43 Rangarajan R., 'On Political Representation of Women | Explained', *The Hindu*, 17 July 2024. https://www.thehindu.com/news/national/on-political-representation-of-women-explained/article68415532.ece

44 'Organisation of Village Panchayat', Constitution of India. https://www.constitutionofindia.net/articles/article-40-organisation-of-village-panchayats/

45 S.Y. Quraishi, *India's Experiment with Democracy: The Life of a Nation Through Its Elections*, HarperCollins, 2023, 393.

46 V.N. Alok, 'Panchayat Elections in India, A Report', Ministry of Panchayati Raj, November 2023. https://cdnbbsr.s3waas.gov.in/s316026d60ff9b54410b3435b403afd226/uploads/2024/07/202407181366823679.pdf

47 'Constitution of India Part IX', Government of India, 6. https://mahasec.maharashtra.gov.in/Upload/PDF/Constitutional%20Provisions%20IX%20-%20Panchayats%20(Rural).pdf

48 E. Sridharan, 'Reforming Political Finance'. https://www.india-seminar.com/2001/506/506%20e.%20sridharan.htm

49 K.N. Wanchoo, *Direct Taxes Enquiry Committee Final Report*, Ministry of Finance, 1971.

50 M.V. Rajeev Gowda and E. Sridharan, 'Reforming India's Party Financing and Election Expenditure Laws', *Election Law Journal* 11, no. 2 (2012), 227. https://casi.sas.upenn.edu/sites/default/files/upiasi/Reforming%20India%27s%20Party%20Financing%20and%20Election%20Expenditure%20Laws.pdf

51 M.V. Rajeev Gowda and E. Sridharan, 'Reforming India's Party Financing and Election Expenditure Laws'.

52 Ibid.

53 E. Sridharan, 'Reforming Political Finance'. https://www.india-seminar.com/2001/506/506%20e.%20sridharan.htm

54 M.V. Rajeev Gowda and E. Sridharan, 'Reforming India's Party Financing and Election Expenditure Laws'.
55 Ibid.

## Chapter 2: Bills to Be Paid: The Costs of Running the 'Mother of Democracy'

1 'Section 34 in the Representation of People Act, 1951'. Indian Kanoon. https://indiankanoon.org/doc/165215034/
2 'Analysis of Criminal Background, Financial, Education, Gender and other Details of Candidates and Analysis of Assets Comparison of Re-Contesting MPs in the Lok Sabha Election 2024', Association for Democratic Reform, 29 May 2024. https://adrindia.org/content/analysis-criminal-background-financial-education-gender-and-other-details-candidates-and-4
3 'Section 29C in the Representation of the People Act, 1951, Declaration of Donation Received by the Political Party', Indian Kanoon. https://indiankanoon.org/doc/163284660/
4 The Public Interest Litigation by Association for Democratic Reform (2017). https://adrindia.org/sites/default/files/ADR_petition_on_electoral_bonds.pdf
5 Raju Gopalakrishnan, 'Indian Journalists Say They Intimidated, Ostracized if They Criticize Modi and the BJP', Reuters, 27 April 2018. https://www.reuters.com/article/world/indian-journalists-say-they-intimidated-ostracized-if-they-criticize-modi-and-t-idUSKBN1HX1EK/
6 Maya Prabhu, 'Is Free Speech Under Threat in Modi's India?', Al Jazeera, 3 August 2017. https://www.aljazeera.com/features/2017/8/3/is-free-speech-under-threat-in-modis-india
7 Poonam Agarwal, 'Exclusive: Will Non-Serialised Electoral Bonds Enable Corruption?', The Quint, 24 March 2018. https://www.thequint.com/news/india/electoral-bonds-sbi-political-party-donation-political-funding
8 Ibid.
9 Poonam Agarwal, 'Secret Policing? When The Quint Exposed Electoral Bonds Carry Hidden Numbers', The Quint, April 2018. https://www.thequint.com/news/politics/hidden-number-on-election-electoral-bond

10 'Government Clarifies the In-Built Security Features of the Electoral Bonds', Ministry of Finance, 2018.

11 Poonam Agarwal, 'Mr. Jaitley, Your Ministry's Statement on Electoral Bond Is Flawed', The Quint, 19 April 2018. https://www.thequint.com/news/india/mr-jaitley-your-ministrys-statement-on-electoral-bond-is-flawedid=1517,3775532&hl=en&sa=X&ved=2ahUKEwj8kKCwoZuAAxUXwzgGHVpQDBQQ6AF6BAgLEAI#v=onepage&q=sophia%20duleep%20singh%20india&f=true

## Chapter 3: The Spectre Of Democratic Backsliding

1 National Press Foundation. "World Press Freedom Day 2024: National Press Foundation Urges Support, Protection of Journalists." National Press Foundation. Last modified January 20, 2024. https://nationalpress.org/newsfeed/world-press-freedom-day-2024-national-press-foundation-urges-support-protection-of-journalists/.

2 Somdeep Sen, 'Big Money Is Choking India's Free Press – and Its Democracy', Al Jazeera, 6 January 2023. https://www.aljazeera.com/opinions/2023/1/6/big-money-is-choking-indias-free-press

3 World Press Freedom Index 2002, Reporters Without Borders. https://rsf.org/en/index?year=2002

4 World Press Freedom Index 2003, Reporters Without Borders. https://rsf.org/en/index?year=2003

5 World Press Freedom Index 2010, Reporters Without Borders. https://rsf.org/en/node/79180?year=2010&data_type=general

6 World Press Freedom Index 2012, Reporters Without Borders. https://rsf.org/en/node/79177?year=2012&data_type=general

7 World Press Freedom Index 2013, Reporters Without Borders. https://rsf.org/en/node/79174?year=2013&data_type=general

8 World Press Freedom Index 2024, Reporters Without Borders. https://rsf.org/en/index?year=2024

9 Reporters Without Borders. https://rsf.org/en/country/india

10 '"Grave Damages": Delhi HC Asks for "Defamatory" Articles on Dhanya Rajendran to Be Taken Down', The Wire, 22 July 2024. https://thewire.in/media/dhanya-rajendran-delhi-high-court-fake-news-disinformation-cutting-south
11 Worldwide Governance Indicators, 2024 Update, World Bank. https://www.worldbank.org/en/publication/worldwide-governance-indicators
12 Sanjeev Sanyal and Aakanksha Arora, 'Why India Does Poorly on Global Perception Indices', Economic Advisory Council to the PM, November 2022. https://eacpm.gov.in/wp-content/uploads/2022/11/Global-perception-indices_Final_22_Nov.pdf
13 World Justice Project. https://worldjusticeproject.org/rule-of-law-index/factors/2023/India/Open%20Government
14 Sanjeev Sanyal and Aakanksha Arora, 'Why India Does Poorly on Global Perception Indices', Economic Advisory Council to the PM, November 2022, 2.
15 Democracy Index 2023, Age of Conflict, Economist Intelligence Unit, 19. https://pages.eiu.com/rs/753-RIQ-438/images/Democracy-Index-2023-Final-report.pdf?version=0&mkt_tok=NzUzLVJJUS00MzgAAAGU0HSmQP5QNc8J-stIuJD2f0FUcCqR74vx4xjfWwt0UnzGypKLRjibk6M5WgKXtUzGg2GxfHXVzJYLXdVCw6hqIw3LEFHYyJM9eLsQDNNNzM2ndg
16 Ibid.
17 Ibid.
18 *Democracy Report 2024*, (V-Dem Institute, 2024). https://v-dem.net/documents/43/v-dem_dr2024_lowres.pdf.
19 Ibid., 25.
20 Freedom in the World 2024, Freedom House. https://freedomhouse.org/country/india/freedom-world/2024
21 Ibid.
22 Ibid.
23 Ibid.
24 Ibid.
25 Arun Kumar, 'Black Economy Persists With or Without Electoral Bonds', The Leaflet, 22 February 2024. https://theleaflet.in/black-economy-persists-with-or-without-electoral-bonds/

26 Poonam Agarwal, 'Exclusive: Electoral Bond May Lead to More Black Money, Warned EC', The Quint, 27 April 2018. https://www.thequint.com/news/india/modi-government-election-commission-electoral-bonds-political-funding#read-more
27 Nitin Sethi, 'Law Ministry Said Modi Govt's Route to Pass Electoral Bonds Was Illegal but Signed Off Anyway', HuffPost, 27 January 2020. https://www.huffpost.com/archive/in/entry/electoral-bonds-rti-arun-jaitley-law-ministry_in_5e2eccb1c5b6d6767fd8733f
28 T.S.R. Subramanian & Ors Versus Union of India & Ors. Writ Petition (Civil), Supreme Court, Indian Kanoon, 31 October 2013. https://indiankanoon.org/doc/183945465/
29 Nitin Sethi, 'Law Ministry Said Modi Govt's Route to Pass Electoral Bonds Was Illegal but Signed Off Anyway', HuffPost, 27 January 2020.
30 Poonam Agarwal, 'Electoral Bonds in Scrip Form Dangerous for Nation: Ex-RBI Guv', The Quint, 9 December 2019. https://www.thequint.com/news/india/rbi-governor-said-electoral-bonds-should-not-be-issued-in-physical-form#read-more
31 Ibid.
32 Ibid.
33 Ibid.
34 T.C.A. Sharad Raghavan and Priscilla Jebaraj, 'Electoral Bonds: Law Ministry, CEC Objected to 1% Vote Share Requirement', *The Hindu*, 28 November 2021. https://www.thehindu.com/news/national/electoral-bonds-law-ministry-cec-objected-to-1-vote-share-requirement/article61617050.ece
35 Ibid.
36 Poonam Agarwal, 'SBI Records Hidden Numbers on Electoral Bonds – Govt Misled Public', The Quint, 25 November 2019. https://www.thequint.com/news/india/sbi-records-hidden-numbers-on-electoral-bonds
37 Ibid.
38 'Salient Points of Press Conference of Senior BJP Leader & Union Minister Shri Piyush Goyal', Bharatiya Janata Party, 21 November 2019. https://www.bjp.org/pressreleases/salient-points-press-conference-senior-bjp-leader-union-minister-shri-piyush-goyal-0

39 Association for Democratic Reforms and Anr. v. Union of India and Ors, Writ Petition Number 333 of 2015, Supreme Court of India Order, 12 April 2019. https://adrindia.org/sites/default/files/16902_2015_Order_12-_Apr_-_2019.pdf

## Chapter 4: Electoral Bonds

1 Association for Democratic Reforms and Anr.Versus Union of India and Ors, The Supreme Court Order, 12 April 2019, 14. https://adrindia.org/sites/default/files/16902_2015_Order_12-_Apr_-_2019.pdf
2 Ibid.
3 Association for Democratic ReformsVersus Ministry of Finance, Ministry of Law And Justice and Election Commission of India, Public Interest Litigation in Supreme Court Order, 2017, 1. https://adrindia.org/sites/default/files/ADR_petition_on_electoral_bonds.pdf
4 Ajoy Sinha Karpuram, 'Key Issue Will Be Back in SC: What Constitutes a Money Bill?', *The Indian Express*, 17 July 2024. https://indianexpress.com/article/explained/explained-law/key-issue-supreme-court-money-bill-9458077/
5 Rangarajan R., 'How and When Can a Bill be Defined as a Money Bill? | Explained', *The Hindu,* 25 July 2024. https://www.thehindu.com/news/national/how-and-when-can-a-bill-be-defined-as-a-money-bill/article68434154.ece
6 Association for Democratic Reforms Versus Ministry of Finance, Ministry of Law And Justice and Election Commission of India, Public Interest Litigation in The Supreme Court Order, 2017, 15. https://adrindia.org/sites/default/files/ADR_petition_on_electoral_bonds.pdf
7 Communist Party of India (Marxist) Writ Petition in the Supreme Court on the Electoral Bonds Scheme, 19 January 2018. https://drive.google.com/file/d/1b9dFuutKpNFZ9dh3VU2ioOyqGjyUEiXp/view
8 Ibid.
9 Press Trust of India, 'Parties Got 99 Per Cent Donations Through Electoral Bonds of Rs 10 Lakh, Rs 1 Crore', *Mint,* 14 April 2019. https://www.livemint.com/elections/

lok-sabha-elections/parties-got-99-donations-through-electoral-bonds-of-rs-10-lakh-rs-1-crore-1555249529052.html

10 The Wire Staff, 'Union Government Spent Rs 14 Crore of Taxpayers' Money on Running the Electoral Bond Scheme: RTI', The Wire, 17 April 2024. https://thewire.in/government/union-govt-spent-rs-14-cr-of-taxpayers-money-on-running-the-electoral-bond-scheme-rti

11 Ibid.

12 Association for Democratic Reform Versus Union Of India & Ors, Writ Petition in The Supreme Court, 5 March 2019, 12. https://adrindia.org/sites/default/files/ADR_Application_05_March_2019.pdf

13 Shreegireesh Jalihal, Poonam Agarwal and Somesh Jha, 'Only 17 Parties in Supreme Court's Sealed List of 105 Got Electoral Bonds, BJP Cornered 68% of Money', The Reporters' Collective, 6 June 2022. https://www.reporters-collective.in/projects/only-17-parties-in-supreme-courts-sealed-list-of-105-got-electoral-bonds-bjp-cornered-68-of-money

14 Shreegireesh Jalihal, Poonam Agarwal and Somesh Jha, 'Debunking a "Sealed" Myth: Only 17 Political Parties of 105 In EC List Got Electoral Bonds', Article 14, 6 June 2022. https://article-14.com/post/debunking-a-sealed-myth-only-17-political-parties-of-105-in-ec-list-got-electoral-bonds-629d7a3bd1d5a

15 Poonam Agarwal, 'Can We Trust EVMs? MP Election Vote Count Shows Huge Discrepancies', The Quint, 2 February 2019. https://www.thequint.com/news/india/evm-hacking-tampering-malfunction-mp-election-2018-discrepancies-vote-count#read-more

16 Ibid.

17 Assembly Election 2018 – Constituency Wise Voter Turnout Report, CEO Madhya Pradesh. https://ceomadhyapradesh.nic.in/Election2018/ACReport.pdf

18 Candidate Wise Votes Details, CEO Madhya Pradesh. https://ceomadhyapradesh.nic.in/Election2018/Form-21%20E%20Candidate%20wise%20Votes%20Details%202018.pdf

19 The Representation of the People Act, 1951, Act No. 43 of 1951', 9 https://ceodelhi.gov.in/WriteReadData/

ManualElectionLaw/REPRESENTATION%20OF%20THE%20PEOPLE%20ACT,%201951.pdf

20 The Representation of the People Act, 1951. https://www.indiacode.nic.in/bitstream/123456789/2096/5/a1951–43.pdf.

21 Handbook for Returning Officer, Election Commission of India, 2023, 1. https://www.eci.gov.in/eci-backend/public/api/download?url=LMAhAK6sOPBp%2FNFF0iRfXbEB1EVSLT41NNLRjYNJJP1KivrUxbfqkDatmHy12e%2FzVx8fLfn2ReU7TfrqYobgIhX2hcHezql%2B6nnk2%2FeqbrIw7XG4Ymo1b5MUat9bvOSUeplspufSrYrPT3q0YbDQfZyuRDbsLdMoGfiLASl33aHkYQNivX5P6biD0TueLJ0i

22 Handbook for Presiding Officer, Election Commission of India, 2023, 2. https://www.eci.gov.in/eci-backend/public/api/download?url=LMAhAK6sOPBp%2FNFF0iRfXbEB1EVSLT41NNLRjYNJJP1KivrUxbfqkDatmHy12e%2FzVx8fLfn2ReU7TfrqYobgIiuXNfXaCGl%2FvBZjsedx9y9%2F1T74fErZadTk033PJJGyk69kQQkKU0sB2BFes6wS%2FqWV5K80PMd4Lc0i1A%2BBPBExEz9r03E0G0ttpKMyzNEk

23 The Representation of the People Act, 1951, India Code, 29.

24 Poonam Agarwal, 'EVM Vote Count Mismatch In 370+ Seats and EC Refuses to Explain', The Quint, 31 May 2019. https://www.thequint.com/news/india/lok-sabha-election-results-2019-mismatch-in-votes-polled-and-counted-in-evm-on-multiple-seats#read-more

25 Ibid.

26 Poonam Agarwal, 'Is EC Misleading Public on How EVM Votes Polled Data Is Compiled?', The Quint, 11 June 2019. https://www.thequint.com/news/india/lok-sabha-2019-ec-press-release-misleading-public-on-evm-vote-counting#read-more

## Chapter 5: Once Bitten Twice Shy: Public Institutions That Enabled It

1 R.K. Anand v. Registrar, Delhi High Court with I.U. Khan v. Registrar, Delhi High Court, Criminal Appeal, Supreme Court

of India, Para – 194, Indian Kanoon, 29 July 2009. https://indiankanoon.org/doc/58440/

2 'Behind Bars: Arrests and Detention of Journalists in India 2010-2020', FreeSpeechCollective, 24 December 2020. https://freespeechcollective.in/behind-bars-arrests-and-detentions-of-journalists-in-india-2010-2020/

3 Avantika Mehta, 'Journalists in UP Face a Flood of Criminal Cases from Yogi Adityanath's Govt', Article 14, 8 March 2022. https://article-14.com/post/journalists-in-up-face-a-flood-of-criminal-cases-from-yogi-adityanath-s-govt-6226b5db6bb7b

4 'मीडियि की घेराबंदी: उत्तर प्रदेश में 2017 से लेकर अब तक हुए मीडयि के दमन पर वसि्तृत रपिोर्ट', Committee Against Assault of Journalists, 10 February 2022. https://www.caajindia.org/2022/02/media%20ki%20gherabandi%20caaj%20report%20uttar%20pradesh.html

5 Tanushree Basuroy, 'News Consumption Trends in India – Statistics & Facts', *Statista,* 27 June 2024. https://www.statista.com/topics/8332/news-consumption-trends-in-india/#topicOverview

6 Bloomberg, 'Billionaire Press Barons Are Squeezing Media Freedom in India', *Deccan Herald*, 26 February 2024. https://www.deccanherald.com/india/billionaire-press-barons-are-squeezing-media-freedom-in-india-2909919

7 Ibid.

8 Paranjoy Guha Thakurta, 'How Modi has Supported Adani's Global Ambitions', Paranjoy.in, 29 October 2024. https://paranjoy.in/article/how-modi-has-supported-adanis-global-ambitions

9 Diksha Madhok, 'Billionaires Alone Won't Turn Narendra Modi's India into a Rich Country', CNN, 8 May 2024. https://edition.cnn.com/2024/05/07/business/india-economy-modi-ambani-adani-influence-intl-hnk/index.html

10 Bloomberg, 'Billionaire Press Barons Are Squeezing Media Freedom in India', *Deccan Herald*, 26 February 2024.

11 Press Trust of India, 'Raghav Bahl Under IT Scanner: Income Tax Department Raids Premises of Quint, Network 18 Group Founder', *Financial Express*, 11 October 2018. https://www.financialexpress.com/india-news/raghav-

bahl-income-tax-raid-i-t-scanner-premises-quint-network18-group-founder-delhi-noida/1345056/

12 Madhu Venkatesh, 'Attempt Made to Colour My Tax Returns as Bogus, Says Media Baron Raghav Bahl', ThePrint, 12 October 2018. https://theprint.in/economy/attempt-made-to-colour-my-tax-returns-as-bogus-says-media-baron-raghav-bahl/133675/

13 Editors Guild of India, 11 October 2018. https://x.com/IndEditorsGuild/status/1050301486050103296?ref_src=twsrc%5Etfw%7Ctwcamp%5Etweetembed%7Ctwterm%5E1050301486050103296%7Ctwgr%5Ee2a1e0813ff4722b059e9a0ce29766e6f975fab7%7Ctwcon%5Es1_&ref_url=https%3A%2F%2Fwww.thequint.com%2Fnews%2Findia%2Fit-officers-search-and-survey-the-quint-raghav-bahl

14 Press Trust of India, 'Income Tax Department "Surveys"', NewsClick, Newslaundry in Tax Case', *The Economic Times,* 10 September 2021. https://economictimes.indiatimes.com/news/economy/finance/it-dept-surveys-news-websites-in-tax-case-say-officials/articleshow/86093859.cms?from=mdr

15 Abhinandan Sekhri, 'Newslaundry's Statement on Income Tax 'Survey' at Our Office', Newslaundry, 11 September 2021. https://www.newslaundry.com/2021/09/11/newslaundrys-statement-on-income-tax-raid-at-our-office

16 Sofi Ahsan, 'Delhi HC Tells IT Dept to Ensure Newslaundry Co Founder's Data Is Protected: "Legally, Morally Wrong to Leak Private Data"', *The Indian Express,* 17 September 2021. https://indianexpress.com/article/cities/delhi/ensure-newslaundry-co-founders-data-is-not-leaked-hc-tells-income-tax-department-raid-7514967/

17 Ibid.

18 Editorial, 'NewsClick's Statement on Income Tax Department "Survey" of Its Office on September 10', NewsClick, 11 September 2021. https://www.newsclick.in/newsclicks-statement-income-tax-department-survey-its-office-10th-september

19 The Wire Staff, 'Income Tax Department Conducts "Surveys" at Offices of NewsClick, Newslaundry in Delhi', The Wire,

11 September 2021. https://thewire.in/media/income-tax-department-raids-offices-of-newsclick-newslaundry-in-delhi

20 Poonam Agarwal (@poonamjourno), 'ED is conducting raids/searches at #newsclick news website's Directors offices in a money laundering case for taking foreign funding from some dubious companies abroad: ED @TheQuint'. Twitter, 9 February 2021. https://x.com/poonamjourno/status/1359046112087166977

21 The Wire Staff, 'Enforcement Directorate Conducts Raids on NewsClick Office, Officials' Residences', The Wire, 9 February 2021. https://thewire.in/media/enforcement-directorate-newsclick-raids#google_vignette

22 NewsClick Team, 'Statement by NewsClick on Oct 3 Raids by Special Cell of Delhi Police', NewsClick, 4 October 2023. https://www.newsclick.in/statement-newsclick-oct-3-raids-special-cell-delhi-police

23 Ibid.

24 Mara Hvistendahi, David A. Fahrenthold, Lynsey Chutel and Ishaan Jhaveri, 'A Global Web of Chinese Propaganda Leads to a U.S. Tech Mogul', *The New York Times*, 5 August 2023. https://www.nytimes.com/2023/08/05/world/europe/neville-roy-singham-china-propaganda.html

25 Abraham Thomas, 'SC Directs AIIMS to Examine NewsClick Founder's Health to Decide His Bail Plea', *Hindustan Times,* 27 February 2024. https://www.hindustantimes.com/india-news/sc-directs-aiims-to-examine-newsclick-founder-s-health-to-decide-his-bail-plea-101709043515225.html

26 Apurva Vishwanath, 'Failure to Follow Procedure: Why SC Said NewsClick Founder's Arrest Was Illegal', *The Indian Express,* 16 May 2024. https://indianexpress.com/article/explained/explained-law/failure-to-follow-procedure-sc-newsclick-arrest-illegal-9330103/

27 'Protection Against Arrest and Detention in Certain Cases', Constitution of India. https://www.constitutionofindia.net/articles/article-22-protection-against-arrest-and-detention-in-certain-cases/

28 'India Top Court Bails NewsClick Editor Arrested in Chinese Funding Case', Al Jazeera, 15 May 2024. https://

www.aljazeera.com/news/2024/5/15/india-top-court-bails-newsclick-editor-arrested-in-chinese-funding-case

29 Ananthakrishnan G, 'NewsClick's Founder Steps Out of Tihar After Supreme Court Says Arrest Invalid', *The Indian Express,* 16 May 2024. https://indianexpress.com/article/india/supreme-court-newsclick-prabir-purkayastha-arrest-release-uapa-9329783/

30 Derek O'Brien, (@derekobrienmp), 'CENSORSHIP @ Twitter @TwitterIndia HAS TAKEN DOWN MY TWEET of the #BBCDocumentary, it received lakhs of views The 1 hr @BBC docu exposes how PM @narendramodi HATES MINORITIES Here's the mail I received. Also see flimsy reason given. Oppn will continue to fight the good fight.' Twitter 21 January 2023. https://x.com/derekobrienmp/status/1616669755938852864?ref_src=twsrc%5Etfw%7Ctwcamp%5Etweetembed%7Ctwterm%5E1616669755938852864%7Ctwgr%5Eb3d2509a247b40732b79a3276e75e98179632 84f%7Ctwcon%5Es1_&ref_url=https%3A%2F%2Fwww.aljazeera.com%2Fnews%2F2023%2F1%2F21%2Findia-asks-youtube-twitter-to-block-links-of-bbc-film-on-modi-gujarat-riots

31 Hannah Ellis-Pertersen and Jim Waterson, 'BBC Offices in India Raided by Tax Officials Amid Modi Documentary Fallout', *The Guardian,* 14 February 2023. https://www.theguardian.com/world/2023/feb/14/bbc-offices-india-raided-tax-officials-modi-documentary-fallout

32 Ibid.

33 Kanchan Gupta (@KanchanGupta), 'Important.Videos sharing @BBCWorld hostile propaganda and anti-India garbage, disguised as "documentary"', on @YouTube and tweets sharing links to the BBC documentary have been blocked under India's sovereign laws and rules. n1.' Twitter 21 January 2023. https://x.com/KanchanGupta/status/1616745166290976769?lang=en

## Chapter 6: The Legal Career Of Political Finance Or No Free Lunches

1 Association for Democratic Reforms and Anr v. Union of India and Ors, Application for Stay, ADR India, 29 November 2019.

https://adrindia.org/sites/default/files/Application_for_the_stay_of_Electoral_Bond_November2019.pdf

2 Association for Democratic Reforms and Anr v. Union of India & Ors, Judgment, Supreme Court of India, 15 February 2024. https://adrindia.org/sites/default/files/ADR_SC_judgment_Electoral_Bonds.pdf

3 Ibid.

4 Ibid.

5 Ibid.

6 Association for Democratic Reforms, Contempt Petition on behalf of the Petitioners, The Supreme Court of India, 6 March 2024. https://www.scobserver.in/wp-content/uploads/2021/10/Contempt-Petition-filed-by-Association-for-Democratic-reforms-against-State-Bank-of-India-SBI-Electoral-Bonds_compressed-1-18.pdf

7 Poonam Agarwal, 'SBI Records Hidden Numbers on Electoral Bonds – Govt Misled Public', The Quint, 25 November 2019. https://www.thequint.com/news/india/sbi-records-hidden-numbers-on-electoral-bonds#read-more

8 Ibid.

9 Association for Democratic Reforms, Contempt Petition on behalf of the Petitioners, The Supreme Court of India, 6 March 2024.

10 *The Economic Times*, 'Supreme Court Live: Hearing on SBI's plea on Electoral Bonds Issue', YouTube, posted on 11 March 2024. https://www.youtube.com/watch?v=HNZ5iXeZI28

11 State Bank of India Versus Association for Democratic Reforms and Others, Miscellaneous Application, Supreme Court of India, 11 March 2024. https://main.sci.gov.in/supremecourt/2024/10382/10382_2024_1_301_51365_Judgement_11-Mar-2024.pdf

12 Ibid.

13 *The Economic Times*, 'Supreme Court Live: Hearing on SBI's plea on Electoral Bonds Issue', YouTube, posted on 11 March 2024.

14 Disclosure of Electoral Bonds, The Election Commission of India, 14 March, 2024. https://www.eci.gov.in/disclosure-of-electoral-bonds

15 Details of Electoral Bonds submitted by SBI Part 1, The Election Commission of India, 14 March 2024. https://www.

eci.gov.in/eci-backend/public/api/download?url=LMAhAK6sOPBp%2FNFF0iRfXbEB1EVSLT41NNLRjYNJJP1KivrUxbfqkDatmHy12e%2FzBiU51zPFZI5qMtjV1qgjFmSC%2FSz9GPIId9Zlf4WX9G9EkbCvX7WNNYFQO4%2FMjBvNyKzGsKzKlbBW8rJeM%2FfYFA%3D%3D

16 Details of Electoral Bonds Submitted by SBI Part 2, Election Commission of India, 14 March 2024. https://www.eci.gov.in/eci-backend/public/api/download?url=LMAhAK6sOPBp%2FNFF0iRfXbEB1EVSLT41NNLRjYNJJP1KivrUxbfqkDatmHy12e%2FzBiU51zPFZI5qMtjV1qgjFmSC%2FSz9GPIId9Zlf4WX9G%2FyncUhH2YfOjkZLtGsyZ9B56VRYj06iIsFTelbq233Uw%3D%3D

17 Ashish Tripathi, 'Supreme Court Raps SBI for Not Disclosing Complete Details of Electoral Bonds; Issues Notice, *Deccan Herald*, 15 March 2024. https://www.deccanherald.com/india/electoral-bonds-case-sc-issues-notice-to-sbi-asks-to-disclose-data-revealing-companies-party-wise-contribution-2937880

18 *The Indian Express*, 'Supreme Court Issues Notice to SBI Over Disclosing Unique Alphanumeric Code of Electoral Bonds', YouTube, posted on 15 March 2024. https://www.youtube.com/watch?v=AaxN4XRIXhs

19 S.N. Thyagarajan, 'SC Refuses to Hear Industry Bodies' Plea Against Revealing Poll Bond Numbers', Money Control, 18 March 2024. https://www.moneycontrol.com/news/business/sc-refuses-industry-bodies-plea-against-revealing-poll-bond-numbers-12479031.html

20 NDTV, 'Supreme Court Constitution Bench on Electoral Bonds Case', YouTube, posted on 18 March 2024. https://www.youtube.com/watch?v=Fv5VsQXAlzg

21 Ibid.

22 Krishnadas Rajagopal, 'SIT Probe into Electoral Bonds: Supreme Court Says "Quid Pro Quo" Through Electoral Bonds Are Now Just "Assumptions"', *The Hindu*, 2 August 2024. https://www.thehindu.com/news/national/sit-probe-into-electoral-bonds-supreme-court-says-it-would-be-premature-inappropriate-to-intervene-at-this-stage-under-article-32/article68476839.ece

23 Subhash Chandra Garg, 'Electoral Bonds | Finance Minister ke knowledge Mein Nahi Tha ki SBI Code Record Kar Raha Hai – Ex Finance Secy', YouTube, posted on 30 March 2024. https://www.youtube.com/watch?v=CXpCkSF87-A

24 Narendra Modi, 'PM Modi's Exclusive Interview with Thanthi TV | Lok Sabha Election 2024', YouTube, posted on 31 March 2024. https://www.youtube.com/watch?v=SyfPGhJzUrM

## Chapter–7: A Biography of the Election Commission

1 Samiran Mishra, 'Supreme Court's 5 Big Quotes on Election Commission Appointments', NDTV, 23 November 2022. https://www.ndtv.com/india-news/supreme-courts-5-big-quotes-on-election-commission-appointments-3545338

2 Ibid.

3 Brut India, 'TN Seshan on How the Election Commission Must Behave', YouTube, posted on 6 June 2019. https://www.youtube.com/watch?v=VgkZJWdSRu0

4 'Constituent Assembly Debates, Volume VIII, Part II, 15 June 1949, Indian Kanoon. https://indiankanoon.org/doc/1336469/

5 Ibid.

6 Part XV, Elections, 324, Ministry of External Affairs. https://www.mea.gov.in/Images/pdf1/Part15.pdf

7 'Part XV Article 324, Superintendence, direction and control of elections to be vested in an Election Commission', Constitution of India, https://www.constitutionofindia.net/articles/article-324-superintendence-direction-and-control-ofelections-to-be-vested-in-an-election-commission/

8 Election Commission of India. https://www.eci.gov.in/about-eci

9 'Limits of Candidate's Expenses Enhanced', Election Commission of India, 6 January 2022. https://old.eci.gov.in/files/file/13928-limits-of-candidate's-expenses-enhanced/

10 'Model Code of Conduct for the Guidance of Political Parties and Candidates', Election Commission of India. https://www.eci.gov.in/mcc/

11 'Section 125 in the Representation of the People Act, 1951', Indian Kanoon. https://indiankanoon.org/doc/28226194/

12 'Details of IPC Sections 153A, 295 & 295A', ADR India. https://adrindia.org/sites/default/files/Details%20of%20 IPC%20Sections%20153A,%20295%20&%2029Apdf
13 'Section 125 in the Representation of the People Act, 1951', Indian Kanoon.
14 Liz Matthew and Abhinav Rajput, 'Minister Anurag Thakur Chants Desh ke Gaddaron ko, Poll Rally Crowd Completes Goli Maaro ...', *The Indian Express*, 28 January 2020. https://indianexpress.com/article/india/ anurag–thakur–slogan–rithala–rally–6238566/
15 Ibid.
16 CJP Team, 'Complaints Mount Against PM Modi: Accused of Inciting Religious Divisions at Banswara Rally', CJP. https:// cjp.org.in/complaints-mount-against-pm-modi-accused-of-inciting-religious-divisions-at-banswara-rally/
17 Ibid.
18 Jay Patel, 'Unequal Watch: ECI Issued 16 Notices Over MMC Violations. BJP Received Just 3', The Wire, 12 May 2024. https://thewire.in/government/unequal-watch-eci-issued-16-notices-over-mcc-violations-bjp-received-just-3
19 'Prime Minister Narendra Modi for Making "Divisive", "Objectionable" and "Malicious" Speech at Banswara in Rajasthan', *The Hindu businessline*, 25 April 2024.
20 Election Commission Issues Notices on Model Code Conduct Violation by Modi, Rahul', *The Hindu businessline*, 25 April 2024.https://www.thehindubusinessline.com/news/ elections/election-commission-issues-notices-on-model-code-ofconduct-violation-by-modi-rahul/article68106288.ece
21 The Wire Staff, 'Without Naming Modi, EC Tells BJP "Star Campaigners" to Stay Away from Divisive Speeches', The Wire, 22 May 2024. https://thewire.in/government/ without-naming-modi-ec-tells-bjp-star-campaignersto-stay-away-from-divisive-speeches
22 E.A.S. Sarma, 'The Functioning of the Election Commission of India During the 2024 Elections Lacked Transparency and Public Accountability', Counter Currents, 18 June 2024. https://countercurrents.org/2024/06/the-functioning-ofthe-election-commission-of-india-during-the-2024- elections-lacked-transparency-and-public-accountability/

23 Ibid.

24 Sukumar Sen, *Report on the First General Elections in India 1951–52*, Election Commission of India, 1955,6. https://cdn.downtoearth.org.in/library/0.61706000_1558592806_first–general–elections–in–india,–vol.pdf.

25 Ibid.,6.

26 Ibid., 24.

27 Ibid., 39.

28 Ibid., 69.

29 Ibid., 30.

30 Krishnadas Rajagopal, 'Supreme Court Calls Out Centre Over Short Tenures of Chief Election Commissioners', *The Hindu*, 23 November 2022. https://www.thehindu.com/news/national/supreme-court-on-election-commission-of-india/article66169513.ece.

31 Tushar Kohli, 'Making Sense of the Election Commissioners' Appointment Case Before the Supreme Court'.

32 'President Gives Assent to Bill for Appointment of CEC, ECs', *The Times of India*, 29 December 2023. https://economictimes.indiatimes.com/news/india/president-gives-assent-to-bill-for-appointment-of-cec-ecs/articleshow/106384610.cms?from=mdr

33 Association For Democratic Reforms versus Union of India, Writ Petition, Supreme Court of India, *ADR India,* 5 January 2024. https://adrindia.org/sites/default/files/Writ_Petition_87_of_2024.pdf

34 Ibid.

## Chapter 8 A Can of Worms: Unpacking Questions Raised about the Election Process

1 Kannan Gopinathan, 'Kannan Gopinathan's Letter to the Election Commission on the Vulnerability of the Election Process', The Polis Project, 23 October 2019. https://www.thepolisproject.com/read/kannan-gopinathans-letter-to-the-chief-election-commissioner-on-the-vulnerability-of-the-election-process/

2 Ibid.

3 Association For Democratic Reforms v. Election Commission of India and Another, Judgment, Supreme Court of India, *ADR India Org,* 26 April 2024. https://adrindia.org/sites/default/files/VVPAT_Judgment_dated_26-04-24.pdf

4 Poonam Agarwal, 'EVM Vote Count Mismatch In 370+ Seats and EC Refuses to Explain', The Quint, 2 April 2024. https://www.thequint.com/news/india/lok-sabha-election-results-2019-mismatch-in-votes-polled-and-counted-in-evm-on-multiple-seats

5 Ibid.

6 'Dr. Subramanian Swamy versus Election Commission of India', Judgment, Supreme Court of India, Indian Kannon, Para- 29, 8 October 2013. https://indiankanoon.org/doc/113840870/

7 Abhishek Sankritik, 'Day 2 Arguments, Increased Vote Verification Through VVPAT', Supreme Court Observer, 8 April 2019. https://www.scobserver.in/reports/n-chandrababu-naidu-union-of-india-vvpat-day-2-arguments/

8 'Legal History of EVMs and VVPATs, A Compilation and Analysis of Case Laws', Election Commission of India, 32. https://www.eci.gov.in/eci-backend/public/uploads/monthly_2022_11/10386732_LegalHistoryofEVMsandVVPATs_pdf.a942a6ed2e36892f92adecb5e88f6d3d

9 'Administrative Standard Operating Procedure (Administrative SOP) Checking and Verification of Burnt Memory/Microcontroller of EVM (Ballot Unit, Control Unit and VVPAT) Post the Announcement of Results', Election Commission of India, 1 June 2024. https://www.eci.gov.in/eci-backend/public/api/download?url=LMAhAK6sOPBp%2FNFF0iRfXbEB1EVSLT41NNLRjYNJJP1KivrUxbfqkDatmHy12e%2FzIv7%2FZQ09etPKoyJV5h%2FcTpRPWpX9OQgP2wHKYqKjmXH5B6xf9Rux5%2FSBRo2hPIttsXQUwCbGU493NshNTgs7UQ%3D%3D

10 '11 Applications Received for Checking/Verification of Burnt Memory/Microcontroller of EVMs for General Elections 2024', Election Commission of India, 20 June 2024. https://www.eci.gov.in/eci-backend/public/api/download?url=LMAhAK6sOPBp%2FNFF0iRfXbEB1EVSLT41NNLRjYNJJP1KivrUxbfqkDatmHy12e%2FzIv7%2FZQ09etPKoyJV5h%2FcTj9Lk68T0pyXxxkkbtoGRDU2%2B8pZcwG8JVNwskIKAMuNsXQUwCbGU493NshNTgs7UQ%3D%3D

11 'Technical Standard Operating Procedure (Technical SOP) for Checking and Verification of Burnt Memory/

Microcontroller of EVM (Ballot Unit, Control Unit and VVPAT) Post the Announcement of Results', Election Commission of India, 16 July 2024. https://www.eci.gov.in/eci-backend/public/api/download?url=LMAhAK6sOPBp%2FNFF0iRfXbEB1EVSLT41NNLRjYNJJP1KivrUxbfqkDatmHy12e%2FzcyjgeFPh4LtAbjL4Y7X74dKYJ7FVrqwMjXZYIIYHZHm1Y0n%2Fli%2Fkl%2BP4pzuTFktysXQUwCbGU493NshNTgs7UQ%3D%3D

12 Subhashis Banerjee, 'EVM VVPAT पर SC में हुए तर्क में कमी, सरिफ 100% VVPAT slips की गनिती की मांग होनी चहिए थी', YouTube, posted on 2 May 2024. https://www.youtube.com/watch?v=p7_3_bTjyzc

13 Association for Democratic Reforms v. Election Commission of India, 26 April 2024, 33. https://adrindia.org/sites/default/files/VVPAT_Judgment_dated_26-04-24.pdf

14 Poonam Agarwal, 'Why Did EC Destroy VVPAT Slips of 2019 LS Polls in Such a Hurry?', The Quint, 2 April 2024. https://www.thequint.com/news/india/why-did-election-commission-destroy-evm-voting-machine-vvpat-slips-of-2019-lok-sabha-polls#read-more

15 Form 17C, Annexure 54, Election Commission of India, https://www.eci.gov.in/eci-backend/public/api/download?url=LMAhAK6sOPBp%2FNFF0iRfXbEB1EVSLT41NNLRjYNJJP1KivrUxbfqkDatmHy12e%2Fzk1vx4ptJpQsKYHA87guoLhDqktw0PNc%2B6xQLr66nAkgO19X1azNg5ATTjKjXh53LcyggoMJ1wBP95xjkxuKvuw%3D%3D

16 'Voter Turnout of 66.14% in Phase 1 and 66.71% in Phase 2 Recorded in General Elections 2024', Election Commission of India, 30 April 2024. https://www.eci.gov.in/eci-backend/public/api/download?url=LMAhAK6sOPBp%2FNFF0iRfXbEB1EVSLT41NNLRjYNJJP1KivrUxbfqkDatmHy12e%2Fzye%2BFD1PRcKxhOuiYZ2Ra30zsZVuncZbKMyY%2FE405%2FpvqQ7hKxk3RS943b6G9oZXTCSv%2B1yJkuMeCkTzY9fhBvw%3D%3D

17 Mallikarjun Kharge, President Indian National Congress, Letter to Election Commission of India, 'Allegation by the President INC Regarding Release of Voter Turnout Data

– Rejection by the Commission Thereof', 10 May 2024. https://www.eci.gov.in/eci-backend/public/api/download?url=LMAhAK6sOPBp%2FNFF0iRfXbEB1EVSLT41NNLRjYNJJP1KivrUxbfqkDatmHy12e%2FztfbUTpXSxLP8g7dpVrk7%2Fda%2BEbTiKk%2FXhgFE8uZCGZfVPGRaeGPqVZA%2F5LjCkbbICSv%2B1yJkuMeCkTzY9fhBvw%3D%3D

18 'Association For Democratic Reforms and Anr v. Election Commission of India and Anr', Writ Petition, Supreme Court of India, 9 May 2024. https://adrindia.org/sites/default/files/Application_for_Direction_in_EVM_case.pdf

19 Association For Democratic Reforms v. Election Commission of India, 33, 26 April 2024. https://adrindia.org/sites/default/files/VVPAT_Judgment_dated_26-04-24.pdf

20 CEO UP, (@ceoup), 'The difference can arise between votes polled and votes counted because there are certain polling stations whose votes polled are not counted as per the extant protocol issued by the Commission and provided in various Manuals and Handbooks (e.g. Para 11.4 of the Handbook for Counting Agent).', X, 6 June 2024. https://x.com/ceoup/status/1798754539069411575?t=arKFDHP175L18iOwlXAcpw&s=08

21 'Lok Sabha Election 2024: Details of Winners and Runner-up', Association for Democratic Reforms, 2 August 2024. https://adrindia.org/content/discrepancies-between-votes-cast-and-votes-counted-2024-lok-sabha-election-multiple-0

22 Sumedha, 'Uncontested Elections and the Surat Walkover Explained', *The Hindu*, 25 April 2024. https://www.thehindu.com/elections/lok-sabha/uncontested-elections-india-polling-unopposed-surat-gujarat-win-explainer/article68097651.ece

23 'Surat Symptoms: On the BJP and the Elimination of Political Contest', *The Hindu*, 25 April 2024.https://www.thehindu.com/opinion/editorial/surat-symptoms-on-the-elimination-of-political-contest/article68102493.ece

24 Mukesh Rawat, 'When Elections Were Won by Just One Vote in India', *India Today,* 22 May 2019. https://www.indiatoday.in/elections/lok-sabha-2019/story/har-ek-vote-jaroori-hota-hai-when-elections-were-won-by-just-one-extra-vote-1498396-2019-04-10

25 Express News Service, 'Civil Society, Citizens' Groups Jointly Launch "Grow Spine" Postcard Campaign Against EC', *The Indian Express*, 12 May 2024. https://indianexpress.com/article/cities/bangalore/civil-society-citizens-groups-election-commission-9322192/

## Chapter 9 One Nation One Election: What Will India Choose?

1 BJP, *Ek Bharat Shreshtha Bharat: Sabka Saath Sabka Vikas*, Election Manifesto 2014, 14. *https://www.bjp.org/images/pdf_2014/full_manifesto_english_07.04.2014.pdf*

2 R.K. Trivedi, *Election Commission of India First Annual Report 1983*, 1984. https://legalaffairs.gov.in/sites/default/files/simultaneous_elections/ECI_FIRST_ANNUAL_REPORT_1983.PDF

3 Law Commission of India, *One Hundred Seventieth Report on Reform of the Electoral Laws*, 1999, https://cdnbbsr.s3waas.gov.in/s3ca0daec69b5adc880fb464895726dbdf/uploads/2022/08/2022082424.pdf

4 Ibid.

5 *Feasibility of Holding Simultaneous Elections to the House of People (Lok Sabha) and State Legislative Assemblies – Seventy-Ninth Report*, Parliament of India, Rajya Sabha, 2015, 4.https://legalaffairs.gov.in/sites/default/files/simultaneous_elections/79th_Report.pdf

6 *Feasibility of Holding Simultaneous Elections to the House of People (Lok Sabha) and State Legislative Assemblies, Seventy-Ninth Report*, Department Related Parliamentary Standing Committee on Personnel, Public Grievances, Law and Justice, Para 9.4, 17 December 2015. https://legalaffairs.gov.in/sites/default/files/simultaneous_elections/79th_Report.pdf

7 Ibid.

8 Bibek Debroy and Kishore Desai, 'Analysis of Simultaneous Elections: The "What", "Why" and "How", A Discussion Paper.' Department of Legal Affairs, *https://legalaffairs.gov.in/sites/default/files/simultaneous_elections/NITI_AYOG_REPORT_2017.pdf*

9 Ibid.

10 IANS, 'Electoral Reforms Necessary to Curb Black Money: Modi', *Business Standard,* 27 June 2016. https://www.business-standard.com/article/news-ians/electoral-reforms-necessary-to-curb-black-money-modi-116062701266_1.html

11 Bibek Debroy and Kishore Desai, 'Analysis of Simultaneous Elections: The "What", "Why" and "How", A Discussion Paper.'

12 Ibid.

13 Law Commission of India, Draft Report, Simultaneous Elections, 30 August 2018. https://legalaffairs.gov.in/sites/default/files/simultaneous_elections/LCI_2018_DRAFT_REPORT.pdf

14 Jagdeep S. Chhokar, 'Simultaneous Elections: Striking at the Roots of Parliamentary Democracy', The Hindu Centre for Politics and Public Policy, no.8 (2018). https://www.thehinducentre.com/publications/issue-brief/simultaneous-elections-striking-at-the-roots-of-parliamentary-democracy/article64935973.ece

15 Ibid.

16 S.Y. Quraishi, 'Desirability and Feasibility of Simultaneous Elections', India Foundation, 24 January 2017. https://indiafoundation.in/articles-and-commentaries/desirability-and-feasibility-of-simultaneous-elections/

17 Jagdeep S. Chhokar, 'Simultaneous Elections: Striking at the Roots of Parliamentary Democracy'.

18 'Lok Sabha Elections 2024: PM Modi Held 206 Rallies; Rahul, Priyanka Gandhi Notched Up Just Over 100', Mint, 30 May 2024. https://www.livemint.com/elections/lok-sabha-elections-2024-pm-modi-held-206-rallies-rahul-priyanka-gandhi-notched-up-just-over-100-11717083634038.html

19 Press Trust of India, '"One Nation, One Election" Saves Costs, But Political Consensus Not Easy to Achieve: Ex-CEC Chawla', *The Economic Times*, 24 January 2024. https://economictimes.indiatimes.com/news/elections/lok-sabha/india/one-nation-one-election-saves-costs-but-political-consensus-not-easy-to-achieve-ex-cec-chawla/articleshow/107118303.cms?from=mdr

20 Ibid.

21 Jairam Ramesh, @Jairam_Ramesh, 19 January 2024. https://x.com/Jairam_Ramesh/status/1748284256755892277

22 Express News Service, '"One Nation, One Election" Is Anti-democratic, Says Sitaram Yechury', *The Indian Express*, 3 September 2023. https://indianexpress.com/article/cities/mumbai/one-nation-one-election-anti-democratic-sitaram-yechury-lok-samvad-programme-india-front-meeting-8921605/

23 'Why "One Nation, One Poll" Needs Greater Consensus', Observer Research Foundation, 27 June 2019. https://www.orfonline.org/expert-speak/why-one-nation-one-poll-idea-needs-greater-consensus-52451

24 P. B. Sawant, 'Keep the Polls Apart', *The Indian Express*, 6 March 2018. https://indianexpress.com/article/opinion/columns/india-lok-sabha-constitution-elections-voters-keep-the-polls-apart-5087305/

25 Rangarajan R., 'The Pros and Cons of Simultaneous Elections | Explained', *The Hindu*, 29 January 2024. https://www.thehindu.com/news/national/the-pros-and-cons-of-simultaneous-elections-explained/article67790554.ece

26 The Union and Its Territory, Ministry of External Affairs, https://www.mea.gov.in/Images/pdf1/Part1.pdf

27 Louise Tillin, 'Simultaneous Elections: What Are the Implications for Indian Federalism?' Scroll, 17 September 2023. https://scroll.in/article/1055859/simultaneous-elections-what-are-the-implications-for-indian-federalism

28 K.C. Tyagi, 'One Nation, One Election: A Blow to Federalism, A Challenge to Implement', *The Indian Express*, 5 September 2023. https://indianexpress.com/article/opinion/columns/one-nation-one-election-blow-to-federalism-8924227/

29 Manuraj Shanmugasundaram, 'The Idea of One Nation, One Election Is Against Federalism', *The Hindu,* 23 January 2024. https://www.thehindu.com/opinion/op-ed/the-idea-of-one-nation-one-election-is-against-federalism/article67766520.ece

30 The Kesavananda Bharati Judgement, Supreme Court of India, 24 April 1973. https://judgments.ecourts.gov.in/KBJ/?p=home/intro

31 Ibid.

32 *Kesavananda Bharati Sripadagalvaru and Others* vs *State of Kerala and Another,* Supreme Court of India, 1973. https://indiankanoon.org/doc/257876/
33 Jagdeep S. Chhokar, 'Simultaneous Elections: Striking at the Roots of Parliamentary Democracy'.
34 P. B. Sawant, 'Keep the Polls Apart'.
35 Shekhar Gupta, 'One Nation, One Election is BJP's "Brahmastra": It Wants State Contests to Be "Modi versus Who", Too', ThePrint, 2 September 2023. https://theprint.in/national-interest/one-nation-one-election-is-bjps-brahmastra-it-wants-state-contests-to-be-modi-versus-who-too/1742807/
36 Himanshu Mishra, 'Centre to Bring Bill on One Nation One Election During Its Current Term: Sources', *India Today*, 15 September 2024. https://www.indiatoday.in/india/story/bjp-nda-government-bill-one-nation-one-election-current-term-sources-2600291-2024-09-15
37 'One Nation One Election Committee: Amit Shah, Adhir Ranjan Chowdhury, Ghulam Nabi Azad Among Eight-Member Panel', *The Economic Times*, 2 September 2023. https://economictimes.indiatimes.com/news/politics-and-nation/one-nation-one-election-committee-ram-nath-kovind-heads-as-chairman-with-amit-shah-and-others/articleshow/103310790.cms?utm_source=contentofinterest&utm_medium=text&utm_campaign=cppst
38 Damini Nath and Ritika Chopra, '"One Nation, One Election" May Only Start in 2034. Here's Why', *The Indian Express*, 13 November 2024. https://indianexpress.com/article/india/one-nation-one-election-earliest-joint-polls-likely-2034-if-no-change-9721986/

# Index

# About the Author

Poonam Agarwal is an Emmy-nominated journalist who has been covering Indian society and politics for two decades. She is a recipient of the Ramnath Goenka Award; BBC News Award for outstanding original investigative journalism; Best Investigative Journalist at The News Television Awards; the CNN Young Journalist Award, among others. Her investigative documentary on the loan app scam with the BBC World Service titled 'The Trap: India's Deadliest Scam' has received wide and critical acclaim. She has also written for the Global Investigative Journalist Network and delivered the prestigious Gavin MacFayden Memorial lecture at the Centre for Investigative Journalism in London in 2024.

Poonam started her career as a TV journalist in 2005 with NDTV. Subsequently, she worked with Times Now and was later the National Editor of Investigations at The Quint. Her award-winning work on elections and electoral bonds made history in helping the Indian Supreme Court deliver a judgement that struck down the Electoral Bonds Scheme. She tweets on X as @poonamjourno

Jai Meher Baba